THE PRACTICE OF
ECONOMIC MANAGEMENT

THE PRACTICE OF ECONOMIC MANAGEMENT

A CARIBBEAN PERSPECTIVE

To Philip Jones —
A new friend whom
I have known for a very
long time.
With best wishes
Courtney

Courtney N. Blackman

Ian Randle Publishers
Kingston • Miami

in association with

Butterfield Bank

Barbados Limited

First published in Jamaica, 2006 by
Ian Randle Publishers
11 Cunningham Avenue
Box 686
Kingston 6
www.ianrandlepublishers.com

National Library of Jamaica Cataloguing in Publication Data

Blackman, Courtney
    The practice of economic management : a Caribbean perspective/
Courtney Blackman

        p.   ;   cm.

        Includes index
        ISBN 976-637-243-8 (pbk)

1. Caribbean Area - Economic conditions   2.   Caribbean Area - Economic
policy   3. Economic development

I. Title

330.9729   dc 21

Cover design by Shelly-Gail Folkes
Book design by Allison Brown
Printed in the United States of America

TABLE OF CONTENTS

LIST OF ILLUSTRATIONS

Tables

Figures

Charts

Diagrams

FOREWORD

I am very pleased to write this brief foreword for Sir Courtney Blackman's book, *The Practice of Economic Management: A Caribbean Perspective.* This volume contains 22 papers which, although dealing with a variety of economic and financial issues, reveal one continuous theme — the crucial importance of sound economic management for securing the development of developing countries, and the greater applicability to dealing with the problems of small countries of what Sir Courtney calls, the *managerial* approach to economic development.

As is well known, Sir Courtney was the first Governor of the Central Bank of Barbados, and served with distinction in this office for three consecutive five-year terms from 1972. Throughout this period, Sir Courtney strongly advocated a *managerial* approach to dealing with the problems of small developing countries in preference to the *economic* approach used by establishment economists, especially those in the Washington-based IFIs such as the IMF and the World Bank, with their 'one size fits all policy prescriptions'. He did this not only through the policies promoted by the Central Bank and in the advice given to government but also in his writings and public addresses.

Sir Courtney was, however, equally critical of those economists from the region who adopted a mainly left-wing ideological approach to the problems of small developing countries, and were blinded by ideology to such an extent that they appeared not to be too concerned about the welfare of the broad masses of people in whose interests they professed to be working.

Sir Courtney, therefore, challenges the practicability of the radicalism of some New World Economists as well as the ultra conservatism and orthodoxy of the economists in the Washington-based IFIs. In so doing he has made an invaluable contribution to economic development theory and practice in the Caribbean, and contributed significantly to successful economic policy making in Barbados. This book should, therefore, prove to be a most interesting and valuable addition to the economics section of university libraries in the Caribbean and other developing countries, as well as those of the Washington-based IFIs, for whose economists it should be compulsory reading.

Sir Neville Nicholls,
Former President of The Caribbean Development Bank

PREFACE

The 22 papers on issues of Caribbean economic development assembled in this monograph were written over three decades, and reflect 40 years of intense study of economics and management. My career as bank economist, university lecturer, Central Bank governor, international consultant, and ambassador, provided the scope to practice those two disciplines, and also involved continuous interaction with decision makers and technocrats in Washington, DC, throughout the Caribbean, and elsewhere.

These essays represent responses to real-life problems facing governments, public and private sector corporations, as well as non-profit organizations. They were certainly not written to impress academicians, although several of them have appeared in learned journals. For this reason, economic jargon is studiously avoided, and diagrams and charts are kept to a minimum. There is only one mathematical equation in the entire book!

Several institutions and individuals assisted with this publication. First there are the various groups which invited me to make presentations, and the clients who sought my services. The Caribbean Centre for Monetary Studies provided me with an opportunity to present papers at their annual conference, some of which are included here. Also, during my tenure at the Central Bank of Barbados, numerous staff members assisted by typing, doing research for, and advising on, the earlier papers. Coming down to the wire, Mrs Aldeen Payne checked out many references on an urgent basis. To her I express my gratitude.

I owe a tremendous debt to Mr Carl Moore who edited the contents of the monograph and prepared them for publication, working under great pressure towards the end. Sir Neville Nicholls, former President of the Caribbean Development Bank, and a long-time friend, kindly agreed to write the Foreword. My computer 'guru', Mr Oliver Cooke, responded readily on numerous occasions when my computer misbehaved. Ian Randle Publishers Ltd, was also most supportive, and Mr Randle himself made several suggestions that greatly improved the quality of the final product.

But there would have been no publication if Mr Mariano Browne, Managing Director of Butterfield Bank (Barbados) Limited, convinced of the social value of this book, had not persuaded his Board of Directors to provide generous financial support.

As always, my wife Gloria both fed the carrot and applied the stick in keeping my nose to the grindstone. She remains an indispensable partner. Finally, my seven grandchildren lifted my spirit with their hugs and kisses, and provided the *raison d'être* to continue. To their parents I dedicate this book.

In spite of the abundance of support and advice, this book contains several imperfections, for which I alone am responsible.

INTRODUCTION

The purpose of this Introduction is to provide the reader with a roadmap for navigating the 22 papers of this book, written on numerous topics over three decades, and in response to various institutional problems and client requests. They were all heterodox at the time of writing. The economic fortunes and challenges of the former British West Indies, spanning three decades or so, have provided the background against which the essays assembled in this volume were written. They are Antigua and Barbuda, The Bahamas, Barbados, Belize, Dominica, Guyana, Jamaica, St. Kitts and Nevis, Saint Lucia, St. Vincent and the Grenadines, Trinidad and Tobago, and Montserrat (still a UK colony), with a total population of less than six million. Since 1978 they have constituted a Caribbean Community and Common Market (CARICOM). Haiti and Suriname, recently admitted into CARICOM, have not been specifically covered in these essays. Former colonies of France and Holland, respectively, these two countries are culturally and politically quite different from the Anglophone Caribbean, and are still only loosely integrated into CARICOM. Nevertheless, lessons from the Anglophone Caribbean experience should not be lost on Haitians and Surinamese.

Compared with the rest of the developing world, the independent Anglophone Caribbean states are quite well off. Of 214 countries surveyed in the 2005 *World Bank Report*, the per capita gross national income (GNI) statistics, calculated on a purchasing power parity basis (PPP), were given as follows for these countries: Antigua and Barbuda at US$9,590.00, The Bahamas at

US$16,140.00, Barbados at US$15,060.00, St. Kitts and Nevis at US$11,040.00, and Trinidad and Tobago at US$9,450.00 are classified as upper middle income; Dominica at US$5,090.00, Grenada at US$3,950.00, Guyana at US$3,950.00, Saint Lucia at US$5,220.00 and St. Vincent and The Grenadines at US$6,590.00 fall in the lower income group. Also, of 203 countries surveyed in 2003 in the *World Bank Atlas*, The Bahamas and Barbados ranked highest in per capita GNI (PPP) at 54th and 57th respectively, and Dominica and Guyana lowest at 115th and 130th respectively.

The group also scores high marks on the 2004 UNDP Human Development Index: Barbados at 29th, The Bahamas at 51st, and Trinidad and Tobago at 55th, place in the high human development category; the others place in the medium human development category, with Guyana bringing up the rear at 103rd. (177 countries were surveyed.)

In spite of these flattering statistics, the group has generally under-performed over the last three decades, especially when compared with the 'Asian Tigers', Hong Kong, Singapore, South Korea, and Taiwan. Jamaica and Guyana are actually poorer than they were 20 years ago; Grenada has not yet recovered from its 1980s Marxist/Leninist aberration, the public finances of Antigua and Barbuda, Belize and Dominica are in disarray, while Trinidad and Tobago's fortunes rise and fall with the price of oil. Even Barbados, arguably the world's most successful predominantly Black nation, was chastised in a recent IMF report for 'complacency' and failure to develop the human potential of its citizens to the maximum. A thread running through the essays in this volume is that the under-performance of the group reflects weak economic management across the board; the intent of the essays has been to suggest policies and strategies for improvement.

My first duty is to disclose the perspectives from which I view the issues under discussion. Secondly, I will set out the groupings into which the essays are arranged, and explain the rationale thereof. Third, I will look back briefly over the three decades spanned by these essays and assess how well their key premises have stood the test of time.

Perspectives

It is proper for social scientists to disclose upfront the ideological filters through which they examine their subject matter, more crudely, their perspective. These essays reflect three main perspectives: a managerial perspective, a small state perspective, and a Caribbean perspective.

Managerial Imperative

Even though 'economic' issues appear to dominate, these essays were written from the perspective of a manager. This is not surprising, since my doctoral studies were done, not in a Department of Economics, but in a School of Business (Columbia University, NYC) where economics, along with several other disciplines, for example, sociology, psychology, anthropology, and so forth, were viewed as the servants of management — a handmaiden, so to speak, not a mistress.

The economist tends to focus on commodities; his world is a world of commodities. As Kenneth Boulding aptly puts it:

> The economist's world is a world of prices, quantities, interest rates, production, consumption, income, etc. He studies the 'behaviour of prices' ... so the economist is really not interested in the behaviour of men. He is aware, of course, at the back of his mind, that prices, outputs, etc., are in fact the result of human decisions. He likes to reduce these decisions, however, to a form as abstract as possible.[1]

The manager, on the other hand, is most conscious that he/she works through people to produce goods and services for the benefit of people. He/she is therefore most conscious of the behaviour of men and women, and the complexity of the societies within which they always live — contrary to Mrs Margaret Thatcher's infamous remark, 'There are no societies, only individuals.' A society is a conglomeration of numerous social groups or organizations — households, churches, schools, small business and large corporations, bureaucracies, political parties, and government administrations. The success of society at large depends on the effectiveness with which the affairs of its various organisations are run. Hence, the emphasis on management throughout this book.

Small State Perspective

The second perspective is that of the citizen of a small country, with limited natural resources, small population and negligible political clout. In the physical world, perspective depends on the position of the observer relative to the object being observed; in the field of economics, the interpretation of statistical data depends on the ideological 'filters' through which economists view reality. 'Free Market' and Marxist economists will therefore observe the same data and come to opposite conclusions. It is therefore important that decision makers in small states view the world from their own perspective, and assert their interests without apology. As my great friend Lloyd Best likes to say, 'Wherever I am is the *First World.*'

By the same token, the directorates of functioning small states are far better qualified to define and consult their own interests than are large states or international organizations, which so often injure when they mean to do good. Indeed, there is no greater national misfortune than to be dictated to by foreigners. Small states must therefore conduct their affairs in such a way as to preserve the maximum degrees of freedom. This implies the religious observance of fiscal discipline, and insistence that their national sovereignty is respected. Indeed, for small states sovereignty is their 'fig leaf', and only they themselves are qualified to determine when sovereignty, and how much of it, should be surrendered in the pursuit of a higher goal.

Perspective of a Caribbean National

The third perspective is that of a citizen of the Caribbean. A common history of colonisation, and especially of slavery, has created conditions in which a unified Caribbean nation may be forged. How we achieve it is a matter of choice, and may very well involve a long period of trial and error — hopefully of less duration than the centuries of internecine struggle leading up to the establishment of the European Union, or the bloody civil war that consummated the union of the United States of America.

But we cannot change the past, for the arrow of time moves in only one direction; we must play with the cards that history has dealt us, and do the best with what we have — and we have a lot! We must certainly rise above the spurious divisions of ethnicity, ideology, religion, politics, and nationality, and focus on our common interests.

Classification of Essays

Three themes bind these essays together. First, sound management in every aspect of our society is imperative. In short, we must cultivate a Caribbean culture of management. Second, since complexity is an increasing function of size, small states are inherently more manageable than large ones, and the returns to superior management correspondingly greater. Third, decision-makers in small states should not accept uncritically alien ideologies and theories, but should think for themselves, and develop strategies rooted in their national interests and aspirations. The essays are also written on the assumption that the Caribbean will persist in the search for a set of cooperative arrangements that will enable us to take our rightful place in the sun — both literally and figuratively.

The essays are arranged within five sections:

Section One: Development and Management: Contending with the 'Left'

The papers in this section take issue with Marxian and 'New World' radical views of the 1970s and early 1980s that promoted autarchy and extensive state involvement in the economy.

Section Two: Debt and the Balance of Payments

This group of papers challenges the policies of the industrialized nations, the international banking community and the IFIs, that forced the less developed countries (LDCs) to shoulder the major burden of the Debt Crisis.

Section Three: The 'Washington Consensus': Contending with the 'Right'

The papers in this section are in sharp disagreement with the 'free market'-based programmes imposed by IFIs in the 1990s on developing countries with balance of payments difficulties, and which came to be known as the 'Washington Consensus'.

Section Four: Critical Caribbean Issues

This section includes a number of important issues which do not fit neatly into any of the other categories.

Section Five: The Barbados Experiment

Having practised management and economics primarily in my
native land, I have exercised the author's prerogative to include
a group of essays on Barbados.

There are two most important areas of economic activity which
have not been specifically covered in the above five groups of
essays: *Trade* and *Regional Integration*. Although I have thought long
and hard on these subjects, I have never had the opportunity to
research and write on either. I must leave it to others to fill the
gap.

The Verdict

These essays should be judged by the extent to which the
hypotheses on which they were based have either been confirmed
or invalidated by subsequent events; they have been confirmed
by at least three criteria.

First, those member states of CARICOM which most zealously
pursued the statist policies promoted by the 'New World' and
Marxist-Leninist paradigms, namely Guyana, Grenada, and to a
lesser extent Jamaica, have suffered grievous economic and social
set-backs. Only those states advanced which, like The Bahamas,
Barbados, the OECS (ex Grenada), and Belize, pursued pragmatic
and conservative economic strategies. By the mid-1980s the 'New
World' school had retreated, while the collapse of the Communist
Bloc in 1989, and the dissolution of the USSR shortly afterwards,
proved that Marxist-Leninist regimes were no longer viable. Only
Cuba and North Korea soldier on!

Secondly, the leaders of the advanced industrial nations, the
so-called G-8, have come to the belated conclusion that the
resuscitation of the most indebted LDCs requires the forgiveness
of their onerous foreign debt, even as they agonize about how
they should go about it. The human suffering resulting from the

Debt Crisis would have been avoided had the approach suggested in my 1983 essay, 'A Heterodox Approach to the Adjustment Problem', reproduced herein, been acted upon.

Thirdly, only those emerging nations prospered which, like the 'East Asian Tigers', rejected the IFI doctrine of free and unfettered markets, and global capital market liberalization. Indeed, it was IMF insistence that LDCs open up their financial markets to unrestricted capital flows that led to the destructive international financial crisis of the late 1990s. Within CARICOM, Guyana and Jamaica, which were pressured into experiments with financial and capital market liberalization, suffered further economic decline.

Most significantly, a number of prominent 'First World' economists, most notably Nobel Laureate Dr Joseph Stiglitz,[2] former chief economist at the World Bank, have begun to write learned papers, replete with mathematical models explaining why the theories of the IFIs, with which these essays have contended for over three decades, did not work out in practice. Hopefully, Caribbean political directorates will not wait another 30 years before the mathematical models of the international economics establishment demonstrate that economic development is, above all, about management.

Notes

1. Kenneth Boulding, *The Image: Knowledge in Life and Society* (Ann Arbor: University of Michigan Press, 1961), 82.

2. Joseph E. Stiglitz, 'Capital Market Liberalization, Globalization and the IMF', *Oxford Review of Economic Policy* 20, no. I (2004).

ABBREVIATIONS AND ACRONYMS

AIDS:	Acquired Immune Deficiency Syndrome
BNB:	Barbados National Bank
CD&W:	Colonial Development and Welfare Act
CAP:	Common Agricultural Policy
CARDI:	Caribbean Agricultural, Research and Development Institute
CARIBCAN:	Caribbean–Canadian Initiative
CARICAD:	Caribbean Centre for Development Administration
CARICOM:	Caribbean Community and Common Market
CARIFTA:	Caribbean Free Trade Association
CARIRI:	Caribbean Industrial Research Institute
CBI:	Caribbean Basin Initiative
CDB:	Caribbean Development Bank
CEO:	Chief Executive Officer
CFF:	Compensatory Financing Facility
CMCF:	Caribbean Multilateral Clearing Facility
COMECON:	Council for Mutual Economic Assistance (Also CMEA; CEMA)
CRNM:	Caribbean Regional Negotiating Machinery
CSME:	CARICOM Single Market and Economy
ECCB:	Eastern Caribbean Central Bank
EDUTEC:	Technical Education Programme
EEC:	European Economic Community
EEZ:	Exclusive Economic Zone
EFF:	Extended Fund Facility

EPA:	Economic Partnership Agreement
ESOP:	Employee Share Ownership Plan
EU:	European Union
FTAA:	Free Trade Area of the Americas
GDP:	Gross Domestic Product
GNI:	Gross National Income
GNP:	Gross National Product
IDB:	Inter-American Development Bank
IDC:	Island Developing Countries
IFI:	International Financial Institution
IMF:	International Monetary Fund
JADF:	Jamaica Agricultural Development Foundation
LDC:	Less Developed Country
MDC:	More Developed Country
NDP:	National Development Plan
NGO:	Non-Governmental Organization
NSP:	National Strategic Plan
OECD:	Organisation for Economic Co-operation and Development
OECS:	Organisation of Eastern Caribbean States
OPEC:	Organization of the Petroleum Exporting Countries
PE:	Public Enterprise
PPP:	Purchasing Power Parity
RNM:	Regional Negotiating Machinery
SARS:	Severe Acute Respiratory Syndrome
T&T:	Trinidad and Tobago
UK:	United Kingdom
UN:	United Nations
UNCTAD:	United Nations Conference on Trade and Development
UNDP:	United Nations Development Programme
USA:	United States of America
USSR:	Union of Soviet Socialist Republics

ABBREVIATIONS AND ACRONYMS

UWI:	University of the West Indies
VAT:	Value Added Tax
WTO:	World Trade Organization

SECTION I

Development and Management:
Contending with the 'Left'

I

TWO LOST DECADES

RETROSPECT AND PROSPECT

In an address to students of the University of the West Indies at the Mona campus in March 1980 (reproduced in *The Practice of Persuasion*), I described the 1970s as the 'Decade of Disaster' in the context of Caribbean economic history. I added, 'If you think the 70s were rough, wait until you see the 80s.'[1] We have navigated the 80s even less adroitly than we did the 70s. The majority of CARICOM residents are worse off than they were at the end of the 1970s. Indeed, Guyanese are worse off than they have been in living memory. Jamaica remains mired in balance of payments difficulties; the habitually better-off Trinidadians have devalued their currency twice in two years, and the traditionally solid Barbadians drift aimlessly into the 1990s. The period 1970–1990 may well go down in West Indian economic history books as 'Two Lost Decades'. The question now is, 'How do we get back on track?'

It is now the habit for political leaders of the more developed countries of CARICOM, when seeking external aid, debt restructuring, or soft loans, to attribute the decline of our economic fortunes to the oil crisis, falling world commodity prices, the protectionism of the industrial nations, and other acts of God and man. There is both truth and deception in these excuses. In fact, the Pacific rim countries of Hong Kong, South Korea, Singapore and Taiwan — variously called the 'four tigers', the 'four dragons' or the 'gang of four' — have flourished over the last 20 years in the same international environment as CARICOM. Furthermore, the least endowed territories in CARICOM, namely the OECS and Barbados, have outperformed the better endowed Guyana, Jamaica, and Trinidad and Tobago. We must therefore look elsewhere than to external factors for explanations of our loss of two decades. Our thesis is that the misfortunes of the last 20 years are, to a large extent, rooted in mistaken development policies reflecting the prevailing Caribbean economic doctrines, and are therefore intellectual in origin.

Some of the leading proponents of that conventional wisdom now claim that their errors are recognizable only with the aid of hindsight. In his book, *The Poor and the Powerless*, the Marxist Clive Thomas pleads that the strategy of 'state ownership and control' of the region's resources neglected important considerations:

> With the vision of hindsight, the importance of these considerations seems self-evident, but at the time they were less obvious and, as a result, a number of serious errors were made.[2]

Similarly, the radical New World economist Norman Girvan, in a review of Clive Thomas's book, concedes the possibility 'that the present position of radicalism ... may, with the aid of hindsight, be exposed to have severe weaknesses as well'[3] In fact, there were a few dissidents whose warnings went unheeded. In a 1975 paper entitled 'The Economic Development of Small Countries: A Managerial Approach',[4] I expressed concern at the trend towards nationalization in the region. In the Mona speech mentioned above I sharply criticized both the Marxists and the New World group:

> I am especially at a loss to understand the attraction of an economic model, conceived in early industrial Britain, and first applied in pre-industrial Russia. Even stranger is that the empirical evidence of its forced application under the Soviet neocolonialist regime

should be completely ignored. Even the Soviets must find it hard to understand.[5]

Of the New World radicals I said:

> Unfortunately, having developed a useful theory of under-development, the scholarship of the New World economists fell apart.... They omitted the next logical step — the development of an operational model of economic development.[6]

Thomas and Girvan therefore beg the question!

This article seeks to identify the main causes of our economic failures during the 1970s and 1980s and outlines a new approach to regional economic recovery during the 1990s.

Pacific Basin and CARICOM compared

The Anglophone Caribbean was a much more likely candidate for economic success in the immediate post-World War II period than the Pacific rim territories of Hong Kong, South Korea, Singapore and Taiwan. All four of these countries suffered grievously under Japanese occupation, while the Caribbean, unscarred by the war, emerged better off than before. The more developed CARICOM countries — Jamaica, Guyana, Trinidad and Tobago, and Barbados — were considerably richer in natural resources than the Pacific countries in question: oil and natural gas in Trinidad & Tobago, bauxite in Jamaica, and bauxite, gold and timber in Guyana; and were far more fortunate in their political and social structure. Two other important Caribbean advantages are proximity to the markets of the US and Europe, and English as the native language.

In his latest book, *The New Realities*, Peter Drucker describes the condition of the four Asian countries in the immediate post-war period:

In 1952, when the Korean War ended, South Korea was even more devastated than Japan had been in 1945; the country had no industries at all and almost no trained and educated people. Hong Kong until the 1960s was a trading port without industries. Singapore was little more than a British naval base. And Taiwan had little except a few plantations that supplied the country's colonial masters, the Japanese, with high-cost sugar.[7]

Yet, from 1970 onwards, these four economies completely outperformed CARICOM (with the sole exception of The Bahamas, itself a most exceptional case). According to the World Bank, real per capita GNP during 1965–1987 grew annually by 6.2 per cent in Hong Kong, 7.2 per cent in Singapore and 6.4 per cent in South Korea. The comparable statistics for the CARICOM MDCs are 1.5 per cent for Jamaica, -4.4 per cent for Guyana, 1.3 per cent for Trinidad and Tobago, and 2.4 per cent for Barbados. The average growth performance for the OECS was approximately 2.0 per cent per annum over the same period.

The approximate per capita incomes of the 'four tigers' in 1987 were US$8,000 for Singapore and Hong Kong, US$6,000 for Taiwan, and US$2,700 for South Korea. For Jamaica, Trinidad and Tobago, and Barbados, the equivalent statistics are US$940, US$4,210 and US$5,350, respectively. Guyana, with a per capita income of US$390, ranked second only to Haiti as the poorest country in the New World. Comparable per capita incomes in the OECS range from US$2,570 for Antigua and Barbuda to US$1,070 for St. Vincent.

The difference in the performance of these two regions has been even more dramatic in the 1980s. The annual real growth rate from 1980–87 was 6.8 per cent for Hong Kong, 6.8 per cent for Singapore and 8.8 per cent for South Korea. Comparable figures for MDCs in CARICOM were -1.1 per cent for Jamaica, -6.0 per cent for Guyana, -5.0 per cent for Trinidad and Tobago and 0.7 per cent for Barbados; for the OECS comparable statistics ranged from 5.9 per cent for Saint Lucia to 1.7 per cent for St. Kitts and Nevis.

Paradoxically, the degree of structural transformation among the 'four tigers' is actually highest in South Korea, where per capita income is lowest. South Korea leads in ship-building, is a major manufacturer of electronic appliances, and successfully exports automobiles and personal computers to the US. All 'four tigers' have chalked up impressive foreign trade records: Taiwan's 20 million inhabitants enjoyed a trade surplus of nearly US$14 billion last year and boast foreign exchange reserves of US$75 billion, the world's largest after Japan.

The major economies of CARICOM, which had successfully established preconditions for 'take-off' by the mid-1970s, have not yet got off the ground. Guyana, having defaulted on all its foreign debts, depends largely on international charity; Jamaica avoids technical default on its foreign debt through a series of acrobatic financial manoeuvres; Trinidad and Tobago has lost much of its economic independence to international creditors, while the Barbadian economy, in the words of Dr Delisle Worrell of the Central Bank of Barbados, 'is going nowhere.' The OECS, through a combination of good sense and liberal UK grants-in-aid, has kept out of trouble and has made modest but steady progress.

CARICOM can hardly use American assistance to Korea and Taiwan as an excuse for its own inferior performance. For one thing, much of the assistance from the United States to Korea and Taiwan was military in character. And if our external debt of US$5 billion is any indication, CARICOM was the beneficiary of considerable capital inflows during the 1970s and 1980s. Besides, Jamaica and Guyana are, on a per capita basis, among the major recipients of foreign aid, both intended and unintended, as defaulted loans may be considered. Furthermore, unlike Trinidad and Tobago, which benefited from a massive windfall of petrodollars, the 'four dragons' imported virtually all their energy needs.

Ironically, it was our own Nobel laureate Sir Arthur Lewis who first articulated the strategy by which these Pacific basin countries achieved their industrial prowess. Influenced by the spectacular early success of Puerto Rico's 'Operation Bootstrap', he suggested that by encouraging foreign capital to establish labour-intensive industries in the region, Caribbean countries could put our growing army of unemployed to work. In time, he argued, local businessmen might learn 'the tricks of the trade' and themselves move into modern industry. He also envisaged that the shift of unproductive labour from the countryside would promote the adoption of more capital-intensive and efficient agricultural methods to feed an expanding urban population.

The pragmatic 'gang of four', unburdened by philosophical misgivings about foreign investment, soon swallowed up the markets for labour-intensive manufactures and moved upstream with deliberate speed. Using the techniques of joint venture and various contractual devices, local businessmen soon became involved in manufacture for foreign markets. Today, high-tech electronics from all 'four dragons', and heavy industrial goods from Taiwanese and South Korean-owned enterprises, have penetrated the markets of the western industrial countries. Indeed, the indigenous South Korean enterprises of Daewoo and Hyundai now rank among the world's leading industrial conglomerates. Moreover, both South Korea and Taiwan, the only two of the 'four tigers' with arable land, have developed vibrant agricultural sectors. It is an amazing fact that Taiwan, with about four times the arable land of Jamaica and ten times the population, is a net exporter of food. Jamaica is a net importer of food.

Roots of Economic Failure in CARICOM

The economic failure of CARICOM in the 70s and 80s derives from three main factors: the inappropriateness of the economic models utilized; the neglect of the management factor and the political failure of the integration process. All three of these issues must be addressed if we are to face the 1990s with any prospect of success.

Marxism and Dependence

The economic strategy of CARICOM governments in the 70s rested essentially on two paradigms — the Marxian ideology and the 'dependence' model. The Marxian ideology, embraced by Guyana and Grenada, called for central planning of the economy, ownership and control of the means of production, including nationalization of foreign-owned enterprises, and counter-trade with the Eastern bloc as against traditional commerce with the West. The 'dependence' model, pushed by radical New World economists of the University of the West Indies, identified 'dependence' on former colonial powers as the root cause of Caribbean underdevelopment. They recommended 'delinking' from the metropoles, 'ownership and control' of indigenous resources, and 'occupation of the commanding heights of the economy'.

One effect of these models in the late 70s was to push Caribbean governments towards a high degree of administrative and political centralization, and extensive state ownership of business enterprises. The Guyana government assumed ownership or control over 80 per cent of the formal economy, nationalizing almost its entire foreign sector: banking, agriculture, mining and telecommunications. The Jamaican government acquired shares in the dominant alumina/bauxite industry, nationalized public utilities, a commercial bank, hotels, sugar plantations and other industries. The Trinidad and Tobago government used its windfall petrodollars to purchase several foreign-owned enterprises, and by the mid-80s had acquired outright, majority or minority ownership in over 60 business enterprises, including oil, hotels, steel and petrochemicals.

Actually, such concentration of economic power in government was understandable in the 1960s. During that time CARICOM MDCs were still in the second stage of economic development when the preconditions were being laid for 'take-off' into sustained economic growth. Governments have traditionally provided the dynamic for such transformation. A high degree of political and administrative centralization was required, firstly, to sweep away obsolete institutions and, secondly, to mobilize the vast sums required to put a modern infrastructure into place — airports, harbours, bridges, public utilities, and other social overhead projects. In addition, development banks, central banks, secondary and technical schools, university colleges, and so forth had to be established. Governments throughout CARICOM invested heavily in infrastructural projects with generally favourable results.

By the mid-70s the preconditions for 'take-off' had been well and truly laid in CARICOM MDCs. The appropriate strategy then was for governments to loosen their centralized control and give full reign to the private sector. The analogy of an army assaulting a defended river is most apposite. First, there is a concentration of forces to create a strong bridgehead. Once a passage is forced, there follows the 'break-out', during which centralized control is relaxed, and individual brigades are permitted to fan out, seeking targets of opportunity. Instead of relaxation of controls in the 70s and 80s, CARICOM states concentrated authority even further in their cabinets, and too often in a prime minister or president. This created serious bottlenecks downstream in the economy and strangled the efforts of private enterprise.

A second impact of the Marxist and 'dependence' models was to promote inward-looking, rather than the outward-looking, strategies favoured by the 'four dragons'. The Lewis strategy was explicitly rejected by the Marxist and New World schools, which both prescribed autarchic economic policies and limited trade with the outside world. Vain attempts were made, especially in Guyana and Jamaica, to maximize the use of local materials, to alter consumption patterns and to practise other forms of 'self-reliance'.

It is conceivable that states as large as Russia and China, or developing countries as large as Brazil or Argentina, might contemplate self-reliant strategies. For CARICOM self-reliance was never really an option. Our resource base is too narrow and skewed to produce the range of products needed to sustain civilized life, and our markets far too small to support economic production of any but the most primitive goods and services. However, some Caribbean economists still regard 'backward and forward linkages' within individual CARICOM economies, and the exploitation of indigenous technologies and materials, as crucial strategies for economic development. Moreover, since most of the capital goods required for economic growth are not produced within CARICOM, we must either earn foreign exchange by exporting goods and services, or making foreign loans to obtain them. In any case, foreign exchange to repay external debt can only be obtained from future export earnings.

More surprisingly, the deleterious effects of closure of the economy for economic growth were not understood by our economists and policy makers. From the mid-70s onward I frequently put forward the open systems model as an alternative to the Marxist and 'dependence' paradigms. In my Mona address mentioned above I said:

> A casual reading of General Systems Theory, too, would have taught that closed systems do not grow; that only open systems grow through the continuous exchange of material and information with their environment. In fact, closed systems demonstrate a natural tendency towards the kinds of disorder which we see developing all around us in the Caribbean — also in keeping with the Second Law of Thermodynamics. The example of economic decline in Guyana, the country which most

assiduously pursued the strategy of closure, confirms the validity of the second law of Thermodynamics.[8]

The Managerial Imperative

The neglect of managerial issues in the region exacerbated the damaging effects of already flawed economic strategies. As Peter Drucker observes in *Management: Tasks, Responsibilities, Practices*, 'Economic and social development means above all management'.[9] Economists had rightly identified the establishment of modern institutions as a prerequisite of economic development in the Third World, but paid very little attention to the management of these institutions. From about the mid-1970s I had the temerity to suggest that management was a critical element in Caribbean economic development. In the 1975 paper quoted above, I spoke of the 'managerial imperative'. I argued that economic development required the diffusion of sound management practices throughout the entire economy — in government, in business, in hospitals, in schools, in churches and even in homes. I opposed nationalization, not so much on grounds of ideology, but because it led to larger and more complex organizations. This increased complexity, I argued, would place an intolerable strain on our already limited managerial resources.

The extensive degree of government ownership made matters even worse. CARICOM governments, without exception, found it impossible to separate political from operational considerations in the management of public enterprises and even in the administration of the public service. Political affiliation and ideological conviction weighed much more heavily in appointments to top managerial positions than professional training, experience and competence. As a consequence, public enterprises throughout the region piled up huge financial losses. Jamaica, and Trinidad and Tobago experienced chronic disruptions in their public services; Guyana, according to The *Economist*, descended into chaos.[10] Barbados and the LDCs were saved only by their limited excursion into state ownership. We in CARICOM have not understood that financial losses represent a destruction of capital and may be seen as 'negative investment'. Positive investment produces growth; negative investment leads to economic decline and a deterioration of living standards.

The most serious stumbling block to improved management in the public sector is the preoccupation of politicians with control over institutions within their responsibility. Only a small proportion of Caribbean politicians have any training or experience in corporate management. Many of them believe that political control is only possible by detailed oversight of the activities within their responsibility. In fact, to control everything is to control nothing! Control is achieved through the determination of objectives, the establishment of performance criteria, the feedback of operating results, and the correction of operating results which deviate significantly from performance criteria. CARICOM ministers should heed the words of Professor John Kenneth Galbraith:

> To subject the behaviours of the individual to the detailed surveillance of another is to obtain debased and inferior performance.... As with the individual personality, so with the corporate personality.[11]

Failure of Integration Movement

Another effect of those two fatal paradigms was to disrupt progress towards regional integration. Under the guise of 'ideological pluralism', Guyana placed much greater emphasis on relations with the Socialist bloc, drawing closer diplomatically to Moscow, Peking and Havana than to Port-of-Spain and Bridgetown, capitals from which she obtained far more subsidies than from the entire Eastern bloc. Michael Manley, distracted by the campaign of the Non-Aligned Movement for an illusory new international economic order, paid much more attention to

Dr Fidel Castro than to Dr Eric Williams. Moreover, the response of the MDCs, Barbados excepted, to balance of payments difficulties, was resort to fierce protectionist measures and beggar-thy-neighbour currency devaluations, leading to the collapse of the CARICOM Multilateral Clearing Facility and to a sharp contraction of intra-regional trade.

The most serious consequence of the setback to regional integration was our inability to develop regional enterprises with the critical mass required to compete in the international marketplace. Whereas Japanese firms merge regularly with American, or German with British, Guyana's insistence on state ownership prevented investment of Trinidadian petrodollars in their economy, and alien land-holding legislation limited CARICOM investment in the Trinidad and Tobago economy. The recent proposals for the integration of CARICOM stock markets have highlighted the numerous obstacles to the movement of capital, goods, enterprise and skills within the region. In his book, *A Grand Strategy for the West*, former German Chancellor Helmut Schmidt argues that West Germany, France and the UK are too small to be economically viable in the long run.[12] Why do CARICOM states think that they are large enough to go it alone?

Getting Back on Track

Redefinition of Development

The road to economic recovery for CARICOM will be long and hard. The first order of business is for us to arrive at a definition of economic development that is realistic and practical. In its most fundamental formulation, economic development describes the process by which more and more citizens are enabled to carry out more and more productive activities in an increasingly effective manner. This requires the multiplication of decision-making centres, in contrast to the concentration of authority that now characterizes economic decision-making within CARICOM. This is precisely what Mr Gorbachev is attempting with his 'perestroika', and what Deng Xiaoping was seeking up to the events of Tiananmen Square.

Role of Government

We need as well to redefine the role of government in economic development. Here the insights of Peter Drucker are most enlightening:

> For almost two centuries, we hotly discussed what government should do. We almost never asked what government can do. Now increasingly the limits and functions of government will be the issue. And government is no longer, as political and social theory still postulate, the only power centre. In the developed countries both society and polity have become pluralist again, in startling reversal of the trends that prevailed since the end of the Middle Ages.[13]

He goes on to say:

> We now understand why there are some things government, by its very essence, cannot do. And even for the things government can do, conditions must be right. A government activity can work only if it is a monopoly. It cannot function if there are other ways to do the job, that is, if there is competition. The post office in the nineteenth century was a true monopoly. And so were the railroads. There were no other ways of sending information or of moving freight and people over land. But as soon as there are alternative ways to provide the same service, government flounders.[14]

The Caribbean experience accurately reflects Dr Drucker's contention.

Need for Decentralization

Recent developments in the international economy also suggest that CARICOM governments should alter their economic and political strategies. Many science-based technological advances are now being incorporated into the production and service sectors of advanced industrial economies — automation, biotechnology, computers, fibre-optics, ceramics, microelectronics, robotics, and telecommunications. A task force set up by the Rockefeller Foundation describes the implications of these developments for developing countries as 'not a welcome view of the future'. I quote from a commentary on the report of the task force:

> It is even possible that as a result of advances taking place in the research laboratories of the richer countries, the poorer countries could lose the few comparative advantages in the world economy that they now enjoy. Automation could reduce the need for natural resources found in developing countries: genetic engineering in agriculture could significantly alter global markets for the products of tropical farms and plantations.[15]

I submit that it is entirely beyond the capacity of the bureaucratic apparatus of CARICOM governments to respond effectively to these variegated, complex and dynamic developments in our global environment. There is a theorem in General Systems Theory which states: 'Only variety can regulate variety.' Our responses, then, to these multiple challenges must emanate not from a monolithic central authority, but must be diffused throughout our society. Decentralization, not centralization, must be the order of the day.

What Government Can Do

The modified role of the state within CARICOM, then, must be to promote the multiplication of private economic activities and rapidly withdraw from those activities which it cannot do well, or which can more effectively be carried out by private economic units. (I recently had to advise a CARICOM minister of housing that neither his government nor any LDC government could build houses for all its citizens.) We are fortunate that the IMF conditionalities now in vogue do push CARICOM MDCs towards privatization of public sector enterprises. Those not under IMF direction should follow suit!

CARICOM governments can do much to establish a supportive macroeconomic framework for the multiplication of private enterprises. This implies appropriate tax and monetary policies, including moderate levels of interest rates. Above all, government must do all it can to keep its foreign payments in balance and so ensure an adequate supply of foreign exchange to fuel economic development. An administration that fails to do so will before long surrender control over its economy to the IMF and other foreign creditors. I can think of few other, more humiliating and unfortunate national fate.

The Culture of Management

CARICOM governments could do much to enhance the culture of management in the region by themselves adopting modern management practices in the conduct of public enterprise and civil service operations. There is now enough accumulated management expertise in the region to carry out the necessary reforms. Ministers in one or two CARICOM LDCs have already participated in management seminars organized by the Caribbean Centre for Administration Development (CARICAD). Cabinets of the MDCs might do likewise. They might then be induced to halt the practice of sending the most trivial matters to cabinet for decision, and so would dramatically increase the national productivity.

Re-integration of CARICOM

The most urgent item on the agenda is the reintegration of CARICOM and the resumption of the movement towards the original goal of a regional common market. Encouraging commitments have already been made to remove restrictions on intraregional trade. These should be followed by a freeing up of the movement of capital, skills and enterprise within the region. Trinidad and Tobago should be persuaded to re-amend its alien land-holding legislation so as to permit the realization of the CARICOM enterprise regime. These would promote the development of region-wide corporations capable of competing in the international market. Such action by the Trinidad & Tobago government would also remove an important obstacle to the establishment of a regional stock exchange on which CARICOM governments have reached agreement in principle. CARICOM might also follow the example of the European Common Market and set a date for the establishment of a monetary union for CARICOM.

To demonstrate their seriousness about the regional integration movement, CARICOM governments should provide adequate funding for their secretariat. The headquarters of the secretariat might be removed from Georgetown; otherwise substantial investment should be made in new offices that reflected the importance of the institution, and a commitment to the future of the regional integration movement.

Finally, the trend towards fragmentation of the University of the West Indies should be reversed as a matter of the greatest urgency. Presently the quality of the services on each campus reflects the economic fortunes of the respective government, making nigh impossible the establishment of institutional goals and programmes. It should be clear by now that governments which were prosperous in the 1970s can very well be poor in the 1980s, and those which were poor in the 1980s can be rich in the

1990s. With centralized funding of the entire university system, individual governments would contribute according to their ability, and individual campuses receive resources according to their need. The university system is only as strong as the weakest campus.

Meanwhile, Guyana should be seduced or coerced into reintegration of the University of Guyana into the University of the West Indies. Neither Trinidad and Tobago, with a population of 1.2 million and a per capita income of US$4,000, nor Guyana, with a population of 0.8 million and a per capita income of under US$400, can support a bona fide university.

The prognosis for mankind in the decade of the 90s is undoubtedly more favourable than it was for the 70s and the 80s. The relaxation of East–West tensions will reduce the likelihood of nuclear war, and a growing perception of interdependence will promote cooperation in many areas of vital interests to us all — arms reduction, the environment, drugs, health, et cetera.

It is not clear, however, that the 1990s will be more favourable for us in the Caribbean. The World Economy will be increasingly characterized by large blocs — the European Common Market after 1992, the US–Canada Free Trade Area, possibly with Mexico added, the Soviet Union, China, and the Pacific basin under the tutelage of Japan. In such a world, the small, developing nation states of CARICOM may very well fall between the cracks. To survive we must jettison the outworn dogmas and slogans of the past, and face up to the new realities of the 1990s. We will have to act quickly since we are already two decades behind.

Submitted to *Caribbean Affairs*, Port-of-Spain, Trinidad, for publication in the special December 1989 issue

Notes

1. Courtney N. Blackman, *The Practice of Persuasion* (Bridgetown: The Cedar Press, 1982), 2.

2. Clive Y. Thomas, *The Poor and the Powerless* (New York: Monthly Review Press, 1988), 200.

3. Norman Girvan, Review article, 'C.Y. Thomas and the Poor and the Powerless: The Limitations of Conventional Radicalism', *Social and Economic Studies* 37, no.4 (December 1988): 262–63.

4. Courtney N. Blackman, 'The Economic Development of Small Countries: A Managerial Approach', in *Contemporary International Relations of the Caribbean*, ed., Basil Ince (St. Augustine, Trinidad and Tobago: University of the West Indies, 1979).

5. Courtney N. Blackman, *The Practice of Persuasion*, 6.

6. Ibid., 3.

7. Peter F. Drucker, *The New Realities* (New York: Harper & Row, 1989), 141–42.

8. Courtney N. Blackman, *The Practice of Persuasion*, 4.

9. Peter F. Drucker, *Management: Tasks, Responsibilities, Practices* (New York: Harper & Row, 1973), 13.

10. *Economist*, August 22, 1987, p.15.

11. John Kenneth Galbraith, *Economic Development* (Boston: Houghton Mifflin, 1964), 89.

12. Helmut Schmidt, *A Grand Strategy for the West* (New Haven: Yale University Press, 1985).

13. Peter Drucker, *The New Realities*, 59.

14. Ibid., 63.

15. 'Rockefeller Foundation in the Developing World' (Rockefeller Foundation, New York, 1986).

2

A SYSTEMS APPROACH TO PLANNING MODELS FOR SMALL DEPENDENT ECONOMIES

WITH SPECIAL REFERENCE TO THE CARIBBEAN

The decade of the 1950s saw the flowering of Caribbean novelists George Lamming of Barbados, Vidia Naipaul and Samuel Selvon of Trinidad and Tobago, Jan Carew of Guyana, John Hearne and Vic Reid of Jamaica, and many others. In a similar fashion the Sixties witnessed the emergence of a new school of Caribbean political economists, who are fast becoming household names in the region. There have been, among others, William Demas and Lloyd Best of Trinidad and Tobago, Alister McIntyre of Grenada, Clive Thomas and Havelock Brewster of Guyana, and George Beckford and Norman Girvan of Jamaica.[1] Writing mainly in the *New World Quarterly*, they were the first scholars to address economic problems from a distinctly Caribbean point of view. Sir Arthur Lewis had, of course, done excellent work on regional problems in the 1950s, but his approach has always been that of a classical economist.

The New World economists focused on the 'dependence' syndrome as the most important feature of Caribbean political economy and blamed it on the colonial experience — an experience they see as essentially replicated by the current development policy of 'industrialization by invitation'. For them the plantation is the villain of the piece, and their policy prescriptions are calculated to undo the effects of the plantation system.

However, the economists of the New World Group have gone off in different directions. Demas and McIntyre have focused on the obstacles to economic development posed by the small size of Caribbean territories, and have emphasized the need for economic integration. They have probably oversold integration as a source of economic growth; at least, they may not have emphasized that the benefits of integration are slow of realization. At any rate, the policies they proposed were always tempered by pragmatism. Girvan and Beckford have been mainly concerned with reducing the dependence of the Caribbean territories on the outside world. They are bent on closing the system, and are strong proponents of the 'ownership and control' of the natural resources of the region. Rabid enemies of the multinational corporation, their stance may be described as one of reactive nationalism and their prescription for economic development is a blend of autarchy and chauvinism.

In a certain sense, Clive Thomas has betrayed the New World School, which promised to view Caribbean problems from a decidedly Caribbean viewpoint. He offers the alien Marxist-Leninist model, and sees central planning and socialization of the economy as solutions to Caribbean economic problems. Both the emphasis of Girvan and Beckford on closure of the economy, as well as Thomas's insistence on central planning and the monolithic organization required for socialist production, reveal a continuing adherence to deterministic and mechanistic models of economic development.

Lloyd Best, perhaps the most fertile and creative New World mind, understands quite well that small size is a parameter of growth and not a variable. Moreover, he recognizes clearly the nature and the limitations of mechanistic economic models, and understands the need for a heuristic approach to economic planning. He rejects the Marxist-Leninist model as being both deterministic and undemocratic. The policies that he proposes may be described as a mild blend of nationalism and anarchism. Generally speaking, the practical contribution of the New World Group to regional economic development planning has been disappointing.[2]

The purpose of this paper is to formulate planning models for small dependent economies, like ours in the Caribbean, from the viewpoint of General Systems Theory. The main thesis of this paper is that the traditional (which includes the Marxist-Leninist) approach to economic planning, based on deterministic theories of economic growth, is certain to lead small dependent countries down false paths. Instead, economies, especially of small dependent countries, are seen as 'open systems' and implications for planning economic development in such economies are drawn from the application of General Systems Theory.

Section I comments on the paradoxes of development planning. Section II sets out the basic propositions of General Systems Theory. Section III examines the implications of General Systems Theory for the consideration of small size, while Section IV deals in similar fashion with issues of dependency. Section V presents in outline an integrated approach to planning models for small dependent economies. The paper concludes on a cautionary note.

Paradoxes of Economic Planning

The most interesting observation of economic planning is that the development of most First World countries occurred without its conscious use. Indeed, Adam Smith, the prophet of the first industrial revolution, taught that the unfettered working of the free market would generate the optimal level of economic activity. There was certainly no conscious economic planning in the United States, although the federal and state governments did make several fortunate interventions into the national economy. The construction of the Erie Canal, which opened up the grain producing Middle West, and the establishment of the land grant colleges, which gave the US its pre-eminence in agriculture, are but two striking examples. On the other hand, it is a moot point whether central planning has accelerated the growth of East European economies or hindered it. In the Soviet Union, central planning certainly appears to have performed unsatisfactorily in the agricultural sector.

The second paradox is that planning for development is much more difficult for small countries, which really need development, than for rich countries that sometimes have too much of it. Arthur Lewis points out that 'without a reasonably competent administrative machine, there is no basis for development planning.'[3] He also stresses the need for reliable statistics but, again, he warns: 'Even in countries which are rich in statistics, forecasts of the economy have usually turned out poorly. In poor countries the econometrician has to invent many of the crucial figures.' He suggests that it is only when economies reach a reasonably advanced state of development that sophisticated mathematical models become useful: 'India is certainly ready for an elaborate mathematical model; whereas in most of the simpler African economies such a model would do no good, and . . . might well do harm, by deflecting attention from the major task of evolving useful policies and institutions.'[4]

Third, the planning process itself poses problems which a country may find insuperable. And as Naomi Caiden and Aaron Wildavsky put it, planning may itself become a part of the decision making problem.[5] There is no certainty that the people best capable of planning will be made planners, and even if they are, that they will be able to persuade the decision makers to accept their criteria for project selection and their hierarchy of operational priorities. There is certainly some evidence in the Caribbean that the planning process, by introducing excessive centralization into the economic system, may very well make things worse than they were before. It was certainly fortunate for early Americans that they did not try to plan their economic development; the vast size of their country and the inadequate means of communication in the eighteenth and nineteenth centuries required a decentralized system of decision making, and this the market system provided!

Planning in small dependent economies is even more hazardous than in the general case. Small countries, by definition, must depend on export-propelled growth — hence the need to make judgments about markets in far away countries and developments over which they have not the slightest control. Dependence may further subject the poor country to the whims of decision makers in metropolitan countries.

The fourth paradox of conventional economic planning is that it omits particular consideration of what most development theorists consider the crucial variables of economic development, especially institutional and psychological aspects. This is specifically brought out in Lewis's discussion of the practical aspects of plans related to foreign trade, foreign aid, taxes and savings, inflation, etc. If he is right in his emphasis on improved administrative performance; if he is right in his observation that 'dynamism in economic affairs may spring from the same deep uncharted sources as activity in literature, painting, music, war or religion';[6] if he is right that sound policies are crucial, why then does not development planning concern itself more with how societies develop administrative capacity, creativity, and wisdom? Why isn't development planning more about the activation of these mainsprings and less about the re-arrangement of their perturbations?

But the above is not a case against planning, and certainly not a case against planning in small dependent economies. However, there is a distinct suggestion that small developing countries should understand the nature of the planning problem, the opportunities which are open to them, the constraints under which they labour, and the processes by which their economic systems may be driven to higher and higher levels of performance.

Planning Models for Open Systems

Most economic plans are stated, explicitly or implicitly, in terms of macroeconomic models. The economy is seen either in terms of national income components, such as consumption, investment, savings, government expenditure, imports and exports, or in terms of various sectors, such as mining, agriculture, services, manufacturing, etc. In either case a change in one variable or one sector is presumed to have a predictable effect upon other variables or sectors, and is therefore deterministic. The Cobb-Douglas growth model in which income is stated as a function of capital and labour ($Y=K^aL^b$), is one example of the first type of model; the Leontieff input-output model, which displays the interdependence of various sectors of the economy through a matrix representation, is a second. Economic growth models programmed into computers are the most elaborate and sophisticated type of these models. The attractiveness of such models is that they facilitate quantification and are relatively easy to manipulate. However, they do not accommodate the phenomena of organic and structural growth.

Kenneth Boulding identifies three different types of growth: simple growth, that is, the growth or decline of a single variable or quantity by accretion or depletion; population growth, in which growth is regarded as the excess of 'births' over 'deaths', and structural growth, 'in which the aggregate which "grows" consists of a complex structure of interrelated parts and in which the growth process involves change in the relation of the parts'. He continues:

> Thus in the growth of a living organism, or of an organization, as the whole grows, the form and the parts change: new organs develop, old organs decline, and there is frequently growth in complexity as well as in some overall magnitudes. Problems of structural growth seem to merge almost imperceptibly into the problems of structural change or development, so that frequently

26

what grows is not the overall size of the structure but the complexity or systematic nature of its parts. [7]

In growth models, then, analogies are properly drawn between economies and organisms, rather than mechanisms. Additions may be made to mechanisms, but they do not grow; only organisms, and by extension organizations and economies, can grow.

The failure of development economists reflects their neglect of the latest scientific advances, especially in the area of thermodynamics. Economists have always aspired to be as 'scientific' as physicists and so, maturing in the nineteenth century as it did, economics took on the mechanistic character of Newtonian physics. Modern physical sciences now perceive natural dynamic systems as organismic rather than mechanistic.

In remarking on this development, N. Jordan writes:

> Much of nineteenth century science shared the idea that all phenomena are ultimately reducible to a mechanical system consisting of unit elements and a push-pull connectivity between them. With the formulation and development of concepts such as the space-time gravitational field, the sub-atomic electronic field, or chemical equilibrium, this idea has been found to be, most probably, wrong. Natural dynamic systems seem to be organismic. One must almost perforce go along with the conclusion reached by Whitehead that all natural dynamic physical phenomena are organismic.[8]

The mechanistic view inclined economists to think of economies as 'closed' systems to which deterministic laws could be applied. Ludwig Von Bertalanffy, the father of modern General Systems Theory, was the first to draw a clear distinction between 'closed' and 'open' systems:

> Conventional physical theory was restricted to closed systems which do not exchange matter with their environment. But organisms are

open systems which maintain themselves by a continual import and export of matter which is built up and broken down.[9]

He goes on:

the concept of the organism as an open system is an essentially new construct in biology. Before its introduction, the explanation of biological order and organization was almost invariably in terms of static arrangement, of machine-like structures in the widest sense. The concept of the organism as a system in continuous flow is a different approach and the elucidation of the laws governing these flows may provide explanations for phenomena unaccountable by mechanistic models.[10]

The essential difference between closed and open biological or social systems is that whereas in the closed system a change in entropy will always be positive, that is, there will be a tendency towards maximum disorder; in the open system entropy can be arrested and may even be transformed into negative entropy — a process of more complete organization and ability to transform resources. As we have seen, this is possible because in open systems resources are continuously imported from an external environment.

Imports from the environment into the open system, and exports therefrom, may operate in such a way as to maintain the open system in a steady state. However, if growth is to take place, open systems must move in the direction of greater differentiation and a higher level of organization.

As Bertalanffy puts it:

In organic development and evolution, a transition towards states of higher order and differentiation seems to occur. The tendency toward increasing complication has been indicated as a primary characteristic of the living, as opposed to inanimate, nature.[11]

This phenomenon is also visible in human organizations. The organization of General Motors is far more elaborate and complex than the corner drugstore. And if the corner drugstore is to develop into a major pharmaceutical corporation, it too will be forced to adopt a more elaborate form of organization.

A final consideration in our discussion of open systems is the capacity of the open system to survive in a hostile environment. To do so, as F.E. Kast and J.E. Rosenweig explain, open systems must have two mechanisms which are often in conflict; namely, maintenance mechanisms and adaptive mechanisms.[12]

Maintenance mechanisms are essentially conservative and serve to prevent the system from changing so rapidly as to throw it out of balance. 'An open system,' Miller and Starr explain, 'appears to be goal-seeking, despite the lack of pervasive cerebral rationality behind it,' because 'an equilibrium exists among its component parts. Any disturbance of this equilibrium initiates compensating reactions which immediately lead to the establishment of a new equilibrium.'[13] Donald A. Schon also comments on the 'dynamic conservatism' of societies which induces resistance to change.[14]

Adaptive mechanisms enable the system to generate appropriate responses to external pressures and are necessary for maintaining the system in dynamic equilibrium with respect to its environment. The development of the adaptive mechanism usually requires an increase in the variety of the system's structure. W. Ross Ashby, in his general theory of adaptive systems, has enunciated a 'law of requisite variety', which states that the variety within a system must match the variety of its environment. Walter Buckley summarizes, 'Only variety can regulate variety.'[15]

In applying this principle to organizations, Buckley goes even further:

A requisite of sociocultural systems is the development and maintenance of a significant level of non-pathological deviance, manifest as a pool of alternate ideas and behaviours with respect to the traditional institutionalized ideologies and role behaviours. Rigidification of any given institutional structure must eventually lead to disruption or dissolution of society by way of internal upheaval or ineffectiveness against challenge.[16]

Of course, the analogy between organisms and economies is not complete. No matter how favourable their environment, organisms are destined by their genetic structure to die and give way to new organisms. Organizations, however, may survive indefinitely. Daniel Katz and Robert L. Kahn explain it in this way:

> Social structures are essentially contrived systems. They are made of men and are imperfect systems. They can come apart at the seams overnight, but they can also outlast by centuries the biological organisms which originally created them. The cement which holds them together is essentially psychological rather than biological. Social systems are anchored in the attitudes, perceptions, beliefs, motivations, habits and expectations of human beings.[17]

However, biological and economic systems share the characteristic that they both represent a number of interacting subsystems and can only be considered in a holistic or synergistic framework.

Once the basic analogy between economies and organisms is accepted, it is not difficult to identify characteristics common to both:

- Organisms are active: 'It is now recognized that the organism, even under constant external conditions, is not inert or resting, but constitutes an active system,' writes Buckley.[18] So does an economy.
- The future of organisms is apparently indeterminate, as Buckley again warns us, 'Today, we are not yet in a position to analyse the enormous complexity of an organism into its individual physiochemical processes and therefore we

cannot predict whether or not biological laws may ultimately be reduced to physical laws.'[19] The same may be said for economies.

+ The principle of 'equifinality' as observed in open systems may be seen to apply to economies as well, that is, the same goal may be reached from different starting points and along different paths.

+ Open systems have a tendency towards 'dynamic conservatism'. So do economies.

+ The processes of open systems are irreversible. The theory of open systems, according to Bertalanffy, is an important generalization of thermodynamics, which essentially is the study of irreversible phenomena.[20]

+ A closed system will tend towards entropy, i.e. increasing disorder, whereas entropy in an open system can be arrested and a higher state of organization reached. Open systems offset entropy by continually importing material, energy and information, transforming them and redistributing them to the environment.

+ Growth in open systems requires the elaboration and increased complication in organization.

+ The variety in an open system must increase in proportion to the variety in the environment if the system is to survive.

Size and the Systems Approach

Until Schumacher, economists had been mostly concerned about the economies of large scale and about market size. They apparently had overlooked the existence of economies of small scale, as well as the diseconomies of large scale. This preoccupation with large size has been inherited by modern development economists, some of whom have come to believe that small countries will naturally find economic development more difficult than large ones. This attitude is incredible when we consider that some large countries, such as India and Zaire, are very poor while some small countries, such as Switzerland and Luxembourg, are quite rich. In his superb work, *Small is Beautiful,* E.F. Schumacher has convincingly exposed the economic, social and cultural ravages of large-scale operations.[21]

To a General Systems theorist the emphasis on size is relatively unimportant. The important thing about a system is its capacity to carry out the function for which it was designed and, especially in the case of open systems, its ability to cope with the environment. To say that the small size of an economy prevents its development is very much like saying that the small size of a hen's egg prevents the chick from developing into an ostrich. The chick's growth is constrained not so much by the size of the egg as by the genetic code which determines that it will grow up to be a hen and not an ostrich. Of course, economies, being contrived systems, are even less constrained than natural systems, since their 'genes' are unstable, and participants in the system, by altering technologies, philosophies and organizational methods, can, in a manner of speaking, produce genetic mutations which enable the social organization to survive in changing circumstances.

Small size is also seen as an especial constraint on the natural resource base, with countries such as Kuwait treated as exceptions to the rule. But again, some countries with few natural resources, like Japan and, even more remarkably, tiny Singapore, have become two of the richest countries in the world. The emphasis on size and resource base is even more surprising, since growth theorists over the past three decades have increasingly come to view human and institutional factors as by far the most important variables in economic development. As Kenneth Boulding observes:

It is not the physical resources of a society which determine the course of economic development ... it is what lies in the minds of men that determines, for the most part, whether a society shall grow in the productive power.[22]

Of course, the potential for development of the human mind is quite fantastic, if not infinite. I have often reflected on the tremendous possibilities for economic growth if an Archimedes, a Benjamin Franklin and a Leonardo Da Vinci should simultaneously take up residence in my native land.

Once it is conceded that economic growth depends on the intellectual rather than the physical resource, the size of an economy can only be viewed as a parameter of growth and not a variable. Barbados's size determines not so much its growth capacity, as the nature and direction of its development. It will never be a major producer of jumbo jets, but it could very well develop into a producer of high technology goods! Faced with small economies then, the General Systems theorist looks instead for the special advantages of small size and creatively exploits any opportunities that circumstances permit.

To begin with, small economies are more manageable than large ones. This is because size largely determines complexity, and complexity increases the problems of management. As Peter Drucker reminds us:

> In social organizations growth in size soon requires disproportionate increase in complexity and more and more specialized organs. Soon organs have to be developed that take care of the "inside", that is, organs that inform and direct the increasing mass and "feedback" to it from the increasingly remote outside and results of its own "inside" activities. The larger any body, physical or social, becomes, the more its energy will be needed to keep the "inside", that is, its own mechanisms, alive and functioning.[23]

Drucker further explains that beyond a certain size some operations are, in fact, unmanageable. 'The United States Department of Defence,' he observes, 'is so big that it defies control', and hospitals beyond 4,000 beds or so 'are clearly too big for effective management and decent patient care'.[24] By choosing its activities carefully, a small country may be even more efficient than large ones and, as the Swiss and the Swedes so clearly have demonstrated, may achieve even higher standards of living than much larger and better endowed nations.

Above all, small countries are capable of greater flexibility than large ones. The limitation of size itself guarantees that such vast resources cannot be sunk in a particular activity as to inhibit a shift to new activities. In the US today the tremendous investment sunk into oil-burning energy plants renders the development of a sensible energy policy horrendously difficult. It will be easier for Barbados to make that adjustment whenever the decision is made.

Perhaps the major problem facing a small system is the problem of survival in a hostile environment. This will depend on the effectiveness of its adaptive mechanisms. In the case of social organizations, this requires the development of social techniques for dealing with the natural, as well as the man-made, environment. In either case an effective feedback mechanism is required to provide accurate and timely information about likely external developments. Secondly, the society's capacity for learning must be developed in order to generate the aptitude for responding to threats from the outside.

As far as the man-made environment is concerned, the society will have to develop the transactional skills to handle conflicts with outside organizations. Weak adversaries may be overwhelmed and accommodation reached with stronger adversaries. In cases where the cost of accommodation is intolerable, alliances may be formed with other systems to repel a strong opponent. In extreme cases, a small system may integrate itself in a larger system to ensure its survival. The cost of such a strategy is the extinction of the system as a distinct unit, and rarely in history have human societies willingly taken this step. To unite with other systems is to sacrifice the flexibility of small systems. This is why political federation, or even economic integration, has proven so difficult in the Caribbean.

From the General Systems viewpoint, the assumption by Caribbean economists that economic integration necessarily leads to economic growth merely reflects adherence to a mechanistic model, which treats the individual islands as if they were inert sections to be fitted together into a complete structure. In fact, they are active organisms, which must learn to cooperate effectively. They may learn or they may not! There are certainly areas in which the various islands may find it useful to cooperate. A successful experience of cooperation provides the incentive for further cooperation, while each failure promotes disintegration. Regional cooperation is essentially a learning process and, for that reason, indeterminate and uncertain of success.

Dependence and the Systems Approach

According to the literature on 'dependence', Caribbean territories are dependent economies par excellence. There is foreign ownership and management of many major industries; the islands depend upon preferential prices for their agricultural goods, and import a major proportion of their essential foodstuffs. New World economists are convinced that structural transformation of the economies is impossible unless the pattern of dependence is altered.

The most articulate proponent of the dependence thesis is found in George Beckford's *Persistent Poverty*. He writes:

> The main thesis of this book is that development possibilities in all countries are determined chiefly by institutional factors that ultimately influence the more proximate growth variables, such as resources, capital accumulation, technological change, and human capital. In the plantation economies of the world these institutional factors derive their flavour from the plantation.... The analysis so far in this study suggests that, on balance, the underdevelopment biases tend to outweigh the development impact, and this explains

the equilibrium of underdevelopment that characterizes all plantation economies of the world at present.[25]

Beckford's solution to the problem of underdevelopment is the destruction of the plantation: 'To put the matter rather bluntly, the plantation system must be destroyed if the people of the plantation society are to secure economic, political and psychological advancement.'[26]

He goes on: 'Destroying the system involves revolutionary change in the institutional structure; that is, the social, economic and political arrangements. It is possible to release the creative energies of people once they have a stake and have confidence in themselves.'[27]

Instinctively, I am reluctant to attribute so complex a phenomenon as under-development to the single institution of the plantation. But even if the thesis is accepted, it requires a remarkable act of faith to be convinced that the destruction of the plantation would 'release the creative energies of people' and lead inevitably to development. It is very much as if a physicist carried out a nuclear experiment in the faith that the chain reaction produced would somehow work to the benefit of those in the immediate vicinity!

Beckford's insistence on the destruction of the plantation betrays an allegiance to the mechanistic model — to a pull-push type of operation, that is, to achieve the opposite result, you simply push the lever in the alternate direction. Although he himself frequently describes the plantation system as an open system, he does not understand the irreversibility of dynamic processes in open systems, that is, that what is done is done; so that we must always start from where we are. In the words of Bertalanffy, 'We live in a world in which time is irreversible and in which causes always precede effects.'[28] Moreover, the plantation system has over the years become so intricately intermeshed with other subsystems of the economy that its destruction must have far-reaching, unpredictable and possibly deleterious effects upon the rest of the society.

There is, in fact, a precedent for the root-and-branch destruction of the plantation system, namely the experience of Haiti. In that unfortunate country, the disruption of plantation agriculture, and the fragmentation of sugar lands, led to economic collapse. It may well be true that the widespread artistic expression visible in Haiti today was released by the destruction of the plantation; it is also true that Haiti remains one of the poorest countries in the world.

Beckford's answer to openness in the plantation is closure. 'The plantation economy,' he argues, 'is far too open for development to take place, and measures to bring about some degree of closure must be included in the bag of policy instruments.' Again, he displays an unfamiliarity with complex systems. In fact, closed systems do not grow, nor do closed economies. Only open systems grow by importing low entropy from the environment, applying work to it and then releasing high entropy into the environment.[29]

Most New World economists have a great partiality for nationalization and state control. Pluralism is seen as an impediment to the execution of centralized planning. In fact, the effect of state control is to reduce the variety of the open system and hence its adaptability to a variegated environment. The Marxist-Leninist approach of Clive Thomas would be even more counter-productive since the political structures associated with that ideology invariably suppress deviant opinion and rigidify administrative structures. This dangerously reduces the capacity of the system to respond to a changing environment. It is not surprising that the most successful small nations of the world, like Switzerland and Holland, are among the most tolerant of deviant opinion and minority groups.

A Systems Approach to Planning

A planning model should reflect the crucial characteristics of the system which it purports to represent. We have seen that deterministic models do not reflect the organismic aspects of economics, as do open systems, whose survival depends on their capacity to adapt to a varied and changing environment. Conceivably, a large economy like the United States, with a low ratio of external trade to GDP, may be regarded as relatively closed. Moreover, because of America's preponderant power shocks from the environment may, for all practical purposes, be treated as being of a stochastic nature. In both respects, therefore, such deterministic models may be quite useful in the short run. However, a deterministic-stochastic model of the United States would not deal adequately with the problem of long-term structural growth.

The management of small open systems then requires the application of heuristic models. Our imperfect comprehension of such systems, the 'aliveness' which endows them with a dynamic conservatism, and the instability of their environment, makes the achievement of optimality most unlikely. Our normal aspiration must be to do better tomorrow than we did today. If we are lucky, we may occasionally achieve a quantum leap of progress. In Herbert Simon's terms, we must seek to 'satisfice' rather than optimise. It is in this spirit that we present the barest outlines of an integrated systems approach to planning in small developing countries.

West Churchman outlines five basic aspects of the systems approach:[30]

- The total system of objectives and, more specifically, the performance measures of the whole system;
- the system's environment; the fixed constraints;

- the resources of the system;
- the components of the system; that is, goals and measures of performance; and
- the management of the system.

This outline will provide the framework within which we may explicitly develop a systems approach to development planning.

Objectives and Performance Measures

Once the economy is seen in terms of the interaction of a number of 'live' sub-systems with frequently conflicting goals, there can be no single objective function. However, we may enumerate the various social states which we would like to alter. We might, for example, wish to improve the average life expectancy of the population, to increase the literacy rate, to modernize the transportation system, etc. In many cases we may be able to assign quantitative measures; sometimes the measures of performance will have to be stated in qualitative terms. Above all, we should not take too seriously quantitative measures of the system's global performance, such as national income, gross domestic product and the like. These various measures of performance will at all times be under review. Only experience will tell us what contradictions exist between the respective targets of the sub-systems.

The planner must try to obtain a resolution of conflicts among the various decision centres in the society. In so doing it might be useful to keep in mind the Pareto criterion — that any change which harms no one and which makes some people better off (in their own estimation) may be considered as an improvement. Unfortunately some form of bargaining process among various interest groups is needed to settle on other criteria for the purpose of conflict resolution.

Environmental Constraints

The major environmental constraints of small dependent economies are small size and extensive relationships with foreign countries. Small size usually implies a narrow resource base and small-scale production, and a high proportion of imports from, and exports to, the rest of the world. In some cases, the constraint of size may be modified by cooperation with other small countries, as we are trying to do in the Caribbean. It must be kept in mind, however, that cooperation is a difficult exercise, and that the constraint of size can only be modified over the very long run, if ever at all.

A greater degree of self-sufficiency may, of course, relax the constraints of dependency. Indeed, it is a highly recommended policy in the Caribbean, especially in the area of garden products. However, be warned that the removal of constraints is costly and time-consuming. The planner must therefore satisfy himself that costs of modifying the constraint does not exceed the returns. Above all, it is most important psychologically that constraints are not seen as impediments. Indeed, they serve the very useful purpose of helping us to focus on our opportunities.

Resources

'I was driving around your lovely island yesterday,' a visiting international civil servant once said to me, 'and saw your two major resources — the sugar cane fields and your beaches.' I protested that these were not really our most important resources, since several other islands had equally fine beaches and many countries had even more extensive sugar cane lands.

In fact, it is not at all useful for small countries to think of natural endowments as their resources, but rather as a part of their environment. Tourists will not come to Barbados if there is no safe airport or if the natives are hostile. The true resources of a country, especially of a small country, are those controllable attributes that contribute to the functioning of the various sub-systems or enable inputs from the environment to be transformed into value.

In addition to natural resources, a meaningful list would include human, historical, cultural and ecological resources. Of these, the human resource is, naturally, the most important and potentially the most productive. It subsumes courage, intellect, perseverance, creativity and the instinct for survival. Above all, it provides the capacity to manage.

The historical resources of a country cover those relationships with other countries which give it a comparative advantage in any field. For example, the fact that Barbados was once British gives it an advantage in a world which is largely English speaking. This attribute must be viewed as a resource rather than a constraint, since Barbadians could willfully decide to teach creole Barbadian in school, and in time diminish the population's facility with spoken English. Our historical association with the Americans has also been most profitable, but it could easily be dissipated if Barbadians broke off diplomatic relations with the United States.

The cultural resource gives a people the capacity to survive in their peculiar environment. It is their accumulated collective experience, their stock of knowledge of how to survive. It makes some nations better able to accomplish some things than others. It is maintained through historical recollection and communication from one generation to the next. It is enriched by appropriate contacts with foreign countries. It can be contaminated by exploitative pressures from abroad.

We would hardly have mentioned the ecological resource before the industrial revolution. Until man began the ruthless exploitation of the world's natural resources, the ecological balance was taken for granted. Indeed, the ecological balance of nature was then viewed as a part of the environment. It must now be treated as a resource, since its disturbance could lead to massive economic losses to the society.

Components

The components are activities which cause the total system to function. A minimal list of sub-systems would include systems maintenance, education, politics, administration and diplomacy, especially in the case of dependent economies. The systems maintenance activity covers the routine tasks of seeing that basic needs are met. These would include medical services, transportation services, distribution services, legal systems, housing, water, and any other tasks needed to ensure the physical survival of the society.

Obvious educational activities are systems for the socialization of children, and the inculcation of attitudes needed to ensure the survival of the nation. The educational component would also include technical and professional education for the effective exploitation of the resources of the community, as well as various forms of adult education for enhancing the human resource.

The crucial function of the educational component is to produce in the various sub-systems a strong inclination towards 'learning'. We have observed the tendency of open systems towards dynamic conservatism. In fact, this tendency accounts for many of the problems of development planning. Dynamic conservatism is countered only by developing in the system the capacity to learn, firstly, that some changes are desirable, and secondly, which changes would be most advantageous.

The political component provides the means for central policy makers to establish goals for the global system, and secure satisfactory compliance on established policies from the various sub-systems. It provides what Boulding calls the 'integrative element' in the system. Broadly speaking, it would include ethical and religious norms, as well as legal constitutional arrangements for governing the society. In short, the political component provides the means by which the linkages between various sub-systems are preserved.

The administrative component subsumes the attitudes, techniques and traditions of regulating the various activities of society. It includes the protocols and procedures for directing groups of workers. This is a crucial component, since it impinges on the efficiency of all other components in the economy.

Extensive contacts with foreigners require the highest development of the society's diplomatic skills. Newspapers in the Caribbean often publish letters to the editor complaining of an excessive number of foreign embassies and representative offices abroad. Such correspondence reflects a widespread misunderstanding of the situation of small countries. It is small nations that need a superb diplomatic corps; they cannot, as is the custom in the United States, 'sell' diplomatic posts to the highest bidder. Except for its representatives to Russia and China, indifferent American representation abroad might be a source of embarrassment, but never the cause of disaster. For Barbados, any bad diplomat can cause irreparable damage.

Management

Management is especially important in small dependent economies since the margin for error is usually slimmer than in large countries. A miscalculation which might cause minor inconvenience for the United States could be disastrous for Barbados. Three main factors shape the broad managerial strategies in small dependent economies: complexity of open systems, small size, and extensive interaction with external entities. It is taken for granted that the planners know the fundamental factors of economic growth; namely, that investment must increase as a significant proportion of gross national product.

The crucial managerial strategy for complex open systems must be the maximum decentralization of authority compatible with the achievement of global objectives. Since we cannot utilize deterministic models in our consideration of such systems, it follows that there can be no all-powerful czar directing the activities of the various sub-systems in minute detail. As each sub-system is 'alive' and possesses a 'personality' of its own, it will, like the individual, react negatively to authoritarian interference and perform below its true potential. John Kenneth Galbraith, in making the same point in respect of the modern industrial corporation, puts it this way:

> The individual or natural personality realizes itself only under conditions of liberty. To subject the behaviours of the individual to the detailed surveillance of another is to obtain debased and inferior performance. As with the individual personality, so with corporate personality.[31]

The functions of the planner, then, in an open system must be that of definition of desirable objectives, specification of targets and their articulation to the various sub-systems. His is also a task of political persuasion and, if absolutely necessary, the development of coercive measures to induce maximum co-operation between the sub-systems.

A necessary condition for successful planning is a thorough understanding of the essential features of each sub-system. An intimate 'feel' for the working of the system in question will enable the planner to devise the techniques best suited for its manipulation.

The efficiency deriving from a deep understanding of the system might very well be impressed upon Third World countries intent on 'ownership and control' of their natural resources. An understanding of the workings of a multinational corporation might suggest strategies for their control far less costly and dangerous than outright nationalization. At any rate, ownership without understanding does not produce effective control.

The basic art of managing small systems is to exploit the economies of small scale. The major advantage of small scale is flexibility; that is, the ability to reallocate resources rapidly in the face of changing circumstances. Firstly, this requires that the planners be extremely well informed of what is going on in the outside world so that the system is seldom surprised by foreign developments. In Systems Analysis we speak of 'feedback'. Secondly, the small country must develop the capacity for swift decision-making so that timely adjustment may be made in changing circumstances. Thirdly, opportunities must be constantly sought out and aggressively pursued. The planners in small economies must behave very much like guerillas seeking targets of opportunity, and moving swiftly once the essential advantage of a situation has been exhausted.

We have already noted that the chief decision makers of small dependent countries need to develop considerable powers of diplomacy. The examples of Switzerland and Finland seem particularly instructive. For small countries dogmatism, sloganeering and chauvinism are especially counter-productive. There must be a rigorous definition of enduring interests, and a recognition that both friends and enemies are temporary.

Indeed, it is useful for small countries to view the world in terms of Game Theory, in which all other nations are seen as opposing players. However, small countries must seek to play positive-sum games, rather than zero-sum games, with other countries, and must studiously avoid negative-sum games with bigger countries. Grievous losses have been sustained by Caribbean nations by their refusal to accept this simple fact of life.

Finally, small dependent countries, like all other countries, must try to arrange that the wisest people in society make the most important decisions. There is no known means of ensuring this situation.

Conclusion

The heuristic approach of General Systems Analysis does not guarantee clean solutions to problems. Even if we achieved the anticipated results, these would constitute only partial and temporary solutions. At best, they would present us with a whole new range of problems. Progress, in essence, is the replacement of old problems by new. (This at least makes life more interesting). Churchman admirably captures the spirit of the systems approach:

> What is in the nature of systems is a continuing perception and deception, a continuing reviewing of the world, of the whole system, and of its components. The essence of the systems approach, therefore, is confusion as well as enlightenment. The two are inseparable aspects of human living.[32]

For this reason, Leonard Sayles concludes that 'only managers who can deal with uncertainty, with ambiguity, and with battles that are never won but only fought well can hope to succeed.'[33]

Originally published in *Planificacion y Desarrollo en Paises Pequenos*, ed. Jose J. Villamil (Buenos Aires, Argentina: Ediciones SIAP, 1979)

Notes

1. For a sample of New World literature, see Norman Girvan and Owen Jefferson, eds., *Readings in the Political Economy of the Caribbean* (New World Group Ltd, 1971).

2. Lloyd Best's policy proposals are frequently carried in *Tapia*, a weekly newspaper published in Trinidad and Tobago.

3. W. Arthur Lewis, *Development Planning* (London: George Allen & Unwin, 1966), 20–21.

4. Ibid., 21.

5. Naomi Caiden and Aaron Wildavsky, *Planning and Budgeting in Poor Countries* (New York: John Wiley and Sons, 1974), 167–203.

6. W. Arthur Lewis, *Development Planning*, 23.

7. Kenneth Boulding, 'Towards a General Theory of Growth', in *Beyond Economics* (Ann Arbor: University of Michigan Press, 1970), 64–65.

8. N. Jordan, 'Some Thinking about System', in *Systems Thinking*, ed. E.E. Emery (Middlesex, England: Penguin Books Ltd, 1981), 29.

9. Ludwig Von Bertalanffy, *Perspectives on General System Theory* (New York: George Brazilier Inc, 1975), 109.

10. Ibid., 136.

11. Ludwig Von Bertalanffy, 'The Theory of Open Systems in Physics and Biology', *Science* (January 13, 1950): 26.

12. F.B. Kast and J.E. Rosenweig, 'The Modern View: A Systems Approach', in *Systems Behaviour*, eds. John Beishon and Geoff Peters (London: Harper and Row, 1972), 22S.

13. David W. Miller and Marin K. Starr, *Executive Decisions and Operations Research*, (Englewood Cliffs,, NJ:, Prentice-Hall Inc, 1969), 43.

14. Donald A. Schon, *Beyond the Stable State* (New York: W.W. Norton & Company, Inc), especially pp. 31–60.

15. As quoted by Walter Buckley in 'Society as a Complex Adaptive System', *Systems Behaviour*, 159.

16. Ibid., 159.

17. Daniel Katz and Robert L. Kahn, as quoted by F.B. Kast and J.E. Rosenweig, 'The Modern View', 20.

18. As quoted by Walter Buckley in 'Society as a Complex Adaptive System', in *Systems Behaviour*, 159.

19. Ibid., 101.

20. Bertalanffy, 'General Systems Theory – A Critical Approach', in *Systems Behaviour*, 40.

21. Ernst F. Schumacher, *Small is Beautiful* (New York: Harper & Row, 1973).

22. Kenneth Boulding, 'Towards a General Theory of Growth', 180.

23. Peter F. Drucker, *Management* (New York: Harper & Row, 1973), 639.

24. Ibid.

25. George L. Beckford, *Persistent Poverty* (New York: Oxford University Press, 1972), 183.

26. Ibid., 215.

27. Ibid., 215.

28. Ludwig Bertalanffy, *Perspectives on General Systems Theory*, 129.

29. George L. Beckford, *Persistent Poverty*, 221.

30. C. West Churchman, *The Systems Approach* (New York: Dell Publishing Co Inc, 1968), 29–30.

31. John Kenneth Galbraith, *Economic Development* (Boston: Houghton Mifflin Co, 1964).

32. C. West Churchman, *The Systems Approach*, 231–2.

33. Leonard Sayles, *Managerial Behaviour* (New York: McGraw-Hill Book Co, 1964), 258–59.

3

THE ECONOMIC MANAGEMENT
OF SMALL ISLAND
DEVELOPING COUNTRIES

A hazard of high office in small island developing countries (IDCs) is exposure to unsolicited and patronizing advice of visitors from big countries, especially officials from international financial institutions like the IMF and World Bank. Such advice usually reflects the prevailing economic fad in the major industrial nations that determine IMF/World Bank ideology. This year the panacea is privatization; a little earlier it was positive real interest rates; before that it was currency devaluation. Completing the cycle during the Carter administration was the establishment of public investment units.

A common feature of this advice is failure to take into account the characteristics of small island states. Indeed, a visiting economist once suggested to me that there were no fundamental differences between the economies of Barbados and Brazil! Intuitively, there must be something wrong with this approach. After all, a separate discipline of paediatrics has evolved in medicine for the treatment of the young; children are not regarded simply as small-scale versions of adults.

My topic derives from a consulting assignment which I carried out a few years ago for the Caribbean Community (CARICOM). I was asked to prepare a position paper justifying special financial aid from donor countries to island developing countries (IDCs). I am not sure how convincing was my advocacy. For one thing, IDCs already receive a disproportionately high level of concessional aid. In 1982 the unweighted average of concessional assistance to IDCs, on a per capita basis, was US$428 (US$510 for small IDCs) as compared with US$14 for all developing countries. Besides, small IDCs are among the most successful countries in the world. For example, the per capita income for Iceland in 1989 was US$21,070, US$10,450 for Singapore, US$11,320 for The Bahamas and US$6,350 for my native Barbados, placing them in the World Bank category of high income countries.

Our purpose is to identify those characteristics that differentiate small island states from major industrial states, and to develop principles of economic management for small island states as a group. Our first task will be to define the special features of insularity, especially in respect of small states. Secondly, we shall explore the economics of small IDCs. This exercise should enable us to construct a decision model appropriate for the economic management of IDCs, and to deduce principles of economic management relevant to small IDC, such as those in the Caribbean.

Features of Small Island Developing Countries

Francois Doumenge, who prepared the UNCTAD paper, *Viability of Small Island States*, provides the most erudite definition of insularity:

> True insularity only exists where (the emerged land area) is entirely exposed to the influence of the sea. "True" islands are primarily areas of land which have emerged at a sufficient distance from the continent to escape direct influence, in terms of physical, as well as human and economic factors.[1]

IDCs include independent members of the United Nations as well as island territories, some of them colonies like St. Helena, others self-governing dependencies like Montserrat, and others like Martinique and San Andres, which are integral parts of a metropolitan nation. UNCTAD lists 31 IDC member states of the United Nations and 38 island territories. There are two features of IDCs which deserve special attention: the geographic and the economic.

Geographic

IDCs vary widely in their geographical characteristics. They range from archipelagos like Indonesia, with an area of 1.9 million square kilometres, to the Seychelles, with an area of 280 square kilometres. There are also numerous single islands, like Barbados with an area of 430 square kilometres. There are high islands derived from volcanoes, from aggregations of continental rocks, or from elevations of reef rock. There are low islands, comprising single islets, or two or more connected by a reef to form atolls of carbonate rocks generally less than 15 feet above sea level. Islands are found in every altitude and in all climates. A few islands occur singly in mid-ocean; but the majority occur in archipelagos, a few close to the mainland.

Small Size

Small size is the most frequently mentioned geographical characteristic of IDCs. Of the 69 IDCs listed by UNCTAD, 59 had populations of less than one million in 1981. In respect of land area, 62 of the 69 have land areas of less than 20,000 square kilometres, and 44 of them less than 1,000 square kilometres.

Remoteness

Remoteness is another characteristic of IDCs. Most IDCs are more than 500 kilometres away from the nearest continent; and the great majority are archipelagic, and located away from frequented shipping and airline routes.

Fragile Ecosystems

The fragility of the ecosystems of IDCs is a consequence of their geographic isolation. Owing to detachment from the evolutionary biological processes that took place on continents, they tend to have primitive and delicate biotic patterns. Indeed, there are many examples of unique species or strains of fauna and flora which have survived on islands. The most famous example, of course, is the Galapagos Islands; Aldabra in the Seychelles is a less famous case in point.

The fragility of ecosystems in IDCs is exacerbated by the intrusion of modern economic activities in a relatively small geographic space. Forests are swiftly cut down to provide firewood, removing cover and promoting erosion. Rare species are deprived of breeding grounds; effluents from industrial activity and passing ships pollute the coastal waters and destroy marine life. The extreme example of ecological destruction is the use of islands in the Pacific by the United States as sites for nuclear tests.

A current assignment with the government of Colombia has brought home vividly to me the ecological fragility of small islands. The pressure of 70,000 inhabitants on 26 square kilometres has created serious problems of slum housing, sewage and waste disposal, inadequate power and water supply, and threatens the economic survival of the island of San Andres.

Proneness to Natural Disasters

For reasons best known to Himself, the Almighty has located IDCs, especially the smallest ones, in the path of natural disasters. Tropical cyclones and volcanoes have caused the greatest damage to IDCs, although droughts are less frequent in small islands. Naturally, the effects of any disaster are more pronounced for a small island than for a large country with a wide variety of products and back-up facilities. Hurricane David in 1979 destroyed 80 per cent of Dominica's housing stock. In Saint Lucia, the damage inflicted by a cyclone in 1980 was estimated at 89 per cent of GNP. In St. Vincent, 16,000 people (15 per cent of the population) were temporarily evacuated when Mt. Soufriere erupted, while in 1961 the entire population had to be removed from Tristan da Cunha, a small island in the South Atlantic.

Economic Possibilities

Insularity imposes limits on the range of economic possibilities open to IDCs. Lall and Ghosh put it very well: 'A large economy can do practically everything that a small one can, but not vice versa.'[2] Even though the per capita income of Barbados is many times that of India, Barbados cannot develop nuclear powered utilities. At the same time, even very small continental countries can participate in the economic activities of large contiguous states. For example, Luxembourg shares the electrical grid of its neighbours.

Limited Land Area

Small land area is the most obvious constraint on IDCs, limiting their opportunities for economic exploitation. Moreover, the volcanic origins of most IDCs render them mountainous, making for reduced arable land and difficult conditions for mechanization and transportation.

Furthermore, most IDCs are located in the tropical or sub–tropical zone where poor soils, intemperate weather conditions, and the proliferation of weeds and insects make agriculture rather problematic. The range of agricultural commodities is also limited by the fact that very few islands span more than one latitudinal zone. Taiwan, which grows wheat in the north, rice in the middle, and sugar and bananas in the south, is a rare exception. A few islands are able to exploit the temperature gradients of different altitudes. For example, Jamaica grows sugar on the plains, and strawberries and coffee in the mountains.

Limited Natural Resources

Insularity also imposes limits on the extent and range of natural resources available for exploitation. Moreover, because of their geological origin (oceanic volcanoes), small islands are unlikely to have minerals of economic importance. Except for those like Bahrain and Trinidad, which are geologically part of a continent, they are also unlikely to have commercial deposits of fossil fuels. A few small islands in the Pacific possess significant reserves of phosphates derived from the droppings of birds.

Water is frequently a severe problem on IDCs. Only the largest and wettest high islands have ample sources of water. Even on some of these there may be seasonal and sometimes serious shortages. Most small islands have few or no permanent streams or lakes, and their aquifers are naturally limited. Wells are easily invaded by salt water, as in San Andres, while deforestation limits the incidence of permanent streams, which are also easily polluted by industrial activity.

Limited Marine Resources

Marine resources, in which islands would be expected to enjoy a comparative advantage, are in fact a considerable source of problems. In general, the coastal ecosystems of the northwest Atlantic, Europe and China support more productive fisheries than do islands in the Pacific, the Indian Ocean, the Caribbean or the Mediterranean. This reflects the significantly smaller volume of run-off of nutrient-rich water from islands, and their limited or absent continental shelves. Although tropical islands may contain coastal coral-reef ecosystems with high biomass productivity, deep tropical oceans are usually ecologically barren. Island fishing activities, therefore, tend to be either minimal or subject to overly intensive exploitation. The declaration of exclusive economic zones (EEZs) gives IDCs nominal title to the resources of large oceanic areas. However, some rights are not recognized by all countries (such as, ownership of highly migratory species of fish), and small islands lack the resources to monitor and police their EEZs. Because of economic costs and technical difficulties, the prospects for early exploitation of deep- sea resources of minerals are not bright.

Demographic Constraints

In absolute terms, the populations of IDCs are usally small — sometimes so small as to make economic viability questionable. Frequently, population size appears to exceed the carrying capacity of the island. Haiti is one example; San Andres is another. The demography of IDCs may also be marked by cycles of swift population changes. The deterioration of the domestic economy may force unemployed workers to seek work abroad; migration opportunities may suddenly open up; for example, for Caribbean emigrants to the UK in the 1950s and to the US in the 1970s. In fact, a high proportion of the natal population of IDCs live away from home, for example, West Indians in New York.

Most problematic of all is the 'brain drain'; that is, the emigration to wealthier countries of persons trained in professional and technical skills at considerable cost to IDCs. A few successful emigrants may return to start businesses, but the most highly skilled seldom do. This situation creates severe problems for the manpower planners. To secure a supply of skilled workers, an IDC must train many more people than its anticipated requirements. Admittedly, there are circumstances in which emigration may benefit the sending island, especially through remittances and relief of unemployment

Political Constraints

Small size naturally imposes serious political constraints upon small IDCs in their dealings with larger neighbours. Even countries as large as Mexico and Canada experience considerable discomfort from their proximity to the United States. IDCs are even more likely to get hurt as major powers throw their weight around in their perceived spheres of influence. For example, at the start of 1985 the US unilaterally revoked its double taxation treaty with Barbados. The next 12 months were spent in intense negotiation and a new treaty signed early in 1986. About six months later the US asked for a renegotiation of the treaty, and later, again unilaterally, revoked a clause which had bestowed an important tax advantage to captive insurance companies operating from Barbados. The US would hardly have acted in this way with Germany or Japan!

Economics of Small Island Developing Countries

The economics of IDCs, especially small IDCs, may be analysed in terms of openness, risk and economies and diseconomies of scale, within the constraints of the special features described above.

Openness

Their narrow and skewed natural resource base incline small IDCs towards economic specialization in their international trading arrangements. The net result is that IDCs tend to rely on one or a few agricultural products or minerals. If they are lucky, they may also possess the basis of a tourism industry.

Their history has also predisposed IDCs towards economic specialization. The mercantilist policies of the colonial era cast IDCs in the role of tropical commodity producers and of other raw materials for processing in the metropole and subsequent re-export to the colonies. This syndrome has been articulated ad nauseam by the 'dependence' school of economists.

Relatively small population size, limited resources, and absolutely small national incomes also limit the availability of capital for the development of IDCs. IDCs therefore have always relied heavily on capital inflows, either as foreign investment, imperial grants or, more recently, foreign loans, both commercial and concessional. Of course, debts must be repaid.

Empirical studies reveal an inverse relationship between the size of an economy and levels of international trade. For small IDCs the ratio of visible exports to GNP approaches 75 per cent, and for some IDCs, sometimes exceeds GNP. Dana Khatkate is essentially correct that 'the economic characteristics of a mini-state are that goods which are produced tend to be exported, goods which are sold in the mini-state tend to be imported, and the commodities which are both produced and consumed within the mini-state tend to be services.'[3] Some IDCs also export services, mostly in the form of tourism or off-shore business facilities.

Risks Facing IDCs

On hearing of its small land area and considerable distance from a continental land mass, a Kenyan in Nairobi once confessed to me that he would never live on my native island, Barbados. 'Suppose there was a tidal wave!' In fact, tidal waves are but one of the several hazards facing small IDCs. Eight major hazards contribute to the risks confronting IDCs:

> ➤ Proneness to cyclones, volcanoes, earthquakes and similar acts of God requires elaborate disaster preparedness measures.
> ➤ The geographical remoteness of IDCs and their relatively extensive coastlines are a constant invitation to intrusion. Smuggling, improper fishing practices, pollution of coastal areas by passing ships, the invasion of EEZs by alien fishermen, and even attacks by guerillas and mercenaries must all be guarded against.
> ➤ In the absence of appropriate conservation policies, the fragile biological, plant and marine ecosystems could be

irreparably damaged and rare and unique species lost forever.

➢ Demographic instability could lead to excessive population pressures and so strain the 'carrying capacity' of an IDC. Alternatively, a haemorrhage of professional emigration might seriously diminish its productive capacity.

➢ Extensive specialization subjects the economies of IDCs to marked fluctuations of foreign exchange earnings.

➢ The indigenous cultures of IDCs are notoriously vulnerable to the intrusion of alien influences. A fine balance must be preserved between the adoption of useful technologies and the insidious penetration of alien influences, such as novel criminal practices, drugs and other socially harmful imports.

➢ New scientific advances in biotechnology and materials sciences could alter the comparative advantages in agriculture and mining that some IDCs now enjoy.

➢ The political decisions of major nations, whether reflecting malevolence, insensitivity or ignorance, may impact adversely on the economies of IDCs.

Diseconomies of Remoteness

Obvious diseconomies facing IDCs are those associated with remoteness. Islands that are isolated from major population and industrial centres are obviously at a disadvantage in terms of freight costs of imports and exports while their service industries, especially tourism, are severely handicapped by scarce or expensive airline services. Archipelagic IDCs have the further problem of intra-island or intra-regional transport. Transport costs frequently determine the viability of industries. For this reason, IDC governments are frequently forced to undertake the operation of airlines, shipping and ferry services in circumstances when private enterprises find the rate of return unattractive. In such circumstances, the currently popular strategy of privatization is hardly relevant.

Narrow Markets

Severe diseconomies derive from the narrow markets of IDCs which reflect small populations and relatively low and maldistributed incomes. This deprives producers of the economies of scale available in large economies, and makes for high unit costs. It also renders competition in the international arena difficult. Producers of tradeable goods lack the domestic markets from which fixed costs may be recovered, allowing goods priced at marginal cost to penetrate foreign markets.

Narrow markets also give rise to monopoly and oligopoly and, in turn, to high transactions costs, since prices always tend to be higher than would prevail in highly competitive markets. This situation is most troublesome for national economic decision-makers who must often choose between intervening themselves in the market place or allowing colluding oligopolies to fix prices.

High Cost of Infrastructure

The small scale of IDCs also condemns them to frightful diseconomies in the installation and maintenance of infrastructure. Runways for 747 aircraft must be as long in Barbados as in London, and deep-water harbours as deep in St. Kitts as in Caracas.

There are also minimal economic scales and standards for certain facilities, such as power and cement plants, and telecommunications systems. However, the costs of such installations in IDCs must be borne by so few taxpayers that the financial burden is much greater than in larger societies with lower per capita incomes. This is the most powerful argument against the application of the per capita income criterion for graduation of IDCs from World Bank borrowing privileges.

The small population of most IDCs also creates tremendous problems in the provision of many services that are considered essential in modern societies. For example, highly specialized professionals; such as brain surgeons, would not have enough clients in Barbados to support themselves, and the scale of production does not allow for crucial research and development. In some instances, common services, like shipping, university education and meteorological services may be provided cooperatively among neighbouring IDCs; however, expensive facilities, like airports and harbours, must often be replicated on each island.

Economies of Small Scale

The diseconomies of small scale should not blind us to certain diseconomies of large scale. As Peter Drucker observes:

> In social organizations ... growth in size soon requires a disproportionate increase in complexity and more and more specialized organs.... The larger any body, physical or social becomes, the more its energy will be needed to keep ... its own mechanisms alive and functioning.[4]

The agony of the USSR in its reform efforts should sensitise us to the extreme difficulties of large nations in bringing about economic change, and remind us that there are also considerable economies of small scale. It is easier for small IDCs to achieve national consensus; to formulate and carry out programmes, and above all, to achieve changes in policy in response to developments in a volatile environment. Flexibility in decision-making is the most important asset of small IDCs and must therefore be a prime consideration in the construction of any operational model for their governance.

A Trifocal Model

Economic Development

An operational model that informs the economic management of small IDCs will presumably address the issue of economic development. The transition from the Industrial Age to the New Information Age, although stressful, has been good news for small IDCs, enabling them to overcome several of the diseconomies of scale, especially as the cost of computing power is in sharp decline.[5]

In this latest revolution, hardly two decades old, information has replaced physical resources, including energy and capital, as the critical input in the economic process. Computers and robotics have trimmed workforces, new materials and technologies have reduced the need for natural resources, and advances in telecommunications have rendered distance increasingly irrelevant. Almost 1,000 Barbadians now process data on the island and transmit the output via satellite to various parts of the USA.

In the modern economy, information is the raw material of knowledge, which subsumes both theoretical understanding and technical know-how. But knowledge without skill is valueless. The skill needed to process knowledge into value is management. In the New Information Age information, knowledge and management supersede the land, labour and capital of classical economics as the basic factors of production.

Open Systems Theory

Our operational model must also accommodate openness, a dominant characteristic of IDCs. An obvious candidate is the open systems model. Open systems, as opposed to closed systems, import inputs from and export outputs into their environment. Their survival and growth depend on their efficiency in adding value to the inputs which they process. Machines, by comparison, are closed systems, and do not carry out similar autonomous exchanges with their environment.

Closed systems obey the Second Law of Thermodyamics and tend towards their most probable state of total entropy or absolute chaos. Closed systems do not grow. However, higher forms of open systems, such as human beings and economies, flourish and grow through the progressive increase in complexity and variety of their processing sub-systems. In this way they may defy, temporarily at least, the inexorable workings of the Second Law of Thermodynamics.[6]

Risk and Game Theory

Finally, our operational model must enable us to deal with risk. There are two basic types of risks that threaten small IDCs. They may both be addressed within the Theory of Games.[7] The first category of risks arises from the probability of acts of God; for example, volcanic eruptions, hurricanes, and so on, as well as sharp fluctuations of commodity prices, highly volatile international interest rates, etc., which are unpredictable and beyond the control of small IDCs. Their authorities therefore face decisions under uncertainty, and in these circumstances are well advised to regard nature and the international economy as adverse intellects which mean us no good. Since the danger of total ruin is so real for small IDCs, they should use the decision criterion of pessimism — the *maximin*. In short, they should be extremely cautious.

The second category of risks arises from our dealings with other nations and institutions which are seldom totally malevolent or totally benign. Here, the authorities in an IDC face decision making under conflict. In these circumstances they should avoid zero-sum games with their large opponents and seek to play positive-sum games instead. That is, they try to make deals from which both sides stand to benefit. Above all, they should avoid negative-sum games — the kind of games that Manuel Noriega and Saddam Hussein chose to play with the US.

My trifocal model is eclectic, drawing on the theories of Economic Development, Open Systems and of Games. It represents small IDCs as intelligent and purposeful open systems operating in an uncertain and difficult environment, frequently pitted against opponents more powerful than themselves. They need to import inputs from their environment, especially information and technology, and must process these inputs into outputs for export. Their economic development will depend on the continued improvement in the quality of management and technology applied to the processing procedures. At the same time they should use the maximum diplomatic skill to promote their survival against mighty opponents who sometimes deliberately seek to injure, and frequently do so even when they seek to be of assistance.

The most obvious implication of the above analysis for Caribbean IDCs is that their extreme exposure to risks requires that economic managers operate with a generous margin for error. In short, they should err on the side of caution. The most potentially catastrophic outcome is the loss of economic sovereignty to the IMF, World Bank or other creditors. There is no reason to believe that they know better than we do, and they certainly will not be as committed to our peculiar interests. Very few countries have effected an elegant exit from IMF/World Bank adjustment programmes.

The following economic management principles recommend themselves:

- ◆ The foundation of successful economic management in any small IDC is a sound currency. For this reason, fiscal and monetary policies should be directed towards the maintenance of an adequate level of foreign exchange reserves.

- Should resort to the resources of the IMF become necessary, the approach should be made in a timely fashion well before the majority of the nation's options have been foreclosed.
- To ensure timely response to international hazards, institutional arrangements must be put in place to monitor developments in the international environment. Central banks are especially well placed to carry out this task, and every effort should be made to staff them with suitably qualified personnel.
- The need to earn foreign exchange to pay for imports, especially intermediate and capital goods, requires the export-oriented strategy implied by Open Systems Theory. We have seen, especially from the Guyana experience, that attempts to close small economies merely invite disaster.
- Small size requires an emphasis on quality rather than on quantity. For this reason the establishment and maintenance of the highest quality infrastructure is absolutely essential if we are to compete internationally with any chance of success. For small IDCs, infrastructure is the equivalent of a natural resource.
- To neutralize or reduce the adverse effects of the diseconomies of small scale, Caribbean IDCs should boost the effectiveness of the CARICOM Secretariat in promoting functional cooperation.
- Caribbean IDCs should nurture an elite and highly professional public service of the highest skill and integrity. In this respect, trends toward the politicization of the civil service and of public enterprises should be reversed.
- Special attention should be paid to the foreign service. This is an area where scarce diplomatic resources might be effectively pooled under the aegis of the CARICOM Secretariat.
- Economic management in Caribbean IDCs should be characterized by swift decision-making processes for maximum flexibility of response to external developments.

The current concentration of policy making in Cabinets should be seriously addressed.

♦ The watchwords of Caribbean IDCs in their economic management should be quality and efficiency. Only super powers can afford the luxury of shoddy and inefficient production.

Submitted to Trinidad Express Newspapers Ltd for publication in *Caribbean Affairs*, November 22, 1991

Notes

1. UNCTAD, *Viability of Small Island States,* prepared by Francois Doumenge, (TD/B/950), 1983, para. 4.

2. S. Lall and Ghosh, 'The Role of Foreign Investments in Industrialization', in *Problems and Policies in Small Economies,* ed., B. Jalan (London: Groom Helm, 1982), 145.

3. D.R. Khatkhate, and B.K. Short, 'Monetary and Central Banking Policies of Ministates', *World Development* 8, no. 12 (1980): 1018.

4. Peter F. Drucker, *Management: Tasks, Responsibilities, Practices* (New York: Harper & Row, 1973).

5. For an excellent discussion of this topic, see Alvin Toffler, *The Third Wave* (New York: Bantam Books, 1971).

6. See Ludwig Von Bertalanffy, *General Systems Theory,* Revised Edition (New York: George Braziller, 1968).

7. For a concise exposition of Game Theory, see Samuel B. Richmond, *Operations Research for Management Decisions* (New York: The Ronald Press Company), 501–526

4

AN ANALYTICAL FRAMEWORK FOR THE STUDY OF CARIBBEAN PUBLIC ENTERPRISE

In any study which seeks to assess performance and make recommendations for improvement, the application of criteria is unavoidable. Criteria can only be derived by means of theoretical analysis utilizing deductive methods of reasoning to arrive at normative conclusions. Given its limited scope, this study must utilize existing theories of political economy, of organization and of management from which to derive normative principles for the assessment of public enterprise in the Caribbean. Our theory, to be made relevant, must be constrained by Caribbean circumstances and experience. Considerable reliance on the section 'Management in Development' of the World Bank's *World Development Report* 1983 is acknowledged.[1]

The proposed analytical framework is predicated on four issues:

Issues of political economy affecting the establishment of public enterprises (PEs); issues affecting the organization of public enterprises, especially in their relationship with government; issues affecting the management and operation of public enterprises; issues of liquidation and divestiture of public enterprises.

Out of this analytical exercise should flow criteria for assessing the performance of public enterprises in the Caribbean.

Issues of Political Economy

Ideology

In developing a normative theory of public enterprise for the Caribbean, we may confidently begin with the premise that the goal of all governments is to maximize the incomes and general welfare of their citizens. (If this is not the objective, then it ought to be.) Public enterprise, then, is seen as an important policy instrument for achieving that goal.

As in any theorizing in the social sciences, we cannot escape consideration of the values of the subjects of our concern, and we must suppress to the maximum extent possible the intrusion of our personal values into the exercise. The values of governments are expressed in their ideological positions — socialism in Guyana and revolutionary Grenada, nationalism in Trinidad and Tobago, socialism/nationalism in Jamaica, capitalism in the case of Barbados, Antigua, and the other OEC states. We do not judge these ideologies to be either good or bad. However, if we assume minimum rationality, we should regard ideology as an input of our value system, and not as the end of economic development. If an ideologically inspired programme leads to the patent decline in incomes and general welfare, it will, presumably, be abandoned or adjusted. There is certainly a strong motivation on the part of democratic governments to place economic development above ideology as a goal, since the impoverishment of the population through the pursuit of ideological goals per se would lead to defeat at the polls or to some other dramatic form of social protest.

Public enterprise may be viewed as an instrument of policy in pursuit of the primary goal of economic development. The extent to which it is employed is determined by the prevailing ideology. It will obviously be used more in socialist Guyana than in capitalist Barbados. At any rate, the effectiveness of public enterprise will depend upon the economic circumstances surrounding its implementation, and on its organizational, managerial and operational efficiency.

Economics

There is considerable consensus among development theorists on the need to concentrate resources in the early stages of economic development. This corresponds to the 'preconditions for take-off' phase in Walt Rostow's *The Stages of Economic Growth.*[2] New institutions must be established and major elements of infrastructure put in place. It is during this stage that public enterprise is most likely to be employed as an instrument of national policy in any developing country, whether socialist or capitalist.

The suggestion of international financial institutions and First World economists that economic development is best achieved by the workings of the free market flies in the face of the history of developed countries which, without exception, have recorded periods of intense state direction of economic activity. This position is even more astonishing in view of the recent successes of Japan, still very much a state directed economy, and the newly industrializing countries of Taiwan, South Korea and Singapore. 'Free market' Hong Kong is an anomaly arising from its history and location.

Public enterprise makes the most sense in circumstances where the private sector comprises small units, and where only the superior fiscal and administrative capacity of government can achieve the critical mass needed to carry out major public works — airports, harbours, utilities, etc. Government may also resort to public enterprise when the entrepreneurship required to launch promising industries is not forthcoming from the private sector, or where the risk of the new venture is beyond the capability of the private sector. In many cases the technological and managerial capacity may be in place but financial markets may be too thin and shallow to absorb the risks of a proposed venture. Even in the case of developed countries, gigantic projects such as the 'Chunnel' linking Britain and France and the space programme in the United States, are beyond the capacity of the private sector, and must either be assisted or totally undertaken by government. Sometimes, government may use a public venture as a catalyst for new industrial expansion. For example, a cement plant could get a construction industry off the ground; a saw-mill could promote an export trade in timber.

The public enterprise is the favoured format when the desired industrial activities are of a dynamic rather than a bureaucratic nature. Operations which are repetitive in nature, and which are carried out in a predictable environment, are generally manageable through the diligent observance of rules, and as such, are best carried out within the framework of the Civil Service. However, successful operations in rapidly changing circumstances, and in a competitive or otherwise unpredictable environment, depend on the technical, managerial and judgmental skills of staff; they cannot be effectively executed through civil service-type procedures, and in the face of bureaucratic practice. This is not meant as a denigration of civil servants. A professional, disciplined, and circumspect cadre of civil servants is as essential to national success as is a cadre of skilful, experienced and dynamic managers. Perhaps, even more so!

The theory enunciated above regards public enterprise as a strategic weapon in the economic arsenal. To apply another military metaphor, public enterprises might be regarded as the panzer divisions of the army — dynamic, elite divisions used to make openings which the slower moving infantry regiments may exploit in a more deliberate and leisurely fashion. Panzer divisions are not efficiently utilized in slogging matches or garrison duties. Similarly, the use of public enterprise to achieve the ideological objective of 'ownership and control' of the commanding or any other heights, could result in the misuse of scarce resources required for the effective operation of an otherwise legitimate public enterprise.

The use of the public enterprise as a means of providing employment for the party faithful or others is also contra-indicated. (In any case, public enterprises are usually quite capital intensive and do not generate many jobs.) To saddle public enterprises with such extraneous duties is to blunt their strategic capabilities. As Peter Drucker reminds us, 'Governments can do well only if there are no political pressures.... And as soon as a governmental activity has more than one purpose, it degenerates.'[3] If the public enterprise is properly conceived from the beginning, its effective operation should create additional job opportunities in the economy at large, far in excess of possible redundant posts or bloated payroll. Even more serious, the unhealthy overweight would reduce its ability to achieve the strategic objectives set for it. Ineffectual and loss-making public enterprises are worse than no public enterprises at all, for they represent the destruction of existing capital rather than the creation of additional income flows.

Organizational Issues

Resources

The first responsibility of any government to a public enterprise is the provision of adequate resources at the time of its establishment. Necessary resources include finance, land space, accommodation and, above all, human resources — technical, professional and managerial.

Too often in developing countries public enterprises are established with inadequate capital resources, especially working capital, which they are expected to borrow from commercial banks. Frequently, funds earmarked from the Treasury are not forthcoming as required and public enterprises are forced to depend on delayed payments, or goods and services purchased on credit from the private sector, as a means of financing their ongoing operations. Such hand-to-mouth financing absorbs an inordinate amount of top managerial attention, and severely prejudices the success of the public enterprise. Niggardly capital financing leads to inadequate public sector accommodation. In developing countries the inadequacy of the public sector accommodation is proverbial, not being perceived as contributing to the achievement of the organization's objectives. Working conditions approaching the quality of that in the private sector are viewed as luxurious. In fact, accommodation should be regarded as a management tool for the promotion of the productivity of the physical, and especially the human assets of the enterprise.

Management

The most important precondition of success is the recruitment of adequate management — this includes an experienced and knowledgeable board of directors and a capable chief executive of impeccable integrity. The CEO and his senior staff should either be familiar with the operations of the enterprise or be capable of learning its operations in a short period of time. In the absence of nationals who fit the bill, there should be no hesitation about calling upon non-nationals to work on contract. The development of competent executives is a long-term proposition and the drop-out rate can be high.

Control

The next problem is that of exercising adequate control over the public enterprise. The public enterprise is established by government to achieve certain objectives in the interests of the community. Government is responsible to the community at large, which is the ultimate owner and provider of its resources. Clearly government has a duty to ensure that the public enterprise carries out its mission efficiently; hence the problem of control. Here, the primary concern of government should be for the results of the organization, not for the detailed steps taken to achieve the results, with the understanding, of course, that the enterprise operates within the law, and within the accepted norms, practices and general guidelines laid down by the Act establishing it.

Control itself is a well-established function in engineering. The principal elements of a control system are:

♦ A criterion of performance, a feedback mechanism and a corrective mechanism. Translated into managerial terms, the controller of an organization must first establish specific criteria for judging the performance of the organization.

♦ Secondly, there must be provision for reporting on the actual performance so that it may be compared with expected or standard performance.

♦ Thirdly, there must exist a corrective mechanism for restoring actual to desired performance. Any attempt by a minister to control the day-to-day activities of a public enterprise not only produces confusion, but removes the responsibility of management for its success.

If an adequate control mechanism is in place, the principle of 'management by exception' may be observed. If the results of the enterprise's operations are consistent with the expected standard of performance, there is no need for the minister to intervene. If results are not satisfactory, there are three appropriate points of intervention. Firstly, the measure of performance may be inappropriate; secondly, the feedback system may be malfunctioning; thirdly, the corrective mechanism may have broken down. In any case it is management which is responsible for this situation, not operators further down the line. It is from the above considerations that we derive the principle of operational autonomy.

For the control system to function then, the mission and objectives of the public enterprise must be clearly defined in advance and the criteria of performance unequivocally established. If there are conflicting objectives, these must be resolved by government and management in advance. If, for example, government insists on a lower-than-market price for the produce of the enterprise or on maximum staffing levels to bolster employment, it should be made clear by management that profits cannot be maximized in these circumstances and that losses are likely to result.

Another requirement is the determination of which operational results are to be monitored, and how often reporting of results should take place. Annual financial and operating reports are a minimum. Quarterly reports of critical indices of performance are normal. In financial operations, for example commercial banks, monthly operational data should be insisted upon. It does not take very long for financial operations to go sour.

Operational Autonomy

The principle of operational autonomy which flows from the arguments above is based on an engineering model. It holds even if we invoke an anthropogenic model of the organization. This approach sees the public enterprise as primarily a group of people with a personality analogous to that of the individual. Professor John Kenneth Galbraith makes the point beautifully:

> Individual achievement is at its best when the individual has a clear set of goals and the means, including of course the knowledge, with which to pursue these goals under the stimulus of his own will. As with the individual personality so with the corporate personality. Autonomy, the independence to pursue specified goals, is equally important for the producing corporation. So are clearly specified goals. Indeed, these are more than important; they are the only administrative arrangements that are consistent with the effective corporate being.[4]

The *World Bank Development Report* 1983, has coined the expression 'control without interference' to describe the appropriate supervision of public enterprises by governments.[5] The corresponding responsibility of the public enterprise is captured by the term 'accountability'.

Monitoring Function

The final organizational issue has to do with the administrative system used by governments to exercise control over public enterprises. This requires the establishment of a focal point in the government bureaucracy for monitoring the performance of public enterprises. The focal point should serve as a channel of communication for the transmission of government criteria and reporting requirements to the public enterprise's directorate. The focal point would also serve to relay feedback on the operational results of the enterprise. However, the focal point should never be cast in the role of big brother overseeing the day-to-day operations of the enterprise. Public enterprises can only be managed from within, never from without.

In small countries with a handful of public enterprises, a single focal point may suffice. However, in countries with, say, ten public enterprises or more, focal points should be distributed among the relevant ministries. Similarly, the auditing function might be distributed among several private sector accounting firms. The concentration of monitoring duties in a single focal point could create serious bottlenecks in the decision-making process, and compromise the very dynamism for which public enterprises were established in the first place.

The establishment of a holding company to supervise the operations of several or all public enterprises is even less desirable. The rationale of the holding company, put forward by the late Adlith Brown, is that it insulates the public enterprises from political intervention:

A holding company is an intermediary between the enterprises it controls and the political directorate and may therefore have the additional function of reconciling, when necessary, the goals of each public enterprise with the public and social goals of government.[6]

In fact, it creates an additional bureaucratic layer of personnel who, because they are spread so thin, have less understanding of the specific operations than does the management which it seeks to supervise. Ignorance always tends to promote unintelligent meddling, violating the principle of 'control without interference'. Besides, if competent personnel are not readily found to manage individual public enterprises, there will hardly be a superfluity to manage the holding company.

In the last resort we cannot have good management of public enterprises unless we have in place a cadre of highly educated, experienced and disinterested professionals. Such a cadre will insist on operational autonomy, and will either nip in the bud attempts by ministers to intervene or will resign. If the best managers in the business fail, the others are not likely to do better.

Managerial Issues

Board of Directors

The responsibility of the board of directors is to oversee management in the pursuit of the objectives of the public enterprise, not of the political objectives of the party in power. Indeed, an important function of the board is to insulate the management from political influence. The board should serve as advisor, supporter, friendly critic and, most important, as the conscience of management. If things are going badly, it will need to pay closer attention to operations, insist on more frequent reporting and, if necessary, replace the management. However, it must never seek to abrogate the operational responsibilities of management. It must be made especially clear whether the chairman is the full-time chief executive officer, or if he is a non-executive chairman of the board of directors.

The Chief Executive Officer (CEO)

The CEO, ideally a managing director with a non-executive chairman to help insulate him from politics, is responsible to the board of directors for the day-to-day management of the enterprise towards the achievement of legitimate objectives. His job is no more political than that of a surgeon. However, the CEO will need to exercise a fine sense of diplomacy so as to reduce the potential abrasion of his insistence on operational autonomy.

The CEO should have the maximum freedom in the choosing of his subordinates. The board is justified in maintaining a veto on senior appointments. However, it should avoid as far as possible the imposition on the CEO of staff he does not wish to employ. Political affiliation should have no weight in the appointment of management as long as such affiliation does not conflict with the operations of the enterprise. Indeed, most constitutions in CARICOM guarantee the right of individuals to join the political party of their choice.

Management

Critical to the success of the public enterprise is a degree of continuity of its top-level staff. This continuity enables management to learn how to run the organization. Such learning is reflected in the collective experience of the organization. This is why insulation from politics is so important. It is most injurious to the enterprise's prospects of success if after each election its top management layer is purged by the incoming administration. This practice damages the morale of the organization as a whole, and dampens the ambitions of promising middle layer staff. Fearing the plight of their seniors, the best of them seek the greener pastures of the private sector, leaving the second-raters behind to run the organization.

Incentive System

This brings us to the question of incentives and penalties. The purpose of incentives is to enable the public enterprise to achieve its objectives. Unless government is prepared to offer salaries which can attract staff capable of doing the job, any salaries paid will be wasted. The level of salaries being paid in the civil service is not very relevant. If it takes x thousand dollars per year to attract a suitable CEO, it could cost a large multiple of x thousand dollars not to have him. The underpayment of top management staff at an enterprise is extremely bad economics. Governments must demonstrate considerable firmness in resisting civil service pressures to maintain a fixed relationship between civil service salaries and salaries in public enterprises. The relevant criterion is the going market price. By the same token, the job security of civil servants should not be available to the management staff of public enterprises. In other words, differentials between market-rate and civil service salaries should be regarded as the premium paid for limited job security. Management staff of public enterprises who fail should be removed, although with the utmost consideration and humanity. Indeed, the directorate might also be liable to penalties for failure to submit timely financial and operational reports to the minister.

Information System

A characteristic of a well-functioning organization is the presence of an effective information system. An efficient information system is needed within the organization to ensure that relevant information is fed back to the management and to the board. Information on financial operations is, of course, the most critical data component. The absence or lateness of financial reports is prima facie evidence of mismanagement. Reporting on operational results is also important. Public enterprises should therefore have on board the professional accountants, engineers, and systems analysts needed to prepare the necessary reports. In particular, an effective information system will compile and store in an economic manner those records which the organization needs to keep in its institutional memory. If the organization is large enough, it should think of engaging a trained librarian.

Non-Civil Service Management Style

Because they usually operate in a dynamic environment, the 'management by regulations' which characterizes civil service operations is quite unsuitable for the public enterprise. Dynamic operations require timely decision-making, and the quality of decisions depends upon the skill and judgment of decision makers who must also be prepared to accept responsibility for the consequences of their decisions. This does not mean that those making decisions are automatically punished for errors. In fact, trial and error is the only means by which experience can be gained. It means that tasks must be so structured that staff may learn decision-making by trial and error within a framework which does not irreversibly compromise the objectives of the organization.

To be successful, a public enterprise must attract enough personnel of the type who are wiling to make decisions, accept the consequences of their decisions, and learn from their errors. This kind of personnel will develop into top-class managers in the years ahead.

The Learning Organization

An organization will not develop a capacity to solve problems and adjust to the environment unless it is able to think and to learn. This capacity is especially useful in the development of strategic plans. To develop this capacity, management must attract and identify individuals who are reflective and willing to put forward new ideas for dealing with existing and new issues. As far as possible, such personnel should be relieved of continuous operational tasks and given an opportunity to explore all aspects of the organization. Such personnel will form the core of the enterprise's brain.

Issues of Liquidation and Divestiture

Privatization has been very much in vogue during the 1980s. The IMF and World Bank, which encouraged public sector investment in the 1970s, now actively promote divestiture. This reflects disillusionment with the performance of public enterprises in the Third World; it also reflects the ideological influence of the Reagan and Thatcher administrations on these international institutions. Third World governments should therefore make sure that they are privatising for the right reasons. For example, the UK is now planning to privatise water supplies. Indeed, much of the French water works system is privately operated. Third World countries should recognize, however, that family incomes in these wealthy countries, whether from employment or from welfare benefits, are high enough to permit the purchase of water without hardship. In most LDCs, unsubsidised water would be beyond the financial capacity of a large part of the population — and water is an absolute essential of life! Furthermore, since water supply is a natural monopoly, the problem of social control will not go away as it may in the case of other commercial operations.

One obvious reason for the liquidation or privatization of a public enterprise is the accomplishment of its mission or the loss of its strategic purpose. For example, a public enterprise involved in urban development may have been established to develop a certain district. At some point after the completion of the project, it would be no longer necessary to maintain such a large organization. The maintenance function might then be passed on to the Public Works Department or to a cooperative comprising the beneficiaries of the development project.

A public enterprise might also be liquidated if it has failed to carry out its mission or if it seems unlikely to do so. Sometimes an enterprise gets off on the wrong foot and is plagued by cost over-runs, misappropriation of funds or other scandals. In such circumstances it makes sense to terminate operations and start all over again. Sometimes the original objective of the enterprise is overtaken by events. At times, even though the project may still have economic value, it might not justify the absorption of scarce national resources. In all such cases privatization offers a sensible solution.

At other times it may become clear that, for one reason or another, the efficient management of an operation is beyond the capacity of management. This may be reflected in low quality outputs which compromise the success of customers who, in turn, suffer substandard profits or heavy losses. If government is satisfied that the operation might be more efficiently run by private operators, divestiture would represent a considerable saving of national resources that might be more efficiently employed elsewhere.

Sometimes governments acquire enterprises for good reasons in times of crisis. For example, it might make good sense in a cyclical downturn to rescue hotels, an airline, a bank, or some enterprise critical to the public interest — for the same reason that Britain bailed out British Petroleum and the US bailed out Lockheed and Chrysler. Government may also find that it has acquired so many public enterprises over the years that it simply lacks the technical and administrative capacity to control them. Systematic privatization would then make a lot of sense.

It is extremely difficult for most developing countries to exercise effective control over more than half a dozen or so public enterprises. By control we mean the process of indicating goals, establishing criteria of performance, determining reporting requirements, and ensuring that corrective action is taken when feedback indicates a departure from predetermined performance standards. Indeed, these preconditions for control require a most sophisticated cadre of civil servants nor readily available in most developing countries. As a result, most public enterprises are not effectively controlled by governments and attract attention only when their inefficiency has reached scandalous proportions. In such instances, it is much better to have such enterprises operate in the private sector and depend on indirect controls to regulate them in the national interest. In other cases, it makes sense to let them operate on a purely commercial basis and tax their profits for application elsewhere in the economy. In Scandinavian countries this approach is encapsulated in the principle of private production and public distribution.

In some cases public enterprises in the Caribbean have been established on the principle of 'ownership and control' of indigenous resources and 'occupation of the commanding heights of the economy'. We have seen from the above analysis that public ownership need not lead to control, but to the overload of government decision-making systems, and ultimately to pervasive economic disorder. Similarly, the attempt to control the 'commanding heights may leave the state mired in the 'valleys' with external entities like the IMF or debt-for-equity swappers in occupation of the 'heights'. It may frequently be more economical to control through less direct and more economical means. At any rate, control is not properly an end in itself, but merely a means of achieving an end. Does it really matter who owns and controls enterprises as long as they are operated efficiently, or at least more efficiently than government itself could? In these circumstances, isn't privatization a more sensible course?

Peter Drucker goes even further:

We now understand why there are some things government, by its very essence, cannot do. And even for the things government can do, conditions must be right. A government activity can work only if it is a monopoly. It cannot function if there are other ways to do the job, that is, if there is competition. The Post Office in the nineteenth century was a true monopoly. And so were the railroads. There were no other ways of sending information or of moving freight and people over land. But as soon as there are alternative ways to provide the same service, government flounders. Governments find it very hard to abandon an activity even if it has totally outlived its usefulness. They thus become committed to yesterday, to the obsolete, the no longer productive.[7]

Normative Principles

The following normative principles may be derived from theoretical discussion conducted above:

- The public enterprise is a legitimate institutional tool in a strategy of economic development.
- The establishment of a public enterprise is indicated when the contemplated economic activity is dynamic in nature, and does not lend itself to bureaucratic-type operations.
- The managerial, technical and professional resources required for the successful operation of public enterprises are, by definition, scarce in developing countries. The use of the public enterprise should therefore be restricted to strategic purposes.
- The number of public enterprises which a government in a developing country can effectively control is quite limited.
- Government control of public enterprises is appropriately and most effectively achieved through (i) the enunciation of clear objectives, (ii) the establishment of clear performance criteria, (iii) performance feedback and (iv) a corrective mechanism, not through ministerial intervention into day-to-day operations.
- Operational autonomy is a sine qua non of organizational effectiveness.

♦ The legitimate objectives of the public enterprise, rather than party-political considerations, are the appropriate concerns of its directorate and management.

♦ The incentive system of public enterprises should be geared towards the recruitment and maintenance of qualified staff, rather than tied to civil service salary sales.

♦ The public enterprise should develop into a thinking and learning organization.

♦ Public enterprises should be privatised or liquidated if: (i) their original purposes have been achieved; (ii) when their services can be provided effectively in the private sector; (ii) if they fail in the achievement of their purpose.

Presented at the XXIII Annual Conference of the Regional Programme of Monetary Studies, Belize City, Belize, November 25–28, 1991, *Social and Economic Studies* 41, no. 4 (1992)

Notes

1. World Bank, *World Development Report 1983* (New York: Oxford University Press, 1983).

2. Walt W. Rostow, *The Theory of Economic Growth* (New York: Cambridge University Press, 1960).

3. Peter Drucker, *The New Realities* (New York: Harper & Row, 1989), 85.

4. John Kenneth Galbraith, *Economic Development* (Boston: Houghton Mifflin, 1960), 89.

5. World Bank, *World Development Report 1983*, 78.

6. Adlith Brown, 'Introduction': *Studies in Caribbean Enterprise, Vol. 1: An Overview of Public Enterprise, Commonwealth Caribbean* (Georgetown, Guyana and Mona, Jamaica: Institute of Development Studies, and Institute of Social and Economic Research, 1983), 9.

7. Peter, F. Drucker, *The New Realities*, 63.

5

CRITIQUE OF 'GUIDELINES FOR ECONOMIC DEVELOPMENT: STRATEGY FOR CARICOM COUNTRIES INTO THE 21ST CENTURY'

Guidelines for Economic Development summarizes the larger work, *Caribbean Development to the Year 2000: Challenges, Prospects and Policies.* When read these two documents provide a comprehensive description of the current state of Caribbean economies, and are required reading for students of Caribbean economics, civil servants, businessmen and educated laymen throughout the region. The statistical tables, charts and bibliography appended to *Caribbean Development* constitute an elaborate economic database on the region.

However, *Guidelines* suffers from the classical shortcomings of consensus documents that must accommodate several conflicting views. This accounts for the comprehensiveness of the study, but leads to the blurring of some critical issues, and the inclusion of others of marginal or doubtful value. For example, the Exclusive Economic Zone takes up a great deal of space even though its meaningful exploitation is at least a decade away. On the other hand, important insights, such as the need for self-reliance and the appropriate roles of government and the private sector, are not adequately developed.

A second weakness of *Guidelines* is that it does not quite escape the statist mind-set which has characterized Caribbean economic policy making over the last two decades, and from which, under the whiplash of foreign creditors and international financial institutions, we are only now slowly emerging. Government is still seen as the dominant agent in development operations, with the private sector as a junior and somewhat inconvenient partner. For example, *Caribbean Development* (p.115) is concerned with 'how not to stifle entrepreneurial development, while preventing the uneven distribution of economic power from having adverse effects on society at large.

Guidelines is understandably polite to the governments that commissioned the study. The policy failures of Caribbean governments during what I have elsewhere called 'The Lost Decades', are glossed over rather lightly. The 15 years of irresolution in the pursuit of Caribbean integration are too readily forgiven, and the capricious observance and non-observance of the CARICOM Treaty is not mentioned at all. The analysis of our recent economic performance is muted and the recommendations of *Guidelines* lack incisiveness.

In its introduction, *Guidelines* asserts that the challenge to the region 'is to conceptualise, formulate, and implement a development strategy', and it undertakes 'to set out the principal conclusions and proposals for economic strategies and policies which have been identified as being the correct ones to guide the deliberations of the Regional Economic Conference.' In fact, *Guidelines,* like its parent *Caribbean Development,* is an educational document rather than a statement of strategic intent. It conveys exhaustive information about the issues related to Caribbean development and, as indicated above, reveals keen insights on the part of the author and his advisors. However, *Guidelines* does not articulate a coherent development strategy for the Caribbean; what social scientists call a 'paradigm'. This is its most serious weakness.

Guidelines appears to use the term 'strategy' interchangeably with 'policy'. In fact, a strategy is a master plan from which consistent policies and programmes are generated. As Kenichi Ohmae observes in, *The Mind of the Strategist,*[1] the strategist focuses on 'the key factors' of the problem; this means that many interesting, and by no means negligible, factors must be omitted, even though they may later be subsumed under one or another element of the strategy. In turbulent times, such as we now face, strategizing must replace central planning and even development planning, which become less and less effectual as the future becomes more and more unpredictable. 'Strategic planning,' observes Peter Drucker, 'is necessary precisely because we cannot forecast.' He continues:

> The question that faces the strategic decision-maker is not what his organization should do tomorrow. It is, "What do we have to do today to be ready for an uncertain tomorrow?"[2]

This paper critiques *Guidelines* within the framework of a long-term strategic planning approach. This leads naturally to the identification of strategic areas of concern, and to specification of the minimum decisions which Caribbean leaders must take today in order to prepare the region for an uncertain tomorrow.
Strategic planning involves:

- Scanning the environment;
- Identification of the systems' resources and constraints;
- Formulation of a vision of the future;
- Analysis of the operational dynamics of the system, bringing to bear both systemic understanding and an imaginative assessment of future possibilities;
- Enumeration of decisions to be taken today so as to get ready for an uncertain tomorrow.

Scanning the Environment

Section II of *Guidelines*, the Global Framework, identifies 'several important trends in the world economy which influence the development prospects of Caribbean economies'. Here, the report lists world economic trends of recent decades: the emergence of the Pacific Rim as a major pole of economic activity; the perverse flow of financial resources from developing to the developed countries; the increased importance of environmental factors; rapid changes in the technology of production and decreasing usage of unskilled labour; the globalization of production and markets; the collapse of Marxist-Leninist political and economic structures; the 'intensification of regional economic zones'; and the 'massive redirection of financial and foreign investment and technical assistance to Eastern Europe at the expense of the Third World'. We would add the sharp rise of services in relation to goods as a proportion of GDP. For example, whereas services in the United States accounted for 57 per cent of GDP in 1945, that proportion had risen to 77 per cent by 1985, and is projected to reach 93 per cent in the year 2001. Appropriately, *Guidelines* also observes some favourable features in our medium-term outlook, especially the prospect of the resuscitation of Latin American economies.

However, by failing to place these economic and political trends in the context of what Alvin Toffler calls the transition from the Industrial to the New Information Age,[3] *Guidelines* understates the seriousness of the problematique of the Third World and the Caribbean. A Rockefeller Foundation study of the implications of the new technologies for developing countries reported 'a not welcome view of the future'. It goes on:

> It is even possible that as a result of advances taking place in the research laboratories of the richer countries, the poorer countries could lose the few comparative advantages in the world economy that they now enjoy. Automation could reduce the need for cheap

labour; the new materials science could produce substitutes for natural resources found in developing countries: genetic engineering could significantly alter markets for the products of tropical farms and plantations.[4]

Jacques Attali's vision of the new order is even more apocalyptic:

> Not everyone will participate in the riches of the new order. Millions in Africa, Latin America, India and China will remain in misery.... With no future of their own in an age of air travel and telecommunications, the terminally impoverished will look for one in the North: they threaten to become nomads of a different kind ... looking for a few drops of what we have in Berlin, Paris or Los Angeles.[5]

In short, our situation is even more desperate than *Guidelines* suggests.

Resources and Constraints

Resources

The key feature of the emerging global economy is that information has replaced energy and commodities as the basic raw material in the production process. Education is required to transform information into technology and knowledge, and management is needed to add value to the activities of knowledge and technology workers. Indeed, Peter Drucker insists that 'the developing countries are not underdeveloped, they are undermanaged.'[6]

Guidelines quite rightly stresses again and again the importance of technology and human resources, which have taken on a dramatically increased value in the global marketplace. Sometimes, however, *Guidelines* lapses: 'By virtue of its natural resource endowments, the Caribbean is capable of establishing and maintaining a strong international market position for selected minerals.' (p.15) In fact, Caribbean returns from the exploitation of natural resources will depend largely on the quality of our technology and management. Here, *Guidelines* might have directed attention more forcibly to the serious under-funding of the University of the West Indies (UWI), which does not generally enjoy as high a priority in government budgets as in the 1950s and 1960s. The Rockefeller Report cited above warns that, whereas the technologies which underpinned the major industries of the late nineteenth and the first half of the twentieth century were the work of 'gifted tinkers', like Thomas Edison, Michael Faraday, Guglielmo Marconi and Alexander Graham Bell, the new technologies of computers, fibre optics, materials science and biotechnology are evolved in the elaborate laboratories of universities and multinationals. Societies that lack top-class university-trained personnel will not do well in the decades ahead.

Strangely enough, *Guidelines* pays little attention to the scarcest human resource of all — entrepreneurship. Indeed, the term is seldom used, and usually apologetically. Yet, without entrepreneurs, few new businesses are established, and the expansion of existing enterprise is limited.

Constraints

Guidelines recognizes the constraints of small size, small markets and the 'limited range of natural resources and the internationalist nature of their consumption demands and production technologies'. Indeed, the call for the development of a regional market (p.32ff) is one of the strongest sections of *Guidelines*. It recognizes the potential of the removal of barriers to intra-regional trade for inducing 'competitiveness and innovation among regional producers of substitutable products', and the creation of 'intra-CARICOM production linkages and clusters'. Such developments, as Michael Porter points out, are important factors for developing the capacity of domestic firms to compete abroad.[7] The report's plea for urgent 'improvements in the arrangements for regional payments and trade reforms', 'the removal of restrictions on the movement of Caribbean labour and capital', and the 'coordination of fiscal and monetary policies' constitutes a *cri de coeur*.

Guidelines fails to focus on the most serious constraint of our fragmented regional economy —the paucity of enterprises with the critical mass required to compete successfully in the global marketplace. For, as Michael Porter points out, enterprises compete internationally, not countries.[8] Economic integration is less important for the regional trade it will promote (although that will also be useful) than for the pooling of capital, human and other resources required for the development of globally competitive enterprises.

At any rate, the constraint of small size will never be overcome until CARICOM states can be cured of the practice of observing those clauses of the Chaguaramas Treaty which suit them and ignoring those which do not. Like the Commission of the European Common Market, the CARICOM Secretariat should be given power to enforce the terms of the treaty and to take the initiative in accelerating the integration process.

Strategic Vision

The strategic vision which comes through in *Guidelines* is somewhat blurred. It concedes that the 'realities of small economic size and narrow resource bases' prevent Caribbean countries from achieving acceptable growth levels 'on the basis of inward-looking strategies', especially in the light of 'the failures of extreme import substitution and autarky in a few Caribbean countries during recent decades.'(p. 26) It therefore calls for 'a vastly improved export performance' in the international economy. Still, it reports a consensus that 'there is considerable scope for economically efficient import-substitution in domestic absorption of consumer goods ... and in labour usage in production.'(p.9) It observes that export-led strategies of economic development would require 'the acquisition of financial capital, technology, and expert human resources from the international community,' (p.7) yet it records worry about 'the political and economic implications such as loss of economic sovereignty and self-determination and the consequences for traditional rights and practices in the labour market.' (p. 21)

In fact, even large societies like the United States have had to accept the diminution of 'economic sovereignty'. American state governors and city mayors now compete for Japanese investment, and American labour unions have considerably adjusted their demands and expectations to the realities of competition in the global marketplace. Presumably, we will have to do the same in the Caribbean as national boundaries lose their relevance in an increasingly borderless world. For this reason the emphasis of *Guidelines* on the development of 'negotiating capability', the accelerated training of nationals, the establishment of comprehensive databases, the sharing of experiences, and the continuous monitoring of the international environment, is especially well taken. (p. 22)

System Dynamics: Towards a New Caribbean Development Paradigm

The search for a new Caribbean development paradigm must begin by answering the question, 'Why have CARICOM economies performed so poorly that six out of 13 are poorer than they were a decade ago and the majority of them now confront persistent poverty, serious unemployment and inadequate services?' The evidence suggests that underperformance in the region is a positive function of government participation in the production of goods and services. A new paradigm must therefore revolve around the role of the state in economic development.

In the early stages of development, Caribbean governments appropriately and effectively played the dominant role. They installed basic infrastructure, established developmental institutions, and even carried out critical productive operations when the private sector was unwilling to take the risk. As development proceeded, increased government expenditures produced diminishing and, in quick order, negative returns. In particular, horrendous losses racked up by inefficient public enterprises proved a heavy burden on the public treasury. Continued attempts to provide goods, services and jobs for the general public soon undermined the fiscal position of government. Runaway fiscal deficits and crushing foreign debts eventually destroyed the balance of payments of some CARICOM states, leading to sharp reductions in the standard of living which the initial public expenditure was calculated to raise.

Jamaica, Trinidad and Tobago, and Guyana, with some friendly persuasion from the IMF and the World Bank, have accepted the inherent limitation of the state and the need to shift the responsibility for commercial and industrial expansion to the private sector. This leaves governments with the 'minimum role' of establishing 'the broad framework of socio-economic development' and of ensuring 'the existence of an adequate social infrastructure'. The reduced burden of loss-making enterprises also enables government to pay greater attention to its key responsibility; that is, to maintain macroeconomic stability, both internally and externally.

Future efforts to promote economic development must involve the multiplication of opportunities for the formation and expansion of business enterprises, whether single proprietorships, partnerships or corporations. For in any mixed economy there are more people employed privately than in the public sector and, increasingly, more people self-employed or employed in small businesses than in the large scale and frequently capital-intensive state-owned enterprises. In failing to recognize this obvious truth, *Guidelines'* elaborate proposals for increased employment mostly miss the mark. (pp. 24–25)

The paradigm of Caribbean development proposed in this paper turns out to be quite similar to what the World Bank has termed the 'Nordic development paradigm', which restricts the role of government to the provision of infrastructure, high quality public administration, and market discipline. It also incorporates consensus-seeking among organized labour, capital and government, the sharing of economic prosperity among all social classes, a foreign trade orientation, and informed public participation in social and economic decision making, all of which features come highly recommended in *Guidelines*. The outline of the Nordic development paradigm is given in the appendix to this paper.

Strategic Agenda

Out of the above discussion we may identify six areas of strategic importance in which political leaders must take specific decisions *today* so that Caribbean peoples will be prepared for an uncertain tomorrow. Several of these recommendations are implicit in *Guidelines*. However, a strategic document should make its conclusions explicit.

Outward-looking Development

> ➤ The regulations governing investment by foreigners should be liberalized – especially those related to alien land-holding.
> ➤ Caribbean enterprises should be facilitated in overseas investment, especially in their attempts to develop new markets or secure their sources of supply.
> ➤ Existing export promotion programmes should be reviewed and upgraded.

Decentralization

> ➤ The conduct of industrial, commercial and professional activities should be deregulated to the furthest extent possible.

- ➤ The commercial and industrial operations of public enterprises should be privatised wherever feasible.
- ➤ Public sector operations, for example, schools should be reformed so as to ensure that authority and competence are located in the same place.

Human Resource Development

- ➤ Governments should cease and desist from those practices and policies that contribute to the emigration of the region's richest human resources.
- ➤ Suitable measures should be taken to enhance the scope of professional educators for the creative application of their skills.
- ➤ A much higher priority should be assigned to the resource needs of the University of the West Indies and other tertiary educational institutions. The University of Guyana should be merged with the UWI to achieve economies of scale.
- ➤ Higher priorities should similarly be assigned to expenditures on libraries, museums, and other artistic and cultural activities.
- ➤ Governments should take urgent steps to enhance health and recreational facilities through a blend of private and public initiatives.
- ➤ Governments should seek the cooperation of the private sector in the establishment of venture capital corporations and other programmes for the identification and promotion of entrepreneurs.

Management Development

- ➤ Governments should give their fullest support to current programmes for the teaching of management at the University of the West Indies.

➤ Urgent steps should be taken towards the professionalization of the civil service.

➤ Governments should take legislative and other steps to eliminate political considerations from the day-to-day operations of statutory corporations and public enterprises.

➤ Legislation should be passed to promote the highest standards of competence and ethical conduct among the professions.

➤ Institutions whose task it is to monitor developments in the global marketplace should be established or strengthened.

➤ Governments should allocate the resources needed to place CARICAD on a financially independent footing.

Technology

➤ A high priority should be assigned to expenditures on research and development institutions such as CARIRI and CARDI.

➤ Fiscal incentives should be offered to private enterprises which carry out in-house research and development, and make substantial investments in productivity enhancing technology.

➤ Governments should promote foreign investment in areas characterized by dynamic technologies; for example, telecommunications, data processing and computers.

Regional Integration

➤ Governments should act swiftly to remove the remaining impediments to the movement of goods, capital, enterprise and skills within the region.

➤ Enterprises owned and controlled by CARICOM nationals or residents should enjoy the same privileges as national enterprises throughout the region.

- ➤ Multi-taxation agreements should be put in place to prevent the over-taxation of enterprises within CARICOM.
- ➤ The merger of enterprises across national boundaries within CARICOM should be actively encouraged, especially among financial institutions, so as to promote viable organizations capable of competing in the global marketplace.
- ➤ In view of the chaotic arrangements that now prevail for intra-regional payments settlements, governments should move swiftly to establish a monetary union.
- ➤ On the achievement of a monetary union, governments should move swiftly to establish a regional stock exchange.

Government

The withdrawal of the state from the arena of commercial and industrial enterprise would free it to orchestrate the complementary functions of its 'social partners', as *Guidelines* felicitously describes the private sector and labour. This will require a new social contract between political leaders and the electorate. With reduced functions and an unpredictable international environment, government can no longer promise the perpetual improvements in public welfare. At best, it can promise to deliver honest and efficient public service in keeping with the long-term interests of the nation, and to provide citizens with the education, training and support which enable them to help themselves.

The Private Sector

The private sector — the second social partner — should move to fill the vacuum vacated by government in an even more comprehensive manner than *Guidelines* suggests. It should define its own programme within the framework of the strategic agenda set out above. It should:

- actively explore opportunities for foreign trade, whether through its own efforts or in collaboration with foreign entities, and strive continually to improve its competitive advantage in the global marketplace.
- offer opportunities within its staff to all sectors of society, without regard to race, religion or class.
- dramatically increase its financial support for the university and other institutions of tertiary education.
- increase its financial support for management training on the three university campuses.
- seek out and apply those technologies which maximize value added to its production, and
- exploit to the fullest the opportunities arising from regional economic integration whenever that elusive goal is achieved.

The acceptance by labour of social partnership with government and the private sector is essential to the efficacy of any Caribbean development model. The emphasis on quality that characterizes the global marketplace requires the full commitment of workers. As the Japanese have taught us, quality is not achievable in conditions of adversarial industrial relations — the British legacy to the Caribbean. But that issue falls outside the purview of this paper.

Commissioned by the Caribbean Association of Industry and Commerce Regional Economic Conference, Port-of-Spain, Trinidad, February 27 to March 1, 1991

Notes

1. Kenichi Ohmae, *The Mind of the Strategist* (New York: Penguin Books, 1982), 42.

2. Peter F. Drucker, *Management: Tasks, Responsibilities, Practices* (New York: Harper & Row, 1973), 125.

3. Alvin Toffler, *The Third Wave* (London: Pan Books, 1981).

4. The Rockefeller Foundation, 'The Rockefeller Foundation in the Developing World' (New York, 1986).

5. Jacques Attali, 'Lives on the Horizon: A New Order in the Making', *New Perspective Quarterly* 7, no.2 (Spring 1990): 5.

6. Peter F. Drucker, *Management*, 14.

7. Michael Porter, *The Competitive Advantage of Nations* (London: The Macmillan Press Ltd, 1990).

8. Ibid.

APPENDIX

Nordic Development Paradigm[1]

In the mid-1800s the Nordic countries were agrarian economies with low income levels. Starting with Sweden around the 1870s, they have all experienced high growth to become advanced industrial economies. In 1987 the five Nordic countries had an average per capita GDP of $19,670, slightly above that of Japan and the United States, and 48 per cent higher than the EC average. Moreover, Scandinavia's social indicators are among the best in the world. Like any other countries, the Nordic countries had their own unique circumstances. However, there are two noteworthy factors behind their success: the relative roles of the state and the market and the pattern of their orientation and regional cooperation.

Roles of the State and the Market

At an early stage of development the Nordic states assumed the role of providing infrastructure, high-quality administration, and social services, while the goods-producing sectors were largely left to private enterprise and market discipline. The state actively promoted universal access to social services, encouraged a harmonious partnership between labour and entrepreneurs, and kept a light rein on the private sector.

This was in sharp contrast to the practice in socialist countries, where government took over ownership and direction of the means of production. It was also in contrast to the planned economies in the Third World, where government tries to capture the 'commanding heights' of the economy in the goods-producing sectors. It also differed from the purely market-oriented systems, where free enterprise, without the state provision of social services, led to large income disparities: great wealth alongside acute poverty. It differed, too, from Japan's and Korea's approach, where the state played lead roles in targeting, establishing, and protecting key industries.

The Nordic countries have consistently sought consensus among organized labour, capital, and government. Sharing economic prosperity was seen as essential for economic development and political stability. Early on the Nordic societies strove for universal literacy, while emphasizing high quality, although limited, higher education. These policies encouraged informed public participation in social and economic decision-making and provided a healthy and well-trained labour force. The public sector's enabling role and respect for market mechanisms allowed the Nordic countries to achieve a high level of economic efficiency. Private entrepreneurship, encouraged but not directed by the state, became the prime mover in the establishment and expansion of the goods-producing sectors and their trading and financial institutions.

Trade Orientation and Regional Cooperation

The Scandinavians have long been open to trade and technical advances from abroad. The patterns of trade orientation emerged as a result of market forces, in contrast to the more top-down mercantilist policies of Japan and Korea, which guided trade. Further, the early expansion of Nordic industrial entrepreneurship was linked to the domestic resource base and to demand arising from the agricultural sector and infrastructure investments. However, exports increasingly became the driving force in industrial expansion.

The small Nordic countries have demonstrated the scope for regional cooperation despite relatively homogeneous resource endowment and competitive, rather than complementary, patterns of production. Stable and peaceful political relations fostered economic cooperation, carried out without expensive institutional structures. Trade within the region grew from 12 to 13 per cent (of total Nordic trade) before World War I to 30 or more per cent thereafter.

The Nordic countries' remarkable transformation from agrarian societies into modern industrial economies offers a distinctive development paradigm. Their success resulted from a social market economy with its combination of free enterprise economic policies and active social policies.

Note

1.   The World Bank, *Sub-Saharan Africa: From Crisis to Sustainable Growth* (Washington, DC: The World Bank, 1989), 187.

SECTION II

Debt and the Balance of Payments

6

THE INTERNATIONAL DEBT CRISIS IN THIRD WORLD PERSPECTIVE

Shortly after my appointment in 1972 as Governor of the Central Bank of Barbados, I was named an advisor to the Committee of Twenty for the Reform of the International Monetary Fund. From 1974 until my retirement last year, I attended biannual meetings of the Interim Committee of the Fund, the successor to the Committee of Twenty, in various capitals around the world. I had a box-seat view, so to speak, of the unfolding drama of the international debt crisis. I can remember vividly the panic among the finance ministers of the non-oil-producing countries, especially of the LDCs, at their first meeting of 1974 held in Rome shortly after the first oil shock.

Naturally, the spectacles through which I watched the drama had a different tint from those of most viewers from the developed world. Speaking in my resident state of Florida in April last year, Mr Michel Camdessus, Managing Director of the IMF, said: 'The debt strategy which the international community embarked upon has achieved much.' With the economies of sub-Saharan Africa now popularly described as 'basket cases'; with the vast majority of Latin American and Caribbean countries trapped in a syndrome of contracting output, falling exports, rising unemployment, collapsing currencies, spiraling inflation and chronic civil unrest, and with the debt of most LDCs even higher than in 1982, I wonder whether Mr Camdessus and I have been watching the same performance.

As you may have gathered by now, I did not like the show. In my view, the long festering sore of the international debt crisis reflects the collective failure of professional economists, especially those in the First World. In spite of the warning of the Brandt Commission[1] and the Lever Report,[2] and the eloquent pleas of our own Sir Shridath 'Sonny' Ramphal at the Commonwealth Secretariat, professional economists were late in recognizing the severity of the debt problem, were casual in their estimates of the capacity of LDC economies for adjustment, and were insensitive to the human costs of the adjustment process. An early and accurate assessment of the situation, followed by a cogent statement of the problem by the world's leading economists, would have hastened a comprehensive attack by politicians on the international debt crisis.

In their frustration and disillusionment, many of my Third World colleagues have read an international capitalist or neo-imperialist conspiracy into the disasters resulting from the international debt crisis. Perhaps it is because of the peculiar circumstances of my own country that I attribute quite human and ordinary causes to these intellectual and moral failures. So far Barbados has not even had to seek the rescheduling of any foreign debt. Indeed, it has itself been a victim of the debt crisis — Guyana defaulted on its liabilities to the CARICOM Multilateral Clearing Facility, with US$65 million owing to Barbados.

I have identified three main causes of the failure of the economics profession in respect of the international debt crisis: a certain ethnocentricity on the part of First World economists, a lack of historical perspective, and a misplaced reliance on market-based policies.

Ethnocentricity

There is an important law in modern physics called the 'Heisenberg Uncertainty Principle' which recognizes the influence of the observer on physical phenomena being observed and measured. A similar and even more difficult problem confronts the social scientist — the problem of observing and analyzing data of which one is a part, and of separating one's own value set from the values of the subjects one is observing. Jacob Bronowski calls it the problem of 'self-reference'.[3] Let's face it. It is the judgment of First World economists that influence the policies of governments of the industrial nations, multinational banks, and international financial institutions like the IMF and World Bank. (Thatcherian monetarism and Reaganite supply-side economics are two recent examples of the persuasive powers of these professional economists.) It is therefore quite natural that the opinions of First World economists should reflect the interests and the points of view of their clients: governments and multinationals in the First World, the IMF and the World Bank.

The enthusiasm of governments of the industrial nations for transferring resources to the developing world weakened considerably in the 80s. Indeed, they made the situation worse by their increasingly protectionist policies. Above all, they were slow to perceive a role for themselves in the solution of the debt crisis. The Reagan administration, in particular, did not want to be seen as 'bailing out' the banks. The IMF and World Bank were primarily concerned with preserving the integrity of the international banking system, and did all in their power to persuade banks to continue lending to debtor nations. At the same time, they imposed the most austere adjustment programmes on debtor countries to ensure continued servicing of outstanding loans, while the international banks insisted on the servicing of LDC loans. Determined to avoid write-downs on their LDC loan portfolios, they did not stop to consider that the burden of debt payments would depress growth in the LDCs and hasten the inevitable default on original loan capital.

Crisis management became the order of the day, as my friend Bill Rhodes of Citicorp and his travelling circus of bankers moved from debtor country to debtor country, pulling off last-minute deals on the rescheduling of old debt and the extension of new loans. This 'no-win' strategy, known as the 'case by case' approach, was heartily supported by the international financial establishment. Last January, a World Bank report described the participants in these negotiations as suffering from 'debt fatigue'. However, as John Williamson observed late in 1985: 'Debt has been renegotiated, reconstructed, rolled over and stretched out, but it has not been forgiven, nor have interest rates been reduced by more than modest cuts in spreads.'[4]

Morris Miller, in his incisive work, *Coping Is not Enough*, wryly remarks on 'the power of short-sightedness' which enabled the financial community to reject any creative departure from the 'case by case' approach.[5] It was such short-sightedness which led William Cline to conclude in September 1983: 'Broadly, the debt problem is one of illiquidity, not insolvency, and if sufficient financial packages can be arranged to tide over debtor countries temporarily, they should be able to return to a sound financial footing within two to four years.'[6]

'Moral hazard' was another manifestation of ethnocentricity which inhibited any extension of debt relief to LDCs. It would be morally harmful for the indebted nations, some insisted, if they did not repay their debts in full. Even as sophisticated a personality as Paul Volcker, former Chairman of the Federal Reserve Board, once argued before Congress against debt relief: 'The debt burden is the result of poorly thought-out economic policies in many Third World countries and the proper solution is fundamental adjustments on their part.'[7]

The *Economist* magazine, once a gung-ho supporter of the 'case by case' approach, would eventually concede that the problems of LDCs 'were caused as much by the profligacy of the banks and by the ill-managed economic policies of the rich as by their own incompetence.'[8] On the occasion when a British economist raised the issue of 'moral hazard', I could not resist the retort: 'I find it remarkable that the citizen of a nation with such an outstanding record of not repaying its debts should raise the issue of moral hazard.'

Of course, a welcome feature of the 'case by case' approach was that it permitted the international bankers' cartel collectively to deal with an individual country with the implied promise that it would get a better deal on its own than as part of a group. It was the classical 'Prisoner's Dilemma' of Game Theory. (The Prisoner's Dilemma describes a situation in which joint suspects are detained incommunicado. Each is then promised a light sentence if he squeals on his partner and a heavy penalty should he remain silent and his partner squeals on him.) That is one reason why the much-feared debtors' revolt never materialized.

Ethnocentricity would reveal itself in a most curious way. At a conference in Mexico City during the fall of 1982 the top economists of Mexico, Brazil and Venezuela explained, with amazing self-satisfaction, the severely deflationary programmes they had devised for their respective countries. The Mexican programme, for example, envisioned that it would take until 1990 before economic output recovered to the level of 1982. I could not help observing that all three gentlemen held doctorates from top American graduate schools of economics where they had apparently lost the capacity of examining problems from their own national point of view.

Historical Perspective

I have been most astonished at the general failure of international economists to place the debt crisis in historical perspective. Last January at a conference held by the Bank of

Jamaica in Kingston, was the first occasion that I have heard economists, from either the First or the Third World, treat the subject extensively in an historical context. My own attempts to do so at earlier conferences had been met, at best, with polite amusement. Just as 'real women don't pump gas' and 'real men don't eat quiche', neither do real economists read history. For the young economist riveted to his or her computer screen, events prior to 1960 are lost in the mist of antiquity. Yet, as the Spanish historian George Santayana reminds us, 'Those who cannot remember the past are condemned to repeat it.'

One of the reasons which induced New York banks in the 1970s to make sovereign loans with such abandon was the conviction that, in the immortal words of the former president of Citicorp, Mr Walter Wriston, 'Countries do not go bankrupt.' In fact, France, Germany and the UK, all found themselves unable to repay their US loans after the First World War, as did the UK again after the Second World War. After the 1929 crash, several Latin American countries, notably Mexico, Brazil and Argentina, also defaulted on their foreign debts. As President Harry Truman once remarked, 'The only thing new in the world is the history you haven't read.'

Yet, the analogy between the current crisis and the German war reparations issue after World War I, as well as the Marshall Plan after World War II, is most compelling and instructive. In both cases the economic interests of debtor and creditor nations were clearly intertwined. John Maynard Keynes warned in *The Economic Consequences of the Peace* (1919)[9] that insistence on war reparations would injure both the Allies and the Germans. By 1932, when the US eventually forgave the German war reparations debt, the German middle classes had already been demoralized by the ravages of hyper-inflation. Hitler came to power the following year! The lessons from the Peace of Versailles were not lost on the Allies after the Second World War. Massive resources were transferred through the Marshall Plan to restore the economies of Western Europe, victors and vanquished alike, to the mutual long-term advantage of both Western Europe and the United States.

By 1983 observers who, like Lord Lever, were not blinded by ethnocentric tendencies, had come to realize that the LDC debt was not a simple problem of temporary illiquidity, but one that threatened the mutual interests of both LDCs and industrial nations. Debt service payments between 1981 and 1983 had involved a dramatic fall in LDC imports, colourfully described as 'import strangulation'. There were also tremendous costs in terms of social and political tensions as well as other human misfortunes. The reduction in LDC imports, in turn, led to a decline in exports to developing countries and, by one estimate, accounted for a loss of about two million work years in the United States.

The threat to the international banking system was serious enough, since total LDC debt outstanding in 1982 far exceeded the capital of the major US banks involved. But even more frightening was the threat posed to the world political order. The emergence of stable and democratic regimes was clearly in the interest of the developed nations. Yet, as the crushing IMF/World Bank adjustment programmes exacerbated social and political tensions, the debt crisis threatened to abort promising democratic movements in countries like Brazil and Argentina, and to overwhelm traditional democracies like Jamaica and Costa Rica.

Most serious of all, the refusal of the international banks to grant debt relief led to a massive transfer of resources to the developed from the developing countries, depressing economic growth in the latter and virtually ensuring default on their original loans. The 'case by case' approach was clearly a strategy doomed to failure. As in the case of the Marshall Plan, only massive intervention by the governments of the industrial nations could have reversed the net outflows of capital from the LDCs. A timely and orderly programme of debt relief, combined with intelligent counseling by the IMF and World Bank, would have minimized the suffering of the debtor countries and maximized the proportion of debt eventually repaid to the creditors.

Reliance on Market-based Policies

It was a great misfortune for LDCs that the debt crisis occurred at a time when 'free-market' doctrine was in its ascendancy. After the failure of the neo-Keynesians to diagnose and prescribe for 'stagflation' in the 70s, the free market economists, led by the arch-monetarist Milton Friedman, were able to launch a successful counter-revolution. The 'free market' model was restored to the central position from which Keynes had temporarily dislodged it. Karl Brunner, another devout monetarist, argues that 'price theory is the crucial paradigm; indeed, the only paradigm, that economists have.'[10]

The 'Rational Expectations' school of economists would later declare markets to be generally 'efficient', thereby dismissing considerations of market imperfection. I am told that graduate students can now obtain their doctorates at reputable economics departments without ever studying the works of Joan Robinson and Edward Chamberlin on imperfect competition. The 'Free marketeers' have also dismissed the validity of a special theory of economic development, the area in which our own Sir Arthur Lewis earned his Nobel prize. The 'magic of the market' is now presumed to cure all problems in both developed and developing countries.

The 'free market' ideology currently permeates the structural adjustment programmes of the IMF and the World Bank that exert tremendous pressure on LDCs to pursue market-based strategies. An adjustment package predictably includes drastic currency devaluation, positive real interest rates, the removal of subsidies, privatization, the liberalization of trade and the freeing-up of capital flows. Incidentally, the 1982–84 IMF stand-by agreement for Barbados fortunately contained none of the above conditionalities. Maybe that is why it succeeded! Ironically too, IMF insistence on the liberalization of capital flows exacerbated capital flight from Latin American LDCs into high interest-paying US securities.

Undoubtedly, policy makers in the LDCs also seriously retarded economic development in their countries by over-centralization and excessive intervention in the marketplace. I have been the most vocal critic of such tendencies in the CARICOM Caribbean. My case against IMF/World Bank economists is that their prescriptions hardly distinguish between industrialized economies with highly developed goods and capital markets and LDCs with poorly developed or collapsed markets. Indeed, the crucial difference between developing and developed economies lies in the degree of market development. We cannot pretend that efficient markets exist when we know very well that they do not. For example, the use of the market-oriented devaluation or interest rate tools makes no sense in Guyana, where financial markets have obviously collapsed. Here, the appropriate strategy, rather, is the restoration of effective markets through a retreat from nationalization and counter-trading, and the removal of other obstacles to the free flow of resources.

In fact, it was the efficiency of their real and financial markets which enabled the western industrialized economies and Japan to adjust with such elegance to the oil shocks of 1974 and 1978. On the other hand, LDCs lacked both the flexibility engendered by efficient markets, and the advanced technology for economizing on the use of energy. It is therefore not surprising that the market-based adjustment strategies of the IMF and the World Bank have achieved so little in LDCs, and have resulted in such economic dislocation and social unrest.

Even in the most advanced economies, market failures sometimes occur with politically and socially unacceptable consequences. Not long ago the American Congress voted massive subsidies to alleviate the distress to farmers caused by the recent drought. A few years ago both Lockheed and Chrysler were rescued from bankruptcy by the US government. In the global economy, economically, politically and socially unacceptable market failures, like the ravages of world wars or the current debt crisis, must similarly be addressed by international political action. The 'free market' cannot be expected to mobilize the massive volume of resources necessary for a satisfactory solution. Dr Rudiger Dornbusch eventually got it right: 'Solving debt problems is mostly politics'; yet today, unlike in the 1920s and 1930s, the problem is made to look as if it were solely an issue of economics.[11]

Conclusion

As in medicine, correct diagnosis and timely treatment would have minimized the costs and discomfort of the debt crisis for both the creditor nations and the debtor LDCs. As it was, it was left to history to impose her penalties in a haphazard fashion — penalties which fell disproportionately on the LDCs.

The break came in the fall of 1985 when US Secretary of the Treasury James Baker eventually realized that a feasible solution required the resumption of economic growth in the debtor countries which, in turn, required the renewal of commercial bank lending to LDCs. The Baker Initiative never took on substance, since he was not prepared to put American treasury funds where his mouth was. However, it was an important ice-breaker.

Secondly, as sane Latin American countries declared moratoria on debt repayments, the international financial community gradually came to the realization that some element of debt relief, whether in the form of interest rate caps, debt-equity swaps, or whatever, was an unavoidable ingredient in any solution, and began laying aside massive reserves against bad debts.

Thirdly, the governments of several industrialized countries are converting some of their official aid loans to sub-Saharan Africa into grants. They have also committed increasing resources to the IMF and World Bank to assist in the restructuring of debt-ridden LDCs.

Fourthly, the IMF and the World Bank have recognized that the time horizons of their structural adjustment programmes have been unrealistically short. Indeed, some rhetoric about 'adjustment with a human face' has recently emanated from the august corridors of these institutions.

Finally, numerous proposals for comprehensive Marshall Plan-type initiatives have been springing from sources as varied and as unlikely as Henry Kissinger and James D. Robinson, President of the American Express Bank. The latter envisages a radical 'Institute of International Debt Development', which would be capitalized by the major industrial nations, especially Japan, and which would purchase the outstanding LDC debts from the commercial banks. Indeed, the Japanese, in the face of puzzling American objections, have put forward a comprehensive plan of debt relief and economic recovery for Third World countries seriously affected by foreign debt — very much along the lines of the Lever Report (1983).

To parody the advertisement for ladies' cigarettes, 'We have come a long way! Maybe Abba Eban is right: 'History teaches us that men and nations behave wisely only once they have exhausted all other alternatives.' Better late than never!

Presented at the University of Colorado, Denver, USA, August 1988 and reprinted in *Caribbean Affairs*, Port-of-Spain, Trinidad October 1988

Notes

1.   The Brandt Commission.
2.   The Lever Report.

3. Jacob Bronowski, *The Identity of Man* (Garden City, NJ: The Natural History Press, 1971), 121–122.

4. John Williamson, as quoted by Morris Miller in, *Coping Is not Enough* (Homewood, IL: Dow-Jones-Irvin, 1986), 136.

5. Morris Miller, *Coping Is not Enough*, 136.

6. William Cline, as quoted by Morris Miller, *Coping Is not Enough*, 59.

7. Paul Volcker, as quoted by Morris Miller, *Coping Is not Enough*, 137.

8. *Economist*, 'World Economy Survey', Sept. 26–Oct. 2, 1987, p. 53.

9. John Maynard Keynes, *The Economic Consequences of the Peace* (New York: Penguin Books, 1995).

10. Karl Brunner, as quoted by Arjo Klamer in, *Conversations with Economists* (Totowa, NJ: Rowan & Allanheld, 1983), 9, 183.

11. Rudiger Dornbusch, as quoted by Morris Miller, *Coping Is not Enough*, 84.

7

THE BALANCE OF PAYMENTS CRISIS IN THE CARIBBEAN

WHICH WAY OUT?

Introduction

The moment I accepted the invitation to speak on this topic, I recalled a recent experience in Holland. My Dutch friend was taking me to a restaurant near the sea when he said to me: 'Look up at that ship.' I had to look up since, as my friend pointed out, our car was more than 30 feet below sea level. Had the dike given way then, as did in fact happen in the early 1950s, many persons, including us, would have been swept away. Yet, I reflected, I had never heard a Dutchman speak of the 'crisis of the dikes'. The breaching of the dikes is a risk that the Dutch take in their stride. Their only protection is the tremendous skill at dike building that they have developed over the centuries. Similarly, that is the way it will have to be in the case of the balance of payments in the Caribbean.

As long as a country trades with other countries it is likely to have balance of payments difficulties. It is unlikely that the value of their exports will always match the value of their imports; sometimes there will be a deficit on foreign transactions, and sometimes there will be a surplus. Even countries as self-sufficient in respect of natural resources as the Soviet Union may experience balance of payments fluctuations. In recent years Russia has on occasion suffered from poor crops, and has had to seek trade credits from the US in order to obtain adequate supplies of grain.

Of course, the balance of payments poses most serious problems for countries with limited or highly skewed natural resource endowments. Most Caribbean countries produce a few major commodities, such as sugar, bauxite in Guyana and Jamaica, and some oil in Trinidad and Tobago, but are totally lacking in iron ore, copper, tin and other basic raw materials. The need to import, then, is an economic fact of Caribbean life. Until the oil shock of 1974, balance of payments crises were the result of civil disturbances, as in the case of Zaire, or extraordinarily bad economic management, as in the case of Ghana in the last years of Nkrumah. However, the four-fold price increase of so essential a commodity as oil posed tremendous difficulties for all non-oil producers, and for countries that depended heavily on imports in general. Except for Trinidad and Tobago, all Caribbean territories were severely affected. Not only did they have to pay four times as much for oil as before, they also had to find more foreign exchange to purchase imported industrial goods whose price reflected increased energy costs.

A cruel irony of the oil crisis is that the country against which the oil embargo was specifically directed, the US, was the one best able to weather it. The reason is that the OPEC nations had no other option than to accept US dollars in payment for their oil. (US dollars are merely IOUs of the US government.) They also had to invest their oil revenues in US securities, since the US is the only economy large enough to absorb such massive inflows of investment capital. Indeed, the health of the US economy is very much the concern of OPEC nations; no one knows this better than Sheik Yamani of Saudi Arabia, who restrains his OPEC partners from further oil increases that would only worsen inflation in the US and erode the value of their American investments. They cannot invest in the USSR.

Furthermore, in an effort to modernize their economies, many OPEC members have made heavy purchases of capital equipment and high technology services from Western Europe and Japan, who, with the exception of the 'sick men' — Britain and Italy — were able to adjust with remarkable swiftness to the oil shock. The main victims were non-oil producing Third World countries whose currencies were not acceptable IOUs, and who could not produce industrial goods to pay for costly oil imports. This paper attempts to lay bare the anatomy of the balance of payments crisis in the English-speaking Caribbean. Firstly, we will review the historical development of the crisis. Secondly, we will set out the mechanics of balance of payments operations. Thirdly, we will develop a model to explain the relationships among the factors affecting the balance of payments and the various policy considerations involved. The special problems of a prolonged and massive balance of payments surplus, as in the case of Trinidad and Tobago, will be considered in the fourth section. The fifth section will deal with long-term aspects of the balance of payments. The paper ends with some general observations on the conditions required for maintaining the balance of payments in equilibrium.

Slide into crisis

A country's decline into balance of payments crisis may be compared to a man on a slippery slope. Once his slide begins, it is extremely difficult for him to reverse the process, which we might term an implosion. Two Caribbean territories, Jamaica and Guyana, provide excellent laboratories for the study of this process. A careful and disinterested study of their experiences should be carried out as soon as possible so that we in the region may draw the appropriate conclusions. In fact, the non-oil-producing more developed countries of CARICOM (MDCs) were better placed than most other Third World non-oil producers. Both Guyana and Jamaica enjoyed heavy foreign exchange inflows in 1975 as a result of favourable bauxite and sugar prices. Jamaica, in particular, extracted considerably increased taxes from the North American bauxite companies. In the Barbadian case, high sugar prices in 1974 brought our foreign payments roughly in balance, while the record sugar prices of 1975 produced a handsome surplus of BDS$37 million. The rest, as they say, is history.

The Government of Guyana was encouraged by the rosy external situation to embark on an ambitious capital works programme, and by the end of 1976 its foreign reserves had fallen to minus G$31.4 million from about G$200 million at the end of 1975. Jamaica's foreign reserves actually increased by J$54 million during 1974 to reach J$130 million; by the end of 1976 her foreign exchange holdings had declined to minus J$181.4 million. In Barbados, the 1975 trade surplus of BDS$37 million was completely eroded by heavy consumer imports in 1976, and a deficit of BDS$34 million was recorded.

The crisis may be dated from 1976. In that year, both Guyana and Jamaica, the latter in particular, undertook heavy Euro-dollar borrowings. Jamaica had already taken advantage of the new oil facility, and both countries made drawings under the oil facility and the compensatory financing facility (CFF) of the International Monetary Fund (IMF). The oil facility was a special fund set up to help countries most seriously affected by the oil crisis; the CFF is a regular facility of the IMF to help countries which suffer a shortfall in their traditional commodity export earnings. Caribbean countries qualified for the CFF because of the sharp reduction in sugar and bauxite earnings in 1976. Guyana, Jamaica and Barbados also negotiated balance of payments support from oil-rich Trinidad and Tobago, but Barbados made no drawings until February 1977.

The conditions attached to CFF drawings are not stringent, and access to the oil facility only required that the member country should first have drawn down its gold tranche position with the Fund. In September 1976, Guyana negotiated a stand-by arrangement with the IMF under which it undertook to follow a specified set of economic policies. Later that year it drew on its gold tranche position. This meant that any further drawings from the Fund, such as the one currently being negotiated, would involve quite stringent conditions. By mid-1977 Jamaica had also drawn down all available 'soft' IMF funds. For ideological reasons, the Manley government had for some time avoided conditional borrowings, but after access to other sources of funds, including OPEC and COMECON, had yielded inadequate amounts, Jamaica concluded a stand-by arrangement with the IMF in August 1977 under which she adopted a two-tier currency arrangement, the equivalent of a partial currency devaluation.

Jamaica failed to satisfy the terms of this agreement and the arrangements lapsed before year-end. New negotiations were set in train during 1978 for a US$240 million loan under the extended fund facility (EFF). The terms included an immediate and massive devaluation of the Jamaican dollar as well as a programme of monthly mini-devaluations, which were agreed upon only after an extended period of difficult negotiations. Under EFF arrangements, further drawings are conditional on countries meeting certain requirements, euphemistically known as 'tests'; for example, wage settlements and commercial bank credit should not increase beyond certain percentages, and imports and the government budget deficit maintained within prescribed limits.

When a country's balance of payments position becomes as desperate as Jamaica's, it can hardly refuse to accept IMF conditions. Without additional foreign exchange it cannot correct the imbalance, while existing foreign debt must be serviced if the country is not to go into default. Furthermore, the ultimate solution of increased export earnings is unattainable without crucial imports of raw material and capital equipment. Even more important, international commercial banks will extend no further credit to a country in balance of payments crisis without the Fund's imprimatur of approval on policy meas-ures being taken to correct the situation.

Chart 1
CARICOM: Foreign Reserves (US$)

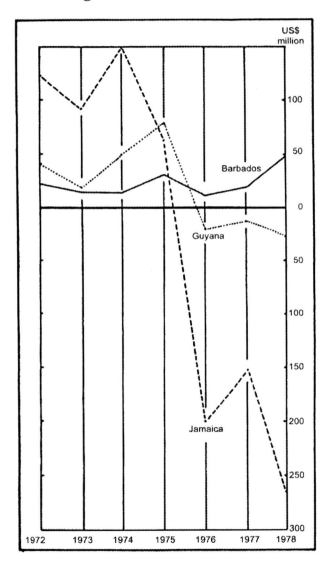

The defensive measures taken by the Barbados government over the period 1976 to 1977 saved Barbados from IMF strictures. The first step was to introduce fiscal measures calculated to dampen import demand; these were later supplemented by direct import controls, particularly of motor cars, by monetary measures to restrict consumer credit, and by a voluntary incomes policy. During 1977 the government took advantage of Trinidad and Tobago's balance of payments support loan, and drew on the IMF compensatory facility. The economy responded well during 1977 and, assisted by excellent tourism earnings in 1978, the balance of payments turned in a handsome surplus of BDS$34 million.

The chief advantage of Barbados was that its social and political institutions were able to absorb the shock of the stern policy measures required to achieve economic adjustment, especially in the area of industrial relations. It is a great tribute to the Barbadian trade union leadership that the island was able to avoid the bitter industrial strife that has characterized Caribbean industrial relations in recent years so that balance of payments problems never reached the same degree of severity in Barbados as elsewhere. In Guyana, political and industrial conflict led to poor economic performance; similarly in Jamaica. Both governments imposed rigorous exchange control restrictions in an effort to conserve foreign exchange and to channel it to the foreign-exchange earnings sectors. But the very scarcity of foreign exchange itself, especially for the purchase of raw materials and capital equipment, has militated against economic recovery in these countries. In addition, significant sums of scarce foreign exchange were exported from both countries, and many professionals and businessmen emigrated.

The lesson of the past few years is that a balance of payments crisis, once it breaks out, feeds on itself. A serious payments deficit makes foreign borrowing difficult; foreign exchange for essential imports and strategic capital investment becomes scarce; attempts to conserve foreign exchange through comprehensive exchange controls create a black market, encouraging further capital flight. In countries whose middle classes are accustomed to North American standards of comfort, shortages of traditional imports become intolerable and lead to the emigration of the most highly skilled; as they take their skills abroad, the economic situation worsens and social strife is exacerbated. In the Jamaican case, widespread social unrest ruined the tourism industry, aggravating the balance of payments problem. As is usual in cumulative processes of this kind, only drastic measures can arrest the decline, and the more prolonged the process, the more drastic are the measures required.

What is more, the balance of payments difficulties of Jamaica and Guyana created hardships for other Caribbean territories. Both Jamaica and Guyana imposed import restrictions against their trading partners within CARICOM, promoting unemployment especially in Trinidad and Tobago, and Barbados. Payments for goods exported to Jamaica and Guyana were also frequently delayed. A prominent University of the West Indies economist at the Cave Hill campus in Barbados has accused me of worrying too much about the balance of payments problem. I plead guilty, and will continue to live in sin.

Mechanics of the balance of payments

Before we can decide on a strategy for dealing with our balance of payments problem, we must first understand the mechanics of foreign trade. As we have seen, the potential for a balance of payments problem always exists when a country trades. One set of problems arises when a country's foreign payments run into heavy deficit with its trading partners; another set of problems arises when, like Trinidad and Tobago, it runs a heavy surplus.

All countries in the Caribbean must import a great proportion of their goods and services. We all import goods such as wheat, flour, machinery, automobiles, and services like air transport and insurance. In 1977 Barbados imported BDS\$546 million worth of goods and BDS\$122 million worth of services, amounting to an import bill of BDS\$668 million. These imports had to be financed in a manner satisfactory to the nations that supplied them. In fact, we financed them by exporting BDS\$182 million of goods, by selling BDS\$361 million of services — mostly tourism services — to foreigners, by gifts of BDS\$32 million (net) — usually from Barbadians living overseas — by borrowings of BDS\$35 million, and by other capital flows (both long and short-term) amounting to BDS\$86 million. Inflows actually turned out to be more than needed, so that Barbados's foreign exchange reserves rose by BDS\$28 million.

The tidiest way of financing imports would be for us to export to each country goods of equal value to the cost of our imports from them. Our payments and our receipts would then match precisely with respect to each of our trading partners, and our overall foreign trade would be in perfect balance. However, we live in an untidy world. The Japanese do not want sugar and tourism services from us in equal value to the motor cars and hi-fi sets we import from them; nor are they willing to accept Barbadian dollars in return for their products since they would not be able to spend them on imports from other countries. What happens then? Fortunately, there are other countries, especially the US, with whom our overall payments are in surplus, and whose currency is accepted by other countries in settlement of international debts. We are therefore able to use our excess US dollars to settle deficits with Japan and other countries. National currencies generally acceptable throughout the world as final payments for goods are said to be 'hard', and include the US dollar, the pound sterling, the French franc, the Swiss franc and the Japanese yen. There are others with limited acceptability, like the Canadian dollar, the Belgian franc and the Dutch guilder, but the ones mentioned first are the hardest. In practice Barbados earns hard currencies abroad wherever it can, and uses them to pay for imports from wherever they come.

There are years like 1975 when our foreign exchange earnings are far in excess of our import needs, and some when they fall short of our requirements, as happened in 1976. In the surplus years we put our excess earnings into a reserve fund managed by the Central Bank; in deficit years we draw down reserves to pay our foreign debts. We may settle foreign payments deficits in one or any combination of three ways: drawing down reserves, borrowing abroad, or from foreign aid, that is, gifts from foreign governments. When these options are exhausted, we will almost certainly experience a balance of payments crisis.

All of us must have observed in our private lives that it is easier to borrow when you have money; similarly with countries! When foreign exchange reserve levels are high, it is easy to borrow abroad; when foreign exchange reserves are exhausted, foreign credit dries up. Trinidad and Tobago, with nearly US$2,000 million of foreign exchange reserves, has been able to incur large foreign debts at favourable rates; Jamaica and Guyana, with negative reserve holdings, are effectively excluded from the international financial markets. As for foreign aid, it is well to remember that there is no such thing as 'aid without strings', whether from socialist comrades or from neo-colonial capitalists. In either case the old adage remains true: 'He who pays the piper calls the tune.'

Clearing Unions

Groups of countries sometimes economize on the use of foreign exchange through the establishment of clearing unions operated by their central banks and monetary authorities. Instead of making a foreign exchange payment for each transaction between any two members of the facility, they pass all entries through a common account; at the end of a given time period, say three months, they settle only the net balances among themselves in hard currency. The CARICOM Multilateral Clearing Facility (CMCF) has been operating since June 1977 with the Central Bank of Trinidad and Tobago acting as agent. This has been a great improvement on the previous method of bilateral settlements in the Caribbean. The benefits to members have also been considerably enhanced by the lengthening of the period between settlements, and by the extension of low-interest credit by members to one another.

In response to balance of payments difficulties in some member countries, each member has been given an increased credit limit in the light of historical trading patterns, and debtor countries have been allowed to settle only half of their credit outstanding at prescribed times for settlement. Debtor members of the facility are thus able to pay for a substantial part of their CARICOM imports with their own currencies, freeing up foreign exchange for the purchase of essential imports from non-CARICOM countries. At the same time, by accepting the currencies of debtor countries, creditor countries, primarily Trinidad and Tobago, and to a lesser extent, Barbados, are able to keep more workers employed in the production of goods and services for intra-CARICOM trade.

The system has not been utilized as much as it should have been especially, I believe, because its potential benefits have not been fully understood. The level of mutual credit could be further extended by funding the accumulated debtor credit for settlement over even longer periods, or even by eliminating settlement indefinitely. The full development of the CMCF would certainly minimize the need for trading restrictions within the region.

A Basic Balance of Payments Model

In an effort to understand how things operate, we frequently have to resort to models. A model is a representation of reality intended to explain the behaviour of some aspect of it. For example, aeronautical engineers make models of aircraft and test their aerodynamic qualities in wind tunnels; ship designers test model ships in tubs filled with mercury to simulate ocean-going conditions, etc. This is much more convenient, much less costly and safer than building the aircraft or ship only to discover later that it does not work. Similarly, economists have resorted to models for exploring the workings of the economy or some aspect of it. Sometimes they represent reality through the use of graphs, sometimes by mathematical symbols. More recently, economists have been building large computerized models; but the vast majority of economic models remain verbal. We shall develop a verbal model to see if we can learn anything about the balance of payments aspects of a typical Caribbean economy.

There are a few things we ought to remember about models before we begin. Firstly, we cannot represent total reality in the model; we therefore must select the factors strategic to our problem or else our model will become too cumbersome. Secondly, only judgment and experience can tell us which factors are strategic. There is no certain method in either the physical sciences or the social sciences for selecting the right factors. Thirdly, the model is not the real world. We will only know whether our model is useful if the principles we extract from its manipulation prove valid when we apply them to the real world. If they prove invalid, we must modify the model in the light of our experience. For that reason we must always be moving back and forth between the model and the real world.

In designing an operational model we must first determine precisely the purpose of our exercise and establish some measure of our effectiveness. Economists refer to this as the 'objective function'. Put another way, we have to know how well or how badly our operation is going. In this instance we will regard ourselves as successful in so far as we are able to reduce our payments deficit to an acceptable level and be in a position to relax various defensive measures, such as bans on imports, exchange controls and import licensing. Even so, there will almost certainly be other desirable objectives that we will have to look at while we grapple with the balance of payments problem; e.g. the control of inflation, the generation of employment and the promotion of economic growth. Economists refer to these secondary objectives as 'constraints'. Sometimes, concern for one of these constraints, will prevent us from using a technique that might otherwise be most effective.

We shall then identify the strategic factors or 'variables', as scientists like to call them, of the balance of payments:

- ◆ Imports
- ◆ Exports
- ◆ Reserves
- ◆ Foreign credit

Since foreign aid to Barbados so far has been negligible, we will omit it.

Before explaining the logical relationships between these strategic variables we must first identify those variables which we can control and those which we cannot. Now, if our international credit is good, we simply borrow either on long-term or short-term to meet the deficit; if our reserve position is healthy, we may draw down from our reserves. However, if foreign credit is increasingly difficult to obtain and our reserves are exhausted, these variables are no longer controllable. Reserves are finite and credit depends on foreigners' assessment of our creditworthiness. Scientists refer to uncontrollable variables as 'parameters'. One solution is to expand exports, but again, this may not be in our hands. Other countries may be unwilling to take our exports because of protectionist measures; for example, Guyana and Jamaica have placed severe restrictions on Barbadian exports; or our crops may fail. At any rate, a significant increase in exports is difficult in the short run since it could take years before an effective export programme is mounted. So in the short run exports may also be uncontrollable. This leaves one variable under our control, namely, imports. We would naturally first try to restrict those imports that we can least do without and pay greater attention to those that are not absolutely essential. We would also focus more on high volume and expensive items, like motor cars, than on items we import in small volume.

Our model leads to the firm conclusion that we should seek to control imports in order to achieve equilibrium in our balance of payments. But before we take such a step, we must go back to the real world and, by reflecting on our past experience, try to work through the implications of direct import controls. We would quickly realize that direct controls on imports of goods and services requires the establishment of a vast bureaucracy to issue licenses to importers, to give exchange control approvals for travel funds and capital transfers, and to police attempts by the public to circumvent regulations. Such controls are not only costly in terms of salaries for the vast army of civil servants but also in terms of social and economic efficiency. Firstly, controls require a large number of decisions, both by senior officials whose time might be better spent in tackling tasks of greater long-run importance, and by junior officials whose powers of' judgment are not highly developed and who are therefore prone to make numerous errors to the extreme frustration of the general public. Secondly, the higher authorities may also make serious errors in the determination of what products should be imported and what should be excluded, leading to shortages of essential goods and to other inefficiencies. Thirdly, rigid controls motivate normally law-abiding citizens to break the law in their attempts to beat the system, and have an extremely demoralizing effect upon the total society.

The above arguments lead to the conclusion that direct controls should be avoided altogether or at least kept to an absolute minimum. Yet, the problem of import control remains and so we must go back to our model to see what further insights are to be gleaned. Let us take another look at imports. In such circumstances, we look behind the controllable variable — imports in this case — to see if there are factors influencing it that might be more easily controlled. If we can influence these secondary factors, we will indirectly influence imports, and our goal of import control might be achieved even more effectively than through the method of direct control.

Imports cannot be purchased unless people have money to pay for them, what economists call 'purchasing power'.[1] Purchasing power stems primarily from disposable income, that is, income available to persons after taxes, rent and other unavoidable outlays are paid. Credit is an alternate source of purchasing power, especially for buying high-priced items like motor cars, refrigerators, etc. If we can control disposable income and credit extended by commercial banks and commercial houses, we will simultaneously reduce imports without the elaborate and costly bureaucracy needed to control imports by direct methods. The control of purchasing power as a strategy for controlling imports is especially attractive in the Caribbean because of the 'openness' of our economies, which spend a high proportion of gross national income (GNI) on imports. As economists put it, our propensity to import is high. In the case of Barbados, five out of every eight dollars spent in 1977 went on imports. To restrict purchasing power, therefore, is to restrict imports.

Once again we return to the real world. Since credit is provided predominantly by financial institutions and is therefore well documented, it is much more readily controlled than disposable income, which has to be estimated. Let us check whether credit control alone will serve our purpose. The classical techniques of credit control in countries with highly developed capital markets, as in the UK and US, are changes in the reserve cash requirements of commercial banks and open market operations by the central banks. However, these techniques are not very effective in developing countries with poorly developed financial markets like Barbados and other member states of CARICOM. But techniques of selective credit control are available which have proven quite effective in Barbados over the last two years.

Credit Control

One such technique is the restriction of consumer instalment loans for the purchase of high-priced consumer durables, such as motor cars, hi-fi sets and washing machines, which have to be imported into the island. Most people need credit to purchase these items. The monetary authorities can limit the availability of instalment credit from commercial banks and retail outlets by requiring consumers to make higher down payments and to repay loans in a shorter time period. By using this technique the Barbadian monetary authorities effectively curtailed the importation of durable goods. To prevent the circumvention of this regulation by banks and commercial houses, the Central Bank of Barbados further directed commercial banks to restrict credit outstanding to the personal and distributive sectors to predetermined levels. In this way banks are effectively prevented from substituting demand loans for instalment loans, while retail outlets cannot increase their bank overdrafts to extend trade credit to consumers.

Curtailment of commercial bank credit to the public would not help very much if government expenditures led to the continued expansion of purchasing power. Government is by far the biggest spender and borrower in any economy. Most Caribbean governments run chronic budget deficits which are financed by the sale of debentures and treasury bills to financial institutions, or through credit from suppliers. In those CARICOM member states with central banks, ministers of finance may require directors to create new money to finance budget deficits. Government borrowing from the Central Bank of Jamaica rose from J$576.8 million at December 1975 to J$5,435.8 million at the end of 1977; central bank credit to government in Guyana over the comparable dates was G$44.5 million and G$5,346.8 million, respectively. Central bank credit to government feeds additional demand for imports. Professor Eltis has rightly pointed to the consequences of a government deficit-financed expansion: 'The ultimate effect of the deficit financed expansion is to destroy the balance of payments.'[2]

Currency Boards and the Balance of Payments

Incidentally, it is the absence of central banks in the less developed countries (LDCs) of CARICOM that has precluded balance of payments crises in those islands of the kind that have occurred in MDCs like Guyana and Jamaica. Under existing currency board arrangements, the individual governments have limited power to obtain credit through the sale of treasury bills and debentures to the East Caribbean Currency Authority, which is statutorily required to maintain at least 60% of its assets in foreign hard currency securities. In these circumstances a decline in foreign exchange earnings will lead automatically to a reduction in the domestic supply of money, and so limit the ability of both consumers and government to purchase imported goods, without any build-up of foreign debt. As higher import prices resulting from the oil crisis have pushed up public outlays, LDC governments have been unable to access 'new' money to close their budget deficits. In particular, they have been unable to satisfy the demand of public workers for increased wages, leading to severe conflict between LDC governments and public sector trade unions.

Chart 2
CARICOM: Central Bank Credit to Government (US$)

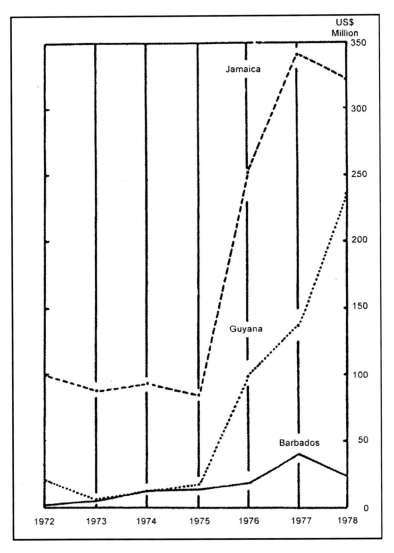

Fiscal policy

Consumers will most likely react to credit control by having their trade unions seek increased wages from employers, including government, so as to restore their purchasing power. If they are successful, they will be able to pay the increased down payments and meet the shortened maturities of consumer loans; as a result, imports will rise once again. In short, consumer credit restrictions will not work if consumers are able to keep increasing their earning power to compensate for the restriction of credit. We must therefore consider other means for restraining the growth of their disposable income.

It is clear then that we must control the level of disposable income if we are to succeed in controlling imports. We can do this in two ways: firstly, we can increase taxes to such an extent that the disposable income of consumers is made consistent with the desirable level of imports; secondly, we can prevent incomes from rising to the levels at which consumers will be able to demand more imports than available foreign exchange can buy. We may describe the first technique as fiscal policy, and the second as incomes policy. The 1975 tax on sugar export earnings, and the five per cent retail tax imposed by the last Barrow administration, were attempts to restrict disposable income through fiscal policy. Recent attempts by the Adams administration to restrain wage increases through moral suasion, what Americans call 'jawboning', falls into the category of incomes policy.

When we move from our model back to the real world once again, we find that both fiscal and incomes policies pose problems of implementation. Taxation is unpopular all over the world, even though many governments, not least that of Barbados, have been able to impose high levels of taxation. Our 'tax effort', to use an IMF euphemism, now exceeds 30 per cent of GDP and is considered quite creditable. Even so, there are practical limits on the level of taxation. Beyond a certain level, high taxes on incomes act as a disincentive to work, and may actually cause a reduction in output. Barbados is dangerously close to that point; some may argue that it is far beyond! On the other hand, indirect taxation has the disadvantage of putting pressure on the general price level.

Incomes Policy

An incomes policy, as the Barbadian experience has shown, is even more fraught with difficulty. I have learned this by experience since as far back as 1974 I was the first person to recommend 'wage-restraint', freely translated by the local press as 'wage-freeze' and bitterly opposed by the trade unions. In fact, an incomes policy need not imply a wage-freeze. By 'incomes policy' we mean a set of arrangements designed to maintain some desired relationship between the rate of increase in incomes and output, especially output for export. (Sir Arthur Lewis argued as early as 1964 for an incomes policy in Jamaica.)[3]

Yet, an incomes policy is potentially the most effective tool of balance of payments control. In the long run it is the only one! Its superiority over fiscal policy lies in that it not only restrains purchasing power at the source, but also suppresses the rate of inflation by dampening the cost of the most important production input, that is, labour.

Like the slide into the balance of payments crisis, inflation feeds upon itself: the more prices rise, the more they rise. The way to fight inflation is not to create a little more inflation, as the late Mr Wendell McLean, an eminent UWI economist once argued, but to strike vigorously at its roots. Lord Kahn sums up the situation this way:

> Keynesians attribute the behaviour of prices to the behaviour of money costs of production, including taxation, together with the behaviour of the prices of imported goods. This largely boils down to the behaviour of money wages. The rate of increase in the price-level is equal to the excess of the rate of growth of productivity, adjusted for the rate of increase in the prices of imports. A reduction in the rate of inflation depends on the willingness of wage earners to accept the downward adjustment of the rate of increase of money wages. This represents one of the really important problems of economic policy.[4]

As increased oil prices led to sharp increases in the price of imports and of local goods, workers quite understandably tried to protect their standard of living and pressed their trade unions to demand more money. The bitter fact of the matter is that nominal increases in wages do not lead to higher living standards; higher standards of living derive from increases in real output.[5] Since real increases in output proportional to increased cost of oil-related goods were not forthcoming even in the medium term, the fourfold increase in oil prices inevitably led to an immediate reduction in our living standards. Indeed, real national income in Barbados declined in both I974 and 1975, even though wages increased by more than 40 per cent over the two years. Wage increases merely fed the inflation, which climbed by 23 per cent in 1974 and 20 per cent in 1975.

Wages are a most important cost of production in most Caribbean economies, accounting for almost 50 per cent of public service expenditures in Barbados. Even a moderate rise in wages can lead to a significant increase in the cost of final goods; increased cost of final goods then leads to further wage demands, and so on.

An effective incomes policy has the added advantage of limiting the rise of unemployment in inflationary times. Increases in labour costs motivate businessmen to contract their work force in order to maintain profit levels, and to substitute capital for labour. There is strong evidence that Barbadian businessmen have laid off large numbers of workers over the past four years or allowed staff attrition from resignations and retirement. Since 1974, government itself has been forced to virtually freeze its permanent work force and reduce the working hours of casual workers, in order to economize on labour costs. Unfortunately, this reduction of new hiring came at a time when large numbers of teenagers were coming on to the labour market. Again, our collective national policy made little sense: we effectively redistributed income from those who were laid off to those who were fortunate enough to keep their jobs. The increase in our crime rate over the past three years, although still quite low by international standards, is attributable in part to higher unemployment and, if not nipped in the bud, could seriously damage our tourism industry and aggravate our balance of payments position.

There is one weakness in an incomes policy to be resolved if we are to maintain a satisfactory rate of economic development. An incomes policy tends to freeze in place the existing relationships among the wages of various categories of workers. If the maximum rate of wage increases is fixed at, say, five per cent per annum, there will be a tendency for the wages of all workers to rise at five per cent per annum. In fact, optimal economic growth may require that wages in the more efficient and expanding sectors should rise more rapidly so as to attract workers from the less efficient and declining sectors. This is a factor that governments, trade unions and employers will have to bear in mind when they negotiate wage increases; they should make some exceptions for the wages of scarce categories of workers to rise more rapidly than others.

Summary of the Model

Let us now try to pull together the various elements of our model. The purpose of the model is to suggest policy measures designed to prevent the economy from sliding into a balance of payments crisis. To do so we must maintain a balance between imports and export earnings. We will continue to experience fluctuations in the balance of payments from year to year, but the degree of fluctuations should be consistent with the level of foreign exchange reserve balances and with the nation's ability to obtain foreign loans. Direct controls on imports involve considerable social costs and should be avoided or kept to a minimum. However, by controlling the purchasing power of consumers and of government, the largest single consumer, we will automatically control the level of imports.

Considerations of national economic development require that we seek first to restrict consumer imports, high-priced durables in particular, rather than capital, intermediate or essential goods. The simplest way to do so is to regulate consumer instalment credit, and simultaneously to impose quantitative restrictions on commercial bank credit to the personal and distributive sectors. At the same time, we must prevent disposable incomes, the ultimate source of purchasing power, from rising too rapidly. One method of keeping disposable incomes from rising is through fiscal policy: taxes are raised to a level where disposable income is consistent with available goods and services at an accep-table price level. Tax increases beyond a certain point lead to economic inefficiency, and so the addition of some form of incomes policy is advisable. Indeed, the inclusion of an incomes policy in any programme of stabilization is now an established tenet of post-Keynesian monetary theory.[6]

Economic Stability and Socialism

Some Caribbean economists profess to see wage restraint policies as repressive of the workers. In fact, the workers undergo even greater suffering during a balance of payments crisis; certainly more than do economists. Ironically enough, this 'pro-worker' group includes 'scientific' socialists and Marxist-Leninists, who constantly applaud the absence of inflation, unemployment and balance of payments crises in socialist countries. In the more restive Soviet satellites of COMECON, inflation is not unknown and workers have been known to riot (strikes are forbidden) against price increases. In the Soviet Union itself the secret of price and balance of payments stability, as well as of full employment, has been to emasculate the trade union movement arid have wage rates fixed by the central planners.

At the beginning of each year the Central Planning Unit in Russia determines how much of the national income will be needed for capital investment and how much remains available for consumption. Wage rates and prices are then fixed at levels to bring about a rough equilibrium between consumption and disposable income, and taxes are imposed at a sufficiently high level to meet government expenditure. If during the year demand threatens to outrun the available supply of goods, taxes are increased to reduce disposable incomes; if supply exceeds demand, then productivity bonuses are paid to provide increased income to mop up excess output. Even so, since prices are regulated, inflationary pressures are reflected in longer queues for scarce goods rather than in rising prices. The government budget is rarely, if ever, allowed to go into deficit. The goal of full employment is also assisted by restricting the free movement of workers.[7]

The Devaluation Tool

A word about the technique of currency devaluation: Devaluation is a classical technique for bringing the balance of payments into equilibrium. Theoretically, devaluation corrects a deficit by effectively reducing the price of a country's exports, thus leading to an increase in foreign demand for them; at the same time, devaluation raises the cost of foreign goods and leads to a reduction in the quantity imported. This model has some validity for developed economies, like the Japanese, where relatively small reductions in the price of manufactured goods, especially of capital goods, produce a significant increase in exports; correspondingly, a small increase in the price of imports calls forth a significant expansion of domestically produced substitutes. Economists describe the responsiveness of the demand and supply of goods to prices as demand elasticity and supply elasticity, respectively.

Even so, exports from some advanced economies; for example, the UK and even the US, have responded slowly and rather insensitively to substantial currency depreciations in recent years. This has led economists to downgrade the effectiveness of the devaluation tool. I have argued elsewhere that the optimal exchange rate level for developing countries with open economies is the highest at which they can dispose of their exports, since the elasticity of foreign demand for domestic exports, and especially of the domestic supply of goods for export, is likely to be negligible. Lower export prices merely result in reduced foreign exchange earnings, and increased import prices lead only to higher domestic and export prices, since a large proportion of inputs into local production must be imported.[8] The main purpose of devaluation in countries like ours in the Caribbean is to reduce the real income of consumers to a level consistent with a sustainable volume of imports after all other measures to achieve balance of payments equilibrium have been exhausted.

I am sure that the CARICOM Secretariat would like to forget that it was once an ardent promoter of devaluation as a tool for 'structural development' in the early part of this decade.[9] It has long since abandoned this crusade. A massive devaluation will become imperative after long years of excessive wage increases; in fact, it will then be a necessary, though not a sufficient, condition for a return to economic growth and price stability. As a technique for short-run adjustments to the balance of payments in developing countries, it is virtually useless, and in developed economies has proven increasingly unreliable. Lord Kaldor, a strong advocate of the 1967 devaluation in the UK, has recently admitted: 'I greatly overstated the effectiveness of the price mechanism in changing the relationship of exports to imports at any given level of income.'[10]

Balance of Payments Surplus Problem

In many respects the problems posed by a chronic balance of payments surplus are more complex and difficult than in the case of a balance of payments deficit. The balance of payments problems of Trinidad and Tobago have resulted from the dramatic increase in oil prices towards the end of 1973. Between December 1973 and December 1977, the country's foreign exchange reserves rose from US$50 million to almost US$2,000 million. In spite of such enormous wealth, the economic problems of Trinidad and Tobago appear to be quite intractable.

The basic problem is that the resource on which these massive export earnings are based, namely oil, is a wasting asset. Whether oil reserves run out in the current estimated 20 years, or whether they run out in 50 years, the quantity of oil in Trinidad and Tobago is finite. Moreover, it is very possible that the major industrial countries will find viable alternative sources of energy, and that the windfall element in the oil price will diminish. The obvious strategy for Trinidad and Tobago, then, is to so invest its resources during the years of plenty that it will possess a highly developed agricultural and industrial capacity to prepare it for the time when its oil resources are depleted. From all indications its government has decided on such a strategy.

The choice of the strategy, however, is much easier than its execution. There are three major difficulties: firstly, the expectations of the public aroused by the knowledge of the country's wealth; secondly, the drive by labour in the non-oil sectors to obtain the same wages as obtain in the oil sector (this phenomenon is sometimes described by economists as the 'demonstration effect'); and thirdly, the limited capacity of the economy to make useful investments for the structural transformation of the economy — what economists term 'absorptive capacity'.

In these days of improved communication it is common knowledge in Trinidad and Tobago that the government is under no budgetary constraint, that in some sense of the word 'money is no problem'. The general public therefore expects to see a dramatic and substantial improvement in its living standards. It will expect civil service salaries, old age pensions and other transfer payments to rise sharply. It will also expect its medical, transportation and educational services to show dramatic improvement. These services will cost money. However, if attempts are made to expand these services too suddenly, their cost will be even greater, and the additional purchasing power unleashed by a surge in government expenditure is almost certain to set off inflation. In these circumstances it is probably better for government to permit a generous level of imported goods in order to give vent to the inflationary pressures.

Even more serious than inflation is the potential damage to non-oil traditional industries, and especially to agriculture. Because of high prices obtainable for oil, trade unions are naturally successful in obtaining greatly increased wages. The oil industry cannot claim inability to pay, and the cost of stoppage from strikes would be intolerable. Management has little choice but to concede generous wage increases. However, oil workers do not live in special compounds but in villages with agricultural workers as their neighbours. The demonstration effect of the oil industry will put tremendous upward pressure on wages in the agricultural sector. Unfortunately, while the price of oil has skyrocketed, the price of sugar on the world market has plummeted; nor have citrus and cocoa prices risen significantly. As a result, the agricultural sector as a whole is unable to pay wages comparable to those in the oil industry, and survives only with massive subsidies from government. This effect is most noticeable in agriculture but is true for other industries as well.

It may well be that the agricultural sector in Trinidad and Tobago will have to be subsidized into the foreseeable future, as indeed it is in Europe, the US and Japan. But it is most important that viable industries should spring up to provide jobs for persons forced out of uneconomic traditional sectors. Government is moving to expand its petrochemical base with products such as fertilizer, and to develop industries such as iron, steel and aluminium, which require heavy energy inputs. But these industries are capital-intensive and will not provide jobs as rapidly as the traditional manufacturing sector. Indeed, Trinidad and Tobago will discover that it is the deficiency in the 'software' that will impose the greatest constraints on its efforts at structural transformation. Before a highway is built, land has to be surveyed, engineering plans drawn up, and the skills of several professions assembled; new buildings require architectural plans, new construction requires carpentry, masonry and building foremen.

Chart 3
Trinidad and Tobago Foreign Reserves (US$)

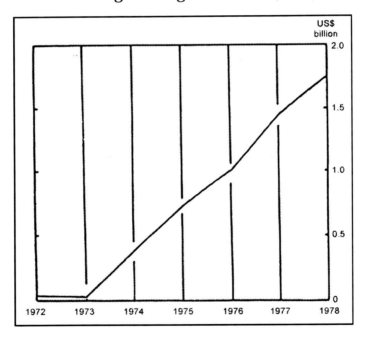

More important than the industrial hardware, that is, plant and machinery and social infrastructure, harbours, roads, airports and so on, is the software, that is, the human, technical, and managerial skills needed for the successful conduct of a modern organization. These skills must be widespread in society. The strength of the world's greatest economy, the US, is due far more to the quality of its software than of its hardware. Indeed, the apparently miraculous recovery of West Germany after its physical destruction in World War II bears out of the validity of this judgment. These skills cannot be developed overnight. To some extent, they can be bought; unfortunately, the expatriates who bring these skills also take them away when they depart, along with the additional experience that they gained.

The Trinidadians too will discover that the rate of wage increases is as crucial in the administration of affluence as it is in dealing with a balance of payments deficit. Wages in the capital intensive oil industry must not be allowed to get too far out of line with those in the agricultural and manufacturing sectors which provide most of the jobs, otherwise, a wage-push inflation spiral will be set off, making local industry uncompetitive and creating a permanent bias towards importation. The resulting inflation will also drain away the capital needed for the structural transformation of the economy. Lord Kahn, writing about the similar British predicament, has painted a frightening scenario:

> I believe that there is a danger that, after we have paid off our overseas debt, our current account balance of payments will be balanced as a result of an oil surplus, our invisible surplus being offset by a non-oil visible deficit. There is a danger that we shall export less and less, and import more and more manufactured goods. The production and refining of oil, and the production of petrochemicals, provide little employment. As our industries wither away — as the result of our failure to be competitive — unemployment will become greater and greater. It will not be Keynesian unemployment, due to lack of demand. It will be the unemployment which is the result of lack of productive equipment.
>
> And when the flow of North Sea oil and gas begins to diminish, about the turn of the century, our island will become desolate. I earnestly hope that this will prove an unduly gloomy forecast. Everything turns on the future of incomes policy, and its success in curbing the upward movement of wages.[11]

Finally, it is also in Trinidad and Tobago's interest that she should be surrounded by economically strong CARICOM neighbours when the oil runs out. She should not only seek to alleviate the short-run problems of her neighbours, as it has so generously done with substantial balance of payments assistance, but to channel both private and public funds for the economic development of the region as well. The lesson of the trade restrictions imposed by Jamaica and Guyana in the last two years is that one weak member of CARICOM injures all the others.

The Balance of Payments in the Long Run

The ultimate solution to the balance of payments is to bring about conditions in which export earnings expand at a rate consistent with the country's import needs. To achieve this, economic development must take place. There are two important problems for our consideration: how do economies, generally speaking, grow, and what strategies should Caribbean economies, in particular, pursue to encourage growth? It was a Caribbean economist, Sir Arthur Lewis, who led the way in the development of models that illuminate the general problems of economic growth. His work, *The Theory of Economic Growth,* is now a classic.[12] His Caribbean successors have failed in a spectacular fashion to devise effective strategies for achieving economic growth for the region.

Lewis and those following him have provided us with some general clues as to how we should go about economic development. There is a general agreement that economic development requires that investment as a proportion of GDP must increase relative to expenditure on consumption. Empirically, the critical ratio of new investment to net national product (gross national product less depreciation) appears to be about ten per cent. This means that an increasing proportion of the national income must be withheld from consumption and channelled into capital investment. It matters little whether capital investment is carried out by private enterprise or by the public sector under a socialist regime. Indeed, a corollary of socialist investment is that public enterprises should be run at a profit, or at a surplus, if that term is preferred. If domestic saving is not realized, there will be no alternative but to attract foreign capital.

In his paper, 'The industrialization of the British West Indies',[13] Lewis put forward a strategy of economic development for the Caribbean as early as the 1950s. He proposed that foreign capital should be invited into the region through a variety of tax incentives, and combined with cheap labour in the manufacture of import substitutes. Lewis was especially concerned with reducing the high levels of unemployment prevailing in the Caribbean, and rightly so! Manufactured goods would then be exported to more developed countries which were no longer cost competitive in the production of labour-intensive goods. Raw materials would be imported if unavailable in the region. This strategy was first used with brilliant success by the Puerto Ricans from the early 1950s into the late 1960s, when it petered out. The British Caribbean islands were slower to adopt the strategy, and less skilful in its execution, even when we allow for Puerto Rico's advantage of association with the US.

The Lewis strategy was later to earn the pejorative soubriquet of 'industrialization by invitation' from a group of brilliant young West Indian economists who viewed it as a modern version of the old plantation system. They were led by the innovative Lloyd Best and included such household names as Clive Thomas, Norman Girvan and George Beckford. They are loosely described as the 'New World Group'.[14]

The consensus of the New World Group was that the underdeveloped conditions of the Caribbean derived from the region's dependent relationship with their former imperial masters. This dependence was characterized by the institution of the plantation, and perpetuated in existing multinational corporations that now exploited the mineral and agricultural resources of the region, and controlled the terms of trade between the dependent Caribbean and the dominant metropolis. The dominance of the metropolis is further exerted through a variety of financial, social and cultural institutions that ensure that the major decisions affecting the region were made in the metropolis and in the interest of the metropolis. They therefore perceived 'industrialization by invitation' as a deepening of the dependence syndrome that had retarded the economy in the past, and undertook to study our situation from a Caribbean perspective. However, the 'dependence' thesis provides a model of economic underdevelopment, not of economic development. It therefore cannot form the basis for an operational model to assist us in formulating a strategy for economic development.[15]

Any operational model we contemplate must deal with openness and the phenomenon of growth. Since the Caribbean economies all lack essential raw materials, they will always have to import a significant amount of the products they use. In order to pay for these imports, they will have to export. Caribbean economies then import materials from the outside world in the form of fuel, commodities, manufactured goods, ideas, technologies and people, and process them for re-export in the form of finished goods, ideas and distinctive people. It is difficult to identify a single export from the Caribbean which does not require some imported input for its production. The typical Caribbean economy, then, is remarkably analogous to what General Systems theorists call an 'open system'. It is not surprising that policies which attempt to reverse our colonial past, to close our economies, to transform them into monolithic and centrally directed systems, and to drive them along dogmatically predetermined paths, should produce such unfortunate human consequences. The Lewis strategy of 'industrialization by invitation', though a 'primitive' operational model, at least recognized the Caribbean economies as open systems, and has proven to be much more useful than the closed models put forward by New World economists.

A Strategy for Economic Development

We come now to the formulation of a strategy for economic growth that would also enable us to deal with the balance of payments problem. Our strategy will rest on three fundamental premises:

The first is the primacy of the human resource, that is, that people are the roots of economic development, the irreducible minima in any social system. Economic development, in its most radical formulation, therefore, describes the process by which more people in a society are progressively enabled to carry out a larger number of productive activities, and in an increasingly effective manner. If my definition is accepted, it follows that intellectual, technical and managerial skills, that is, human skills, are far more important than natural resources and physical structures. Much more important than a nation's hardware is its software. This term subsumes the quality and appropriateness of our educational institutions, the integrity of our legal system and of our public and private administrators, the responsibility of our trade unions and the reasonableness of our community at large.

The second fundamental premise is what I have elsewhere termed the 'managerial imperative'. There is a cliché among West Indian officials that people are our most important resource. If this is so, then certainly the deployment of this resource, that is, its management, must also be of crucial importance. As Peter Drucker, the great American writer on management, has put it, 'Savings and capital investment do not produce management and economic development. On the contrary, management produces economic and social development and with it savings and investment.'[16]

The third fundamental premise is that 'openness' is a necessary condition for economic growth and, indeed, for economic survival. This implies that our continued economic development must rest on our ability to so process foreign inputs in such a manner that our exports will earn us increasing amounts of foreign exchange. In short, we must continuously deepen our technology and improve the efficiency of our economic system.

Based on these three premises, I should like to put forward the following programme:

- The most urgent item on the agenda is to reverse the trend of the past two decades towards closure of our economies. We must be far more willing to permit the entry of new ideas, new capital, new technologies, and new people, especially academicians, who have a different perspective from ours. In particular, we must try to attract home those West Indians who have obtained good experience abroad.

- We must develop in our various institutions the capacity to monitor developments in the wider world so that we can anticipate coming events and make the necessary adjustments to deal with them. In particular, our businessmen must continually search for new markets, new sources of supply and new technologies to improve their ability to compete with foreign industries.

- We must reverse the current trend towards centralization of decision making in the hands of government, and the establishment of large and complex parastatal organizations. Economic development implies an increasing number of decisions, and a larger number of decisions require not fewer decision makers, but more. In fact, management is the art of decentralization, provided that the necessary feedback mechanisms are instituted for control. Decentralization imparts flexibility; centralization reduces flexibility. Large organizations, as Schumacher writes, should be managed as if they were small.[17]

- We must maintain our public utilities and life support systems in superb working order so as to provide external economies for both our public and private enterprises. In countries that possess limited natural resources, efficient public services take on the characteristics of a major resource.

- Finally, we must improve the quality of management throughout the economy. Good management is as necessary in the trade union or the school as it is in the manufacturing plant. In this respect, the society should be much more willing to reward those in positions of managerial responsibility. Good management is also crucial in the key economic institutions of government, and in this respect we in the Caribbean must learn to keep operations and politics apart from each other. Operational autonomy is the only status compatible with the effective functioning of the corporate organization.

The programme set out above provides the essential basis for a strong export performance. Only by increasing our exports at a faster rate than our imports can we expect to emerge in the long run from the crisis in our balance of payments. Our export strategy must be outward looking. Our businessmen must go out into the international markets to discover for themselves what products are needed, what technologies are available and feasible in our type of economy, and which are the best sources of supply. In short, we must shift our emphasis to a positive search for new methods, new products and new markets and gradually move away from our current defensive import control strategies. This is an area where attack is the best form of defence. We should learn to manage our institutions, both public and private, much better than we now do.

Conclusion

As I suggested in my opening remarks, the balance of payments problem will always be with us, but wisdom and skill in the management of our affairs will more often than not keep us out of crisis. The first need is for a clear understanding of the dynamics of the balance of payments, and a continuous review of technical and theoretical developments in these areas. In particular, we must keep in close touch with events going on in the outside world so that we may recognize the shadows of coming events. This exercise requires the recruitment and training of a highly skilled and dedicated cadre of economists, diplomats and professional businessmen. We at the Central Bank are working feverishly on the construction of a computerized econometric model of the Barbadian economy which should enhance our analytical and forecasting capabilities. Having been forewarned about impending difficulties, government decision-making should be swift in its response to external threats. Great political courage will be required when tough measures have to be taken. In this respect, the more timely the measures, the less bitter the medicine needed. This is especially true in the area of the balance of payments. It makes much more sense to exercise a little restraint in consumption and wage increases in the early stages than to have to undergo the humiliation of an IMF-imposed devaluation in the end.

This brings us back to the incomes policy. Its importance obtrudes in every discussion of the balance of payments. In an open developing economy the failure to keep wage increases compatible with foreign exchange earnings will result in inflation, imbalance in foreign payments, unemployment and economic stagnation. It is a bitter fact which, I am afraid, Caribbean economists refused to face until circumstances forced it upon them. The success of an incomes policy depends on the institutional arrangements within which wages are determined. Since we do not have the Soviet option of suppressing the trade union movement, our only alternative is to promote an even greater sense of responsibility among trade unions. They must become as versed in balance of payments matters as the government technicians and even more responsible than the politicians.

As the British experience has shown, the worst kind of wage restraint policy is of the mandatory variety; the bitter industrial relations thus engendered are perhaps worse than the balance of payments crisis itself. The most effective incomes policy is rooted in a deep understanding of the economic issues by both the leadership and the rank and file of the trade union movement, and their acceptance of the responsibility required of individuals and groups who wield great power.

We at the Central Bank of Barbados believe that our modest efforts at improving the quality and timeliness of economic intelligence reaching the Barbadian public have contributed to the atmosphere of relative reasonableness in recent wage negotiations in Barbados. Although protesting loudly against wage restraint, our trade union movement has, in fact, exercised considerable restraint — though not always enough! The bank will be stepping up its efforts in the area of public education.

In the long run our success in coping with the balance of payments problem in the Caribbean, even when we are enjoying massive windfall export earnings, will depend on how effectively we organize for development. The appropriate response to the condition of dependency in the Caribbean is not closure of our economic systems, but the enrichment of our political, technical and administrative systems so that we may be able to transform and enhance the inputs that we obtain from the outside world. Only in this way will we earn adequate foreign exchange. In this respect, the performance of our key public sector institutions will be vital. A determined effort must be made to improve their management.

First delivered at an interdisciplinary seminar sponsored by the
Guild of Graduates of the University of the West Indies, Cave
Hill campus, Barbados, February 5, 1979 and reprinted in Vincent
R. McDonald, ed., *The Caribbean Issues of Emergence: Socio-Economic
and Political Perspectives* (Washington, DC: University Press of
America, 1980)

Notes

1. Professional economists will note that I have not used the
   expression 'money supply'. First, I did not wish to confuse my
   lay audience with the technicalities of M_1, M_2, M_3 and so on.
   Secondly, economists at the Central Bank of Barbados have
   concluded that in an open ceremony with underdeveloped
   markets, commercial bank credit is a more appropriate control
   variable than the money supply.

2. Walter Eltis, 'The Failure of Keynesian Conventional Wisdom',
   Lloyds Bank Review, no. 122 (October 1976): 5.

3. Sir Arthur W. Lewis, *Daily Gleaner, Special Supplement*, September
   1964.

4. E. Kahn, 'Mr. Eltis and the Keynesians', *Lloyds Bank Review*, no.
   124 (April 1977): 9.

5. By 'real output', we mean output after allowance has been made
   for price increases; for example, if output expressed in dollars
   rose by ten per cent while prices rose by five per cent, then real
   output would only have risen by five per cent.

6. Basil J. Moore, 'A post-Keynesian Approach to Monetary Theory',
   Challenge (September/October 1978).

7. See George Garvey, *Money, Financial flows and Credit in the Soviet
   Union* (National Bureau of Economic Research, 1977).

8. Courtney N. Blackman, 'Managing Reserves for Development',
   Columbia World Journal of Business (Fall 1976).

9. CARICOM Secretariat, 'Economics of Devaluation Under West
   Indian Conditions' (Georgetown, Guyana, June, 1972).

10. Nichols Kaldor, *Further Essays on Applied Economics* (London: Duckworth, 1978). As quoted in *Economist,* January 20, 1979, p. 111.

11. E. Kahn, 'Mr. Eltis and the Keynesians', 12.

12. Sir Arthur W. Lewis, *The Theory of Economic Growth* (London: George Allen & Unwin Ltd., 1955).

13. ———, 'The Industrialization of the British West Indies', *Caribbean Economic Review* II, no. I (May 1950).

14. For a sample of New World literature, see Norman Girvan and Owen Jefferson, eds., *Readings in Political Economy of the Caribbean* (Kingston, Jamaica: New World Group Ltd, 1971).

15. For a more detailed critique of New World Economics, see Chapter 2, 'A Systems Approach to Planning Models for Small Dependent Countries, with special Reference to the Caribbean'.

16. Peter Drucker, *Management* (New York: Harper & Row, 1973), 13.

17. Ernst F. Schumacher, *Small is Beautiful* (New York, Harper and Row, 1973).

8

A HETERODOX APPROACH
TO THE ADJUSTMENT PROBLEM

In preparing for this lecture, I read through as many of Adlith Brown's papers in *Social and Economic Studies* as I could find. First, I was struck by her prolificity. Adlith wrote more papers in one year than some of her contemporaries have written in an entire career. Secondly, she left no doubt in my mind that she had mastered the theory and techniques of her profession. But most of all I have been touched by her concern with policy issues. What is more, her passion to improve the lot of her community glowed through her writings, which reminded me of an observation by the great economist Kenneth Boulding:

> In consideration of economic policy ... the ends of society cannot be left out of the picture, and the abstractions of pure economics can only carry us a small part of the way.[1]

These memorial lectures should help ensure that the good that Adlith has done will live on after her.

In selecting a topic for today's lecture I asked myself which issue appeared closest to her heart. I observed that two of her papers touched on the adjustment problem. Her paper, 'Economic Policy and the IMF in Jamaica', is marked by penetrating insight into practical problems which still confront us; for example, 'As capital outflows continue, given the unresponsiveness of direct flows to interest rate changes, the usual priorities of monetary policy become less relevant.'[2] The conclusions of her paper, 'Issues of Adjustment and Liberalization in Jamaica: Some Comments,' were indeed prophetic. She ended it with these remarks:

> These issues raised here suggest that there are inconsistencies in the stabilization and liberalization programme; that foreign exchange uncertainty and a slow recovery of capital inflows and, therefore, of domestic investment, are likely to continue. In effect, in the absence of a windfall which raises the available flow of foreign exchange, the basic strains are ever present. These are continuing high levels of unemployment and slow investment and output growth.[3]

These issues of adjustment with which Adlith grappled with such insight and tenacity, still haunt us, and so I have chosen as my topic: 'A Heterodox Approach to the Adjustment Process.' I think she would have approved of this selection even though she would have done far greater justice to it than I ever could.

The perspective of my lecture reflects my experience as a contributor to economic policy making in Barbados over the past 13 years. Although there have been broad areas of agreement between the IMF and the Barbadian authorities, our policies throughout the last 15 years have been based on economic principles which, from the conventional IMF–World Bank perspective, must be viewed as distinctly heterodox. The major source of departure from the IMF–World Bank economic doctrine over the years has been over the concept of stable equilibrium and the efficacy of the 'free market', both in the adjustment process and in the promotion of economic development. For example, upon realigning our currency from the pound sterling to the US dollar in July 1975, the Barbadian authorities revalued upwards by ten per cent. We went on to enjoy five of the most prosperous years in our economic history and have maintained that parity ever since. In the high inflation years of 1973 and 1974 we rejected the prescription of positive real interest rates: by 1976 inflation had fallen to six per cent. Since 1977 we have rejected the approved global credit controls and applied selective credit controls which discriminate in favour of the productive sectors, I think we have done much better than many who did otherwise.

After the failure of the neo-Keynesian school to diagnose and prescribe for the stagflation of the 70s, the monetarists, led by Milton Friedman, were able to launch a successful counter-revolution. The 'free market' model has now been restored to the central position from which Keynes had dislodged it. Indeed, the arch monetarist Karl Brunner argues that 'price theory is the crucial paradigm — as a matter of fact, the only paradigm — that economists have.'[4] Most professional economists in the North, including those in the IMF and World Bank, now subscribe to this school. The prolonged agony of LDCs involved in IMF programmes, euphemistically described as structural adjustment, suggests that we should take a new hard look at the economics of adjustment.

The next section of this paper explores the mechanics of the balance of payments adjustment process. The analysis is intended to shed light on the differences between adjustment in developed and developing economies. The third section points out the limitations of the market system in the adjustment process. Section four discusses the issue of equity in the adjustment process, both on the domestic and international fronts. Section five grapples with the contradictions of economic growth and the adjustment process to which Adlith first directed our attention. Finally, some practical suggestions for approaches to the adjustment problem are put forward.

The Balance of Payments Adjustment Process

As long as countries trade with each other they must make continual adjustments to changes in the international trade environment. The prices of various commodities constantly fluctuate; national currencies continuously change their value in relation to each other; for example, weather conditions and other acts of God produce variable crop sizes, and new technologies continually create new products and render old ones obsolete. Some changes are seasonal and predictable; other business fluctuations show a cyclical though unpredictable pattern over time. Sometimes economies are assaulted by random and violent shocks that can have disastrous effects on their productive capability.

Most countries adjust satisfactorily to minor changes in international trade. In the major industrial countries the depth and efficiency of real and financial markets bring about considerable adjustments to external shock almost automatically. Robert Solow explains this process in an argument that he attributes to Axel Leijonhufvud:

> There is an equilibrium path that is surrounded by a corridor, a range above and below the equilibrium path. If the economy is disturbed off the equilibrium path and remains within the corridor, normal market forces can bring the economy back; if the disturbance moves the economy outside the range, then inflationary and contractionary expectations and assumptions may become so strong that the normal market forces are unable to push the economy back to a satisfactory state. Physically, it would be like the cup on the desk. If you tilt a little bit, it will go back to upright, but if you tilt it too much, it will fall.[5]

If the economy is pushed outside the corridor, intervention into the market will be needed to restore equilibrium. The classical form of intervention in these circumstances is through some combination of fiscal, monetary and interest rate policies.

It may further be noted that in major industrialized countries government policy measures are expected to take effect primarily through the market mechanism. General equilibrium theory tells us that changes in any market price will be transmitted throughout the economy through the Walrasian process of *tâtonnement*. Sometimes the Central Bank operates on some variable such as the quantity of money or the price of securities; sometimes the national Treasury operates through taxation or other price incentives to induce households and firms to change their behaviour.

Countries with highly developed markets show a tremendous resilience in the face of external shocks. With the exception of Italy, the western industrial economies and Japan adjusted with remarkable elegance to the two oil shocks of 1973 and 1978. In both instances they experienced balance of payments deficits for only one or two years before swinging sharply into surplus.

However, severe shocks may create circumstances that require extra-market measures. For example, in times of war, when a country is blockaded or resources are pre-empted for military purposes, governments regularly have resorted to non-market measures. Rationing, price controls, incomes policies and other administrative measures are then used to allocate strategic resources. In these circumstances no one pretends that the market is an optimal allocator of resources, or relies on market-oriented policy instruments. Rather, the economics of disequilibrium is substituted for the economics of equilibrium.[6] In short, we do the best we can. In extreme cases, for example, when economies are devastated by war as in the case of post-war Western Europe and Japan, it is recognized that extra-market intervention must be even more drastic and extensive. A massive introduction of resources from without then becomes necessary to enable the economy to be restored to a new equilibrium path when the market system may once again be used to facilitate adjustment.

Limitations of the Market System

From the above examination of the mechanics of adjustment in highly industrialized countries, four principles can be extrapolated for adjustment management in developing countries. First, since markets in LDCs lack the depth and sophistication of those in developed countries, the corridor around a stable equilibrium path in developing countries will be much narrower than for developed countries (see fig. I). This situation has been exacerbated by the propensity of several LDCs for autarchy, economic centralization, and extensive state-ownership of production. This approach, besides being prejudicial to economic progress, has stifled the development of the market system in LDCs and so limited the flexibility of their economies in response to external shocks. We might say that the corridor of those LDCs, like Singapore, Hong Kong, South Korea, Taiwan and Barbados, which have generally pursued open sys-tems policies, has proven to be wider than in the case of those countries that have pursued closed-system strategies.

The second principle of adjustment management is that in LDCs market-oriented measures will be less efficient in pushing the economy back within the corridor than in developed countries. Modifications that take into account market imperfections must be made in policy measures designed to push the system back into the equilibrium corridor. In particular, the global approach favoured by the IMF and the *Economist* will have to be tempered by considerations of rigidities and imperfections of markets in LDCs.

Market imperfections will be especially marked in small economies, such as those of the Caribbean, where the law of large numbers is hardly operative. As Kenneth Boulding so elegantly explains:

In the mass human behaviour is fairly regular — which explains, incidentally, why so much of economics assumes the mass-interactions of perfect competition and why indeterminancy appears in the theory of oligopoly — i.e. in the interaction of few exchanges.[7]

Figure 1(a)
Corridor for Developed Countries

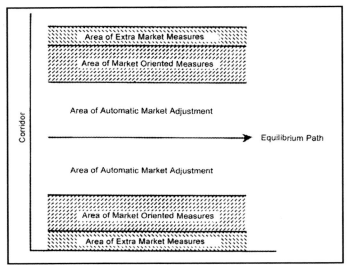

Figure 1(b)
Corridor for Developing Countries

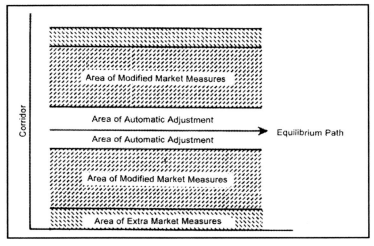

The policy maker in Barbados or Antigua can never contemplate leaving the determination of interest rates to a 'free market' in which three or four commercial banks control 80 per cent of the market.

Thirdly, when violent shocks cause structural damage to the real system leading to the collapse of the market, resort to extra-market measures becomes necessary. The two oil shocks, followed by the deepest recession since the 1930s, have dislocated real and financial markets in several LDCs. Some of them have been driven to the edge of bankruptcy by a staggering debt burden. Others find it extremely difficult to maintain their populations above starvation levels. The plight of many LDCs is similar to that of Western Europe and Japan after World War II and requires similar treatment.

The fourth principle is that the absence of a sophisticated market system will prolong the time required for restoration to a satisfactory growth path. A major problem is that the time horizon of policy makers in developed countries is too short for the circumstances of LDCs. They think in units of years, forgetting that the development of their own countries took place over centuries.

The case against contemporary economists is that their prescriptions hardly distinguish between industrialized economies with highly developed markets and LDCs with underdeveloped and sometimes non-functioning market systems. Most of them appear never to have heard of the work of Joan Robinson and Edward Chamberlin on imperfect competition! They believe that the perfect markets of their models actually exist in real life.

What is more, as itinerant practitioners, the economists of international financial institutions must travel light. They carry a few patent medicines which must fit all the diseases encountered. The standard medicine bag includes devaluation, the economic penicillin; positive real interest rates; the reduction of fiscal deficits; and credit control.

Devaluation is the most frequent prescription for restoring equilibrium in LDCs. A recent issue of *Development Finance*[8] gave several reasons why overvaluation was so harmful. I have never read anywhere about the evils of currency undervaluation!

The impression given is that an LDC can never have too large a devaluation! The most ridiculous exposition of the virtues of devaluation appeared in the *Economist* of August 31, 1985: It went something like this: President Shagari was thrown out in 1983 because the Nigerian naira was overvalued; General Buhari was thrown out because he propped up an overvalued naira; Major-General Babanguida would be wise to instantly devalue the naira or else he, too, will be overthrown. How would the *Economist* explain the failure of massive devaluations to bring about economic recovery in Jamaica? Perhaps it is the frequent devaluations that have averted military coups in Kingston!

Devaluation is the classical technique for bringing the balance of payments into equilibrium. Theoretically, devaluation corrects a deficit by effectively reducing the price of a country's exports thus leading to an increase in foreign demand for them; at the same time, devaluation raises the cost of foreign goods and leads to a reduction in the quantity imported. This model has some validity for developed economies, like that of Japan, where the volume of exports is responsive to relatively small reductions in prices. Even so, exports from some advanced economies, for example, the UK and even the US, have responded slowly and rather insensitively in recent years to substantial currency depreciations. Lord Kaldor, a strong advocate of the 1967 devaluation in the UK, later admitted: 'I greatly overstated the effectiveness of the price mechanism in changing the relationship of exports to imports at any given level of income.'[9]

In LDCs the elasticities of foreign demand for exports, and especially of the domestic supply of goods for export, are likely to be negligible. Lower export prices merely result in reduced foreign exchange earnings; increased import prices lead only to increased domestic and export prices, since a large proportion of inputs into domestic production must be imported. I have argued elsewhere[10] that the optimal exchange rate level for developing countries is the highest at which they can dispose of all their exports. Devaluation as a tool of short-term balance of payments adjustment is contra-indicated; successive mini-devaluations make even less sense. To be effective such devaluations must be sharp enough to preclude the possibility of wage catch-up by trade unions. The true purpose of a devaluation in LDCs is to reduce the real income of consumers to a level consistent with a sustainable volume of imports and/or to reduce real domestic labour costs after wage increases have so outstripped productivity gains as to make exports unsaleable abroad.

Positive real interest rates are another prescription in current vogue with IMF and World Bank economists. Positive real interest rates are needed the argument goes, to stimulate savings which may then be transformed into investments and economic growth. There is an obvious confusion here between financial savings and real savings. At any rate, empirical evidence suggests that savings are more likely to be a function of income and of custom than of interest rates. Deena Khatkate observes:

> The evidence for developed and developing countries alike is not quite conclusive in regard to the interest elasticity of savings. For the United States, income and wealth are found to have a more predominant influence on personal savings than interest rates. For less developed countries, even allowing for the dubious nature of statistics, the evidence points toward the same kinds of doubt about the interest elasticity of savings.[11]

I would also argue that negative interest rates are distinctly desirable in circumstances where powerful trade unions are able to extort wage increases in excess of productivity gains. In this case negative interest rates restore to investors some of the excess wage tax imposed upon them by the trade unions. Moreover, in countries where capital is scare the commercial bank overdraft is frequently a substitute for equity finance that attracts no interest charge in developed countries unless firms are profitable.

Once markets have collapsed, market-oriented policy instruments like devaluation and interest rates lose their efficacy and may even do a lot of harm. By market collapse, I mean a situation where markets do not clear, and are unlikely to clear in the immediate future. In Jamaica and Guyana, for example, foreign debt arrears are so huge that it would require an inconceivably large devaluation to bring about the equalization of demand and supply of foreign exchange. By which time the domestic inflation engendered by the massive increase in the cost of intermediate and consumer goods would have extinguished both domestic production and the consumers themselves.

Fig. 2(a) shows the situation that exists in a functioning foreign exchange market. Note that a movement up the supply curve from P_i to P_{ii} — that is, currency devaluation — results in a restoration of equilibrium. Figure 2(b) shows the situation that exists in a foreign exchange market which has collapsed. The supply of foreign exchange is realistically portrayed as being inelastic; the demand for foreign exchange is shown as far over to the right, signifying that markets are not clearing. The shaded part shows the extent of the disequilibrium. In this situation, a movement up the supply curve from P_i to P_{ii} does not move the system to equilibrium; devaluation merely forces citizens to give up increasing units of output for decreasing quantities of imports without any visible improvement in their welfare. It is most reminiscent of the prescription of bleeding in primitive medicine; usually only those patients who removed the leeches survived the cure.

Figure 2(a)
Functioning Foreign Exchange Market

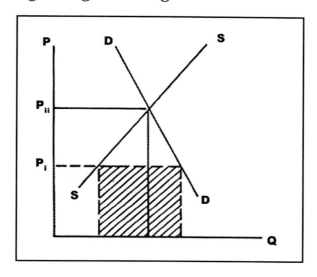

Figure 2(b)
Collapsed Foreign Exchange Market

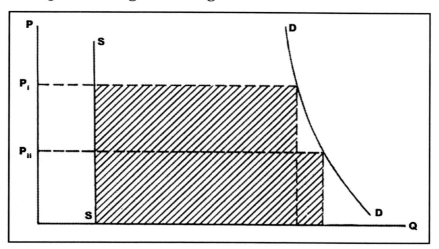

Privatization and deregulation are currently the 'in-thing' among international economists, based on the dubious premise that whatever appears to work for the US must be good for everyone else. In fact, deregulation has led to a dangerous instability in the American airlines industry. Fierce price-cutting wars have driven some airlines out of business and the others to the brink of collapse. It is merely a matter of time before desperate cost-cutting measures begin to compromise safety. Small developing countries cannot afford the luxury of such dislocations.

Equity in the Adjustment Process

The commitment to free market solutions has led conventional economists to neglect issues of equity in their adjustment programmes. Fiscal and monetary measures are applied in a global fashion and the chips allowed to fall where they may. Almost invariably they fall with greater severity on disadvantaged groups in the community. Severe deflationary measures are imposed, requiring widespread lay-offs, sharp cuts in subsidies on basic foodstuffs, and deep currency devaluations which trigger spiralling inflation. Indeed, conventional economists seem far more concerned that the aggregates in their econometric models approach equilibrium than with the welfare of the population. This approach is an excellent demonstration of what philosophers describe as the 'fallacy of misplaced concreteness'— the mistaking of the model for the real-life system it purports to explain.

The above approach is in marked contrast with that taken by John Maynard Keynes in his much neglected tract 'How to Pay for the War', published in 1940. In it Keynes set out an economic strategy for the conduct of war against the Nazis. The rationale of his strategy was that the sacrifices necessary in the conduct of war should not fall primarily on those least able to bear them. Keynes proposed an extensive programme of family allowances as well as a system of rationing and price controls. In this way he established a floor under the general welfare and ensured that the rich could not bid scarce goods away from the poor as would have happened in a free market situation.

The consideration of equity is also absent from the current approach to the international debt crisis. In the first place, it is forgotten that the most serious effects of the sharp rise in oil prices were deflected from the developed economies to the less developed non-oil exporting countries. At the same time, the inequality between developed and developing countries worsens as the international order operates to transfer a massive volume of resources from the developing to the developed world. Expanding US deficits suck vast capital resources into the American economy that serve to maintain high positive real interest rates. When we consider that positive real interest rates in the US have traditionally been between one and two per cent, the positive real rates of five to six per cent paid in recent years by developing countries on Eurodollar debt represent a rate of exploitation not achieved even at the height of the British Empire.

Once again we might learn from Keynes that equity is an essential element of sound policy. Keynes warned in *The Economic Consequences of The Peace*[12] that insistence on war reparations would damage both the Germans and the Allies. By 1932, when Germany was finally forgiven her war reparations debt, it was too late. Hitler came to power in the following year. The lessons from the Treaty of Versailles were not lost on the Allies after the Second World War. Extra-market measures were taken in the form of the Marshall Plan to restore the economies of Western Europe, victors and vanquished alike, to the mutual long-term advantage of both Western Europe and the US.

It is astonishing that the politicians and economists of the developed nations have not perceived the current international debt crisis as analogous to the German War Reparation issue or the Marshall Plan. The current approach purchases the integrity of the banking systems of developed countries at the expense of painful declines in the living standards in the debtor nations. Those less able are required to bear the major share of the adjustment burden. To anyone with the slightest knowledge of the Prisoner's

Dilemma in Game Theory, case-by-case negotiations are an obvious manoeuvre by a creditor cartel to maintain its leverage over individual debtor nations.

Considerations of equity require a shift in emphasis from structural adjustment in the debtor nations to the refinancing of the debt in a manner whereby the creditors bear a fair share of the burden. The situation calls for extra-market measures that bring into being an international lender of last resort along the lines suggested by the Lever Report. Such a programme should promote a positive flow of real resources back to the LDCs, restore them rapidly to a real growth path, and enhance their ability to repay their debt over the long-term.

What is more, this approach is in the enlightened self-interest of the developed nations. The worldwide terrorism and political turmoil which now exercise the political leaders of the First World can only be alleviated by the emergence of stable and democratic regimes. At this very time major Latin American countries, like Argentina and Brazil, are in danger of stumbling into democracy. Some traditionally democratic societies are also in danger of collapse. Prolonged social unrest occasioned by crushing adjustment programmes could very well abort promising democratic movements and create new tyrannies — to the peril of us all.

Economic Development, the Market and the Adjustment Process

It was accepted by the economics profession in the 1950s and 1960s that the analytical tools required for the analysis of developing economies differed from those applicable to developed economies. Joan Robinson wrote in her book *Economic Philosophy:*

> In this situation both static neo-classical analysis of the allocation of given resources between various uses, and Keynesian short period

analysis of how given resources are employed, appear quite in-adequate. A dynamic long-run analysis of how resources can be in-creased is now what we require.[13]

In his celebrated *Theory of Economic Growth,* Sir Arthur Lewis also argued:

> But if we are concerned with long-term studies of changes in propensities, or if we wish to account for difference between groups or countries, we have usually to look beyond the boundaries of contemporary economic theory.[14]

Some time ago, President Reagan, reflecting the attitudes of his economic advisers, recommended that LDCs should rely on the 'magic of the market' in their quest for economic development. As if market forces constructed the Erie Canal, laid the railroad across America, established the Land Grant Colleges, or pioneered the space age!

In an issue early this year, the *Economist* suggested that developing countries had merely to trim their deficits, devalue their currencies, and hit their monetary targets and, presto, growth would follow. The notion that economic development was achievable through a pure market strategy was carried to its logical conclusion in Chile by General Pinochet. The results have been disastrous. The 1983 World Development Report suggested that weak economic growth in a number of LDCs during 1970 to 1980 was related to price distortion, as indicated by exchange rates, and factor and product pricing. One of the countries included in the exercise was Ghana, which in the decade of the 1970s had experienced sundry military coups and counter-coups. These upheavals must certainly have had a greater effect upon Ghanaian growth prospects than any price distortion. As a matter of fact, the price distortion may well have resulted from the military coups!

The history of developed nations reveals that in the early stages of their economic development their governments invariably made critical interventions in the market place. Sometimes, as in the case of Japan, intervention was more systematic and comprehensive. As economic development proceeded the market for goods and services became deeper and more extensive and governments, even in communist countries, found it possible and beneficial to reduce the extent of market intervention or to shift their attention to new areas. The Japanese are only now relaxing their controls over the flow of international capital. The trick in economic management is to make intelligent, rather than unintelligent, interventions into the market place.

The theory of economic development is properly concerned with the processes by which stable and progressive political systems evolve; how efficient public services are developed; how economic enterprises are effectively organized and managed, and how entrepreneurship is made to flourish. Economic development has little to do with positive real interest rates, monetary targets or exchange rates. As societies develop, so too will their capacity for the management of these economic variables.

The trickiest aspect of adjustment, as Adlith so clearly recognized, is how to promote the necessary structural changes in the economic system without undermining the capacity for future growth. Current programmes of adjustment being imposed by international institutions on LDCs have the effect of depressing investment, which is the engine of growth, and even of producing negative growth.

An analogy from aeronautics is instructive. An aircraft must maintain a minimum stability while in flight. If the pilot is unable to control pitch and yaw, the plane is in danger of falling out of the sky. At the same time, he must maintain forward propulsion. If his engines fail he will certainly come to grief. And it matters little whether his plane hits the ground right side up (in perfect equilibrium, if I may use economic jargon,) or upside down.

There is a slight ray of hope. Secretary James Baker has discovered that economic growth is essential to the adjustment process. Let us hope he will soon come to understand that the reverse flow of resources from developed to developing countries is also indicated. Then the rest will be up to us!

Recommendations

There is an urgent need for contemporary economists to review their ideology about adjustment in LDCs. I would make the following suggestions.

- A more rational and non-ideological view of the role of the market system in the functioning of an economy must be developed. The market has no magical attributes. It is merely an ingenious social device for the inexpensive allocation of resources. Like all such devices, it can be used or misused, depending on the circumstances. The circumstances of developed countries are clearly more appropriate to its usage than those of developing countries. In the latter, a fine judgment is required to determine what adaptations are necessary and when extra-market measures are required. However, it is readily admitted that whenever the results of market allocation are tolerable, we should accept them; when the results are unacceptable or perverse, we will have to design extra-market measures to the best of our ability.
- Economic theorists should move towards a systems rather than a generalized approach to LDC problems. The systems approach treats each country as a peculiar system and focuses on its unique characteristics. In this respect, much greater attention should be paid to the opinions of local officials, especially those who have been around for sometime. We should heed the advice of John Dickenson that 'experience must be our guide. Reason may mislead us.'[15]
- Modern economists should refocus their attention away from their econometric models to the human problems of the society. A programme that sharply increases unemployment,

significantly increases the price of food, and threatens the cohesiveness of the society, cannot be viewed as a success. The more serious the adjustment problem, the more time will be required for LDCs to adjust. The IMF must begin to think of structural adjustment periods of five years and more. Moreover, much more concessionary financing must be mobilized by the World Bank, as was done for Europe under the Marshall Plan.

- A new look at the theory of economic development is also required which places greater emphasis on institutional factors and less on 'free market' theoretical formulations. We ought not to behave as if efficient markets exist when, in fact, they do not. Since the development of efficient markets is a prolonged process, a theory of disequilibrium will be necessary. While we are at it, greater attention should be paid to the Theory of Games, especially those aspects which deal with transactions among unequal players.

- It should he recognized that 'non-economic' factors, such as political stability, social cohesion, educational levels, technical and managerial skills are much more critical to long-run development than interest rates, exchange rates and monetary targets. Economists should try to incorporate these factors into their models.

- The current case-by-case approach to the international debt crisis ought to be abandoned by the international financial community. Indeed, the IMF and World Bank should place their prestige and resources squarely behind the implementation of the Lever Report.[16] The most urgent item on the agenda is to reverse the massive flows of resources from LCDs to the developed countries.

One final observation: A group of countries with linked markets is likely to be more resilient in the face of external shocks than if they face the international environment as individuals. The propensity of Caribbean governments over the last decade to try to go it alone, frequently without regard for the interests of each other, has weakened us all. We should draw the appropriate conclusions.

First Adlith Brown Memorial Lecture **delivered on the occasion of the 17th Annual Regional Monetary Studies Conference in Nassau, Bahamas, November 29, 1985, Institute for Social and Economic Research 1986**

Notes

1. Kenneth E. Boulding, *Beyond Economics* (Ann Arbor: University of Michigan Press, 1970), 192.

2. Adlith Brown, 'Economic Policy and the IMF in Jamaica', *Social and Economic Studies* 30, no. 4 (December 1981): 44–45.

3. ——, 'Issues of Adjustment and Liberalization in Jamaica: Some Comments', *Social and Economic Studies* 31, no.4 (December 1982): 200.

4. Karl Brunner, as quoted by Anjo Klamer in *Conversations with Economists* (Totowa, NJ: Rowman and Allanheld, 1983), 183.

5. Robert M. Solow, as quoted by Anjo Klanier in *Conversations with Economists*, 133.

6. See John Kenneth Galbraith, *A Theory of Price Control* (Cambridge: Harvard University Press, 1980), especially Chap. 4, 'The Disequilibrium System'.

7. Kenneth E. Boulding, *Beyond Economics*, 193.

8. Guy Pfeffermann, 'Overvalued Exchange Rates and Development', *Development and Finance* (Washington, DC: IMF– World Bank, March 1985), 17–19.

9. Nicholas Kaldor, *Further Essays on Applied Economics* (London: Duckworth, 1978, as quoted by the *Economist*, January 20, 1979), 111.

10. Courtney N. Blackman, 'Managing Reserves for Development', *Columbia Journal of World Business* (Fall 1976).

11. Deena Khatkate, 'Analytic Basis of the Working of Monetary Policy in Less Developed Countries', in *Money and Monetary Policy in Less Developed Countries,* eds., W.J. Coats Jr. and D.R. Khatkate (Oxnard: Pergammon Press, 1980), 134.

12. John Maynard Keynes, *The Economic Consequences of the Peace* (New York: Penguin Books, 1995).

13. Joan Robinson, *Economic Philosophy* (Garden City, NY: Doubleday, 1964), 101.

14. A. Lewis, *Theory of Economic Growth* (New York, NY: Harper & Row, 1970), 13.

15. John Dickenson, as quoted by Henry Steele Commager in 'Meese Ignores History in Debate with Count', *New York Times,* Wednesday, November 20, 1985.

16. *The Debt Crisis and the World Economy* (report by Commonwealth Group of Experts, Commonwealth Secretariat, Marlborough House, London SW1).

9

FACTORS IN THE CHOICE OF AN EXCHANGE RATE REGIME

WITH SPECIAL REFERENCE TO THE CARIBBEAN

The exchange rate is the most important price in any country; it determines the terms of trade with foreigners as well as relative prices within the economy. 'Establishment' economists are quick to point out the negative implications of an over-valued exchange rate; they are silent about the deleterious effects of an under-valued exchange rate. However, the profession is unanimous about the benefits of exchange rate stability, that is, an exchange rate to whose fluctuations or trends the domestic economy can adjust with relative ease.

In the 1950s and 1960s 'free market' economists, led by Milton Friedman, argued that free-floating exchange rates would promote exchange rate stability worldwide and so welcomed the collapse of the Bretton-Woods fixed exchange rate system in 1971. Instead of the promised stability, there has been such widespread and sharp exchange rate volatility that West European industrialized nations sought refuge in a common currency. Emerging economies in Latin America and Asia have been most severely affected by exchange rate instability. Succumbing to pressure from the 'Washington Consensus', they deregulated their financial markets, floated their currencies and opened their financial markets to unfettered global capital flows. When international financial crises struck and foreign capital inflows were reversed, their financial markets collapsed, leading to deep currency devaluations, high inflation and unsustainable accumulations of foreign debt. Only those escaped who retained an element of capital control, or were prepared to intervene intelligently and pragmatically in their capital markets.

CARICOM member states have at various times employed the fixed exchange rate, the currency board, the peg to a basket of currencies, the foreign currency auction, the interbank market, the cambio system, the free float and the managed float. This paper reviews the CARICOM experience with various exchange rate regimes over the past three decades, with special attention to foreign exchange markets in conditions of chronic disequilibrium. A number of lessons are extracted which should be especially helpful to other small LDCs in the choice of an appropriate exchange rate regime.

In conclusion, the paper summarizes the factors relevant to the choice of an appropriate exchange rate regime. The chief consideration is the quality of financial markets, that is, their breadth, depth and competitiveness.

Lessons from the Anglophone CARICOM Experience

The Anglophone member states of CARICOM provide an excellent laboratory for the study of exchange rates.[1] Four of them operate fixed exchange rate regimes — The Bahamas, Barbados, Belize, and the Organization of Eastern Caribbean States (OECS), comprising Antigua and Barbuda, Dominica, Grenada, St. Kitts and Nevis, Saint Lucia, St.Vincent and the Grenadines, and the two remaining British colonies of Anguilla and Montserrat. Guyana and Jamaica have operated floating exchange rate regimes, with the latter intervening periodically after 1994 in the foreign exchange market; Trinidad and Tobago (T&T) has conducted a managed float operation since 1993.

All CARICOM Central Bank Acts include currency stability among their objectives, and all have at their disposal the traditional powers to set reserve requirements, interest rates, and to employ selective credit controls as deemed necessary. All Central Bank Acts also include limitations on central bank lending to government, but in some countries these regulations have been more honoured in the breach than in the observance. Guyana, Jamaica, and Trinidad and Tobago have liberalized capital flows, but exchange control restrictions on capital account remain in force in The Bahamas, Barbados and Belize. Belize has recently modified its exchange control regime by the introduction of cambios.

Fixed Rate Regimes

The Bahamas

From its establishment in 1974, the Central Bank of Bahamas has operated a fixed exchange rate regime, with B$1.00 = US$1.00. The Bahamian economy is mainly service-based, with more than 40 per cent of the national income linked either directly or indirectly to tourism; another 15 per cent is derived from banking and financial services. The financial sector is two-tiered — a domestic sector and an offshore sector. The domestic financial sector is subject to exchange regulations, while the offshore sector is largely free of controls.

The fixed exchange rate regime has served The Bahamas well. The economy delivered average growth rates of over three per cent in the 1970s and 1980s, but fell flat in the 1990s. However, living standards have continued to rise, with The Bahamas enjoying the highest per capita GDP (US$14,960)[2] of independent countries in the Western Hemisphere, after the USA and Canada; inflation has mostly remained in the low single-digits as successive administrations have kept government debt/GDP ratio below two per cent in all but two of the last ten years.

The secret to Bahamian economic success is that both its main industries have been riding a secular economic upswing. Tourism is frequently described as a fickle industry. In fact, tourism is the fastest growing global industry, and its fortunes have been nothing so volatile as those of oil or bauxite. Oil prices, in particular, have moved from highs of US$40 per barrel in 1981 to less than US$10 a barrel in 1986! It has taken the events of September 11, 2001, the most horrific shock to the capitalist system since World War II, to stop the tourism industry in its tracks. The Bahamian monetary authorities have therefore been able to treat the fall-off in tourist arrivals during global recessions as temporary, and to defend the exchange rate by drawing down foreign exchange reserves or by borrowing abroad until the international economy recovered.

The pursuit of conservative fiscal policies during the economic upswings has ensured the healthy foreign exchange reserve holdings and good credit ratings needed during recessionary times. However, the years immediately ahead will be testing times for The Bahamas because of short-term uncertainty in the tourism industry and the aggressive attempts of OECD countries to put tax havens out of business.

There is one foreign exchange institution peculiar to The Bahamas. The Central Bank maintains a market in investment currency, prescribed for the purchase of foreign currency securities from non-residents and the making of direct investments outside The Bahamas. This market has its origins in the UK following World War II and was established in The Bahamas in 1972. The Central Bank began support for the currency pool from its own foreign reserves in 1986, and assumed responsibility for its administration from London dealers in 1989. In 1995 total purchases amounted to about US$200,000 and sales to about US$270,000, with an end-of-year balance of US$1.3 million. Most sales were for portfolio and real estate investments overseas.

Barbados

The Barbadian economy is based primarily on tourism, which earns two-thirds of the island's foreign exchange. The offshore financial sector is also growing in importance but the once dominant sugar industry now makes but a minor contribution to GDP and foreign exchange earnings. Exchange control restrictions on capital flows, although liberally administered, remain in force, but foreign payments on current account are freely made.

The Barbadian monetary authorities consider the fixed exchange rate to be the centrepiece of national economic policy. The Barbados currency was pegged to the US dollar in 1975 at a rate of BDS$2.00 = US$1.00, and has remained unchanged since then. Except for a brief period (1991–92) the Central Bank has been able to supply adequate foreign exchange to the market so that a parallel market has never emerged.

Monetary policy in Barbados has been conducted mostly within the context of fiscal responsibility, with the fiscal deficit/GDP ratio usually at the three per cent level or below. However, on two occasions (1982 and 1991) following huge election-related fiscal deficits, Barbados was forced to enter IMF structural adjustment programmes, barely avoiding devaluation the second time by legislating an eight per cent cut in civil service salaries and laying off about 3,000 civil servants.

The fixed exchange rate has also worked well for Barbados, delivering a steady average real growth rate of between one and two per cent over the last three decades, with inflation usually in the low single digits. During the 1990s, growth in GDP averaged three per cent, and Barbados, with a per capita GDP of US$8,600, moved into the category of a middle income country, ranking thirty-first in the world and first among nations of the Americas (after the US and Canada) in the 2002 UNDP human development index.

Barbadian monetary authorities, like the Bahamian, have opted to defend the fixed exchange rate during recessionary times by drawing down foreign exchange reserves and borrowing abroad until good times return. Barbados has also added the weapon of an incomes policy to its armoury. Government, Business and Labour have formally instituted a 'social compact', especially for setting appropriate parameters for wage increases. So far it has worked well.

Belize

Unlike that of The Bahamas and Barbados, the Belizean economy is broad based, with a variety of industries — bananas, citrus, sugar cane, rice, fishing and shrimping, lumbering, and tourism, especially eco-tourism. The economy, although less vulnerable to international economic recession, is occasionally devastated by hurricanes and floods. Belize also shares a common border with Mexico, with whom it conducts significant trade, making its foreign earnings sensitive to fluctuations of the Mexican peso.

The Belizean currency was already pegged to the US dollar at a rate of B$2.00 = US$1.00 when the Central Bank of Belize was established in 1981. The Bank is required by law to hold foreign exchange reserves of not less than 40 per cent of currency in circulation and deposit liability. Belize, with a per capita GDP of US$2,910, has enjoyed a more rapid growth rate than any other CARICOM state, averaging more than five per cent per annum over the 1980s and 1990s. However, the trend of growth has been uneven. For example, real GDP in the second half of the 1980s averaged a record 8.6 per cent per annum, but only 4.4 per cent annual in the first half of the 1990s, and has weakened since then.

Belize has been more prone to periods of fiscal excess than either The Bahamas or Barbados. Fiscal deficits in 1992 and 1993 were 6.6 and 6.1 per cent of GDP, and fiscal policy has been especially loose in recent years with the ratio of fiscal deficit/GDP registering 10.2 per cent, 9.8 per cent and 11.7 per cent in 1999, 2000 and 2001, respectively. Not surprisingly, therefore, the Belizean economy is currently undergoing balance of payments stress; the authorization of cambios in 2001, the only instance among countries with fixed-rate regimes, does not augur well.

OECS

The Eastern Caribbean dollar has been pegged to the US dollar at EC$2.70 = US$1.00 ever since the Eastern Caribbean Currency Authority, predecessor of the ECCB, untied from sterling. The controls on foreign exchange flows in the OECS have differed considerably from those of other CARICOM states in that the exchange control authority is vested in the Minister of Finance in each member state, and is not delegated to the Eastern Caribbean Central Bank (ECCB). Moreover, access to foreign exchange by businesses and individuals, including commercial banks, is much more liberally administered than in most other CARICOM states. Furthermore, the legal provision that the ECCB should maintain foreign exchange reserves of at least 60 per cent of its outstanding liabilities has been scrupulously observed.

Ironically, the OECS, collectively termed 'less developed countries' (LDCs) and so entitled to concessions under the CARICOM agreement, have outperformed the 'more developed countries' (MDCs) in some important respects. For most of the 1980s the OECS economies grew in real terms at six per cent per annum, with growth in Antigua and Barbuda, and Montserrat exceeding ten per cent per annum, but slowed to an average of three per cent during the 1990s — still strong in relation to the rest of CARICOM. The per capita incomes of independent OECS now range from US$9,070 for Antigua and Barbuda to US$2,690 for St. Vincent and the Grenadines, while the per capita incomes of three MDCs, namely, Trinidad and Tobago, Jamaica, and Guyana, are US$5,540, US$2,270 and US$840, respectively. However, the OECS has been a beneficiary of substantial grant and aid flows, mostly in response to the frequent hurricanes and occasional volcanic eruptions that afflict the region.

The secret of OECS currency stability is the 'unanimity rule' whereby major monetary policy decisions require the approval of all eight ministers of finance. This means that no individual minister of finance has the power to transgress the rules establishing minimum foreign exchange backing for currency issues or limitations on central bank credit to governments. For this reason no member state government is empowered to finance fiscal deficits through central bank credit, the most travelled path to currency debauchment. Individual member states, especially Antigua and Barbuda, are sometimes guilty of fiscal indiscipline. They must make the inevitable adjustments through taxation or debt operations — not through money creation. This explains why the ECCB, though lacking the authority of other CARICOM central banks, has been able to maintain foreign exchange reserves at well above the legally required level. Finally, individual member states negotiating structural adjustment programmes with international financial institutions cannot commit the ECCB to a currency devaluation.

Floating Rate Regimes

Guyana

Guyana is an extreme example of a foreign exchange market in chronic disequilibrium. In 1975 Guyana untied from sterling and fixed to the US dollar at the rate of G$2.55 = US$1.00. At that time Guyana was the best placed of CARICOM non-oil exporters to withstand the first oil-shock of 1974. It possessed four strong foreign exchange earners in alumina/bauxite, sugar, rice and timber, and produced much of its food. Bumper sugar earnings in 1975 lifted foreign exchange reserves to a healthy US$85 million. In that same year, however, Guyana declared itself the Cooperative Republic of Guyana, and took the first fateful steps down the dead end road of 'cooperative socialism'.

Government launched an over-ambitious social welfare programme, and nationalized the strategic industries, including bauxite/alumina and sugar. Three major foreign commercial banks were also indigenised. By 1976 government was firmly in control of the 'commanding heights' of the economy, and by 1986 the public sector accounted for almost 90 per cent of total claims on the banking sector, up from 40 per cent in 1970.

The vastly increased public expenditures were financed primarily by the Bank of Guyana, whose claims on the government increased from G$45 million at year-end 1975 to G$346 million at the end of 1977, wiping out the country's foreign exchange reserves. The sharp fall-off in export earnings in 1976 and 1977 compounded the problem, as the government relied increasingly on foreign loans and trade credits. As a result, Guyana's foreign debt moved from US$206 million in 1975 to almost US$700 million in 1985, while the Bank of Guyana's foreign exchange reserves declined to less than negative US$500 million. Guyana would become the second poorest nation in the western hemisphere, with a per capita income of US$840 in 2001, US$360 ahead of Haiti.

In spite of increasing balance of payments pressures, no action was taken on the exchange rate until 1981 when, on entering an IMF arrangement, the Guyanese dollar was devalued to G$3.00 = US$1.00, and again in 1984 to G$4.12 = US$1.00 at a time when the Guyana dollar was pegged to a basket of currencies. From the mid-1970s the Guyanese authorities resorted to the most draconian measures, including personal searches at the airport and a travel allowance limitation of US$15.00, in an effort to staunch a haemorrhage of capital flight accompanied by massive emigration of its most skilled citizens — all to no avail.

The emergence of a thriving parallel market, with rates diverging sharply from the official rate, prompted a further devaluation in 1986 to G$10 = US$1.00. With the parallel rate fluctuating between G$14–20 per US dollar, the Bank of Guyana established a 'free foreign exchange market', a second legal rate to compete with the parallel market. The 'free' rate was set at G$20 = US$1.00, while the official rate remained at G$10 = US$1.00. Between 1984 and 1986 the modal rate of the fluctuating Guyana dollar was about G$40 = US$1.00.

When the parallel rate reached G$50 = US$1.00 in 1989, the Bank abolished the free foreign exchange window and returned to a single official rate of G$33 = US$1.00. Another devaluation quickly followed to G$45 = US$1.00, and the government set up the 'cambio system' as a means of eliminating the black market for currencies. Even commercial banks were allowed to set up cambios as separate units of their organizations. The cambio rate quickly jumped to G$90 = US$1.00, and in 1990 a floating rate was formally introduced for the entire economy, and foreign exchange controls formally abolished.

At first, the exchange rate appeared to have stabilized, but by 1996 it had fallen to G$145 = US$1.00 and currently fluctuates around G$200 = US$1.00. In addition to the foreign exchange market scheme and the cambio system, the Guyanese authorities experimented, to no avail, with several devices to restore currency stability, most notably barter trade with other socialist states.

In default on a foreign debt of US$1.5 billion, the government turned to the IMF and the World Bank in 1989, and a classic monetary and market programme was attempted, including real positive and market-determined interest rates, and other demand management measures. The programme was assisted by the government's abandonment of the failed 'socialist' experiment, the divestment of loss-making enterprises, and the wooing of foreign investors. Some measure of economic growth was restored, but repeated devaluations have not made the Guyanese economy any more competitive; nor has persistent ethnic-based political and social unrest helped the situation.

Jamaica

Jamaica pegged its currency to the US dollar in 1971 at the rate of US$1.20 = J$1.00. In the light of increasing balance of payments pressures, a modest devaluation was made in 1973 to US$1.10 = J$1.00. But Jamaica's serious difficulties started in 1975 when, in the name of 'democratic socialism', the government embarked on massive social expenditures, financed primarily by Central Bank credit — reminiscent of the Guyanese experience. During 1977 and 1978 the government increased its loans outstanding from the Central Bank from J$77 million to J$346 million. The Bank of Jamaica's foreign exchange reserves were quickly exhausted and the government resorted to heavy foreign borrowing. Jamaica has since been forced into a series of painful foreign debt reschedulings, barely avoiding technical default. Like Guyana, Jamaica has never recovered from the toxic injection of new money in 1975.

Jamaica started to experiment with multiple exchange rates in April 1977. A 'basic' rate of US$1.00 = J$1.00 and a special rate of US$0.80 = J$1.00. The basic rate applied to: (a) payments for imports of basic foods, petroleum products, drugs, fertilizers and animal feeds; (b) receipts and payments on government account, and (c) receipts and payments related to the mining sector. In October of the same year, new 'basic' and 'special' rates were established; in 1978 the dual exchange system was discontinued when Jamaica entered an IMF extended facility. In 1983, Jamaica returned to the dual exchange system, with an official rate of J$1.78 = US$1.00, and a formal parallel market determined by commercial banks on the basis of demand and supply. A third rate of J$2.25 = US$1.00 was introduced in May. The exchange rate system was soon after unified, and an auction system for foreign exchange established. The Jamaican authorities, like those of Guyana, also put in place fierce foreign exchange restrictions to curb foreign exchange outflows, with similar lack of effect.

In 1990 Jamaica embarked on a programme of financial liberalization with the introduction of an inter-bank foreign exchange system, under which responsibility for the purchase and sale of foreign currency, at market determined rates, was transferred to authorized dealers, who were required to sell a percentage of their purchases to the Central Bank. Pauline Bachelor et al., in 'The Evolution of the Financial Sector in Jamaica' concluded:

> It was anticipated that with the implementation of the inter-bank foreign exchange system there would have been a substantial increase in foreign exchange inflows into the banking system. This, however, did not materialize.[3]

Since 1990 Jamaica has essentially operated a freely floating exchange rate regime.

Liberalization of the foreign exchange market culminated in the removal in 1991 of exchange controls, except that trading in foreign currency was restricted to authorized dealers. In 1994, a system of cambios was established in an effort to marginalize the black market. At year end 1990 the exchange rate was J$8 = US$1.00; by the end of 2001 it had fallen to J$45 = US$1.00. In addition, high rates of inflation have prevailed: the average annual GDP deflator from 1990 to 2001 was 22 per cent. Since the early 1990s the Bank of Jamaica has intervened from time to time in the foreign exchange market to preserve some measure of exchange rate stability.

To make matters worse, the programme of financial liberalization, launched in 1990, was implemented in the context of loose bank and non-bank supervision, and collapsed in the second half of the 1990s when all indigenous commercial banks, representing 60 per cent of liabilities in the banking system, along with the two largest life insurance companies, failed and had to be rescued by the government. The Jamaican story is compelling proof of the ineffectiveness of orthodox financial policies, and the futility of bureaucratic measures to interdict capital flight, while the foreign exchange market remains in a condition of chronic disequilibrium.

Trinidad and Tobago

Trinidad and Tobago has been a significant oil exporter for decades, and more recently a major world producer of natural gas and its derivatives. Indeed, the energy sector represents 25 per cent of GDP, and earns about 60 per cent of the country's foreign exchange. The oil shocks of 1974 and 1978, which created major problems for other CARICOM economies, led to boom conditions in Trinidad and Tobago. Between 1974 and 1982, GDP grew at an average rate of 6.3 per cent, with correspondingly high levels of government revenues and a strong build-up of foreign reserves, which rose from less than US$50 million in 1973 to over US$300 million in 1974, and peaked at US$3.2 billion in 1981. Government expenditures also rose sharply, leading to a significant reduction in unemployment. As a result there was an unprecedented improvement in the general standard of living and vastly increased imports of consumer goods.

The adverse movement in terms of trade brought about by falling oil prices, from a peak of US$40 a barrel in 1981 to less than $10 a barrel in 1986, led to shrinking government revenues and rising fiscal deficits; as a percentage of GDP, the fiscal deficit grew from 1.4 per cent in 1978 to 13.1 per cent in 1983. The instinctive reaction of the authorities was to defend the existing exchange rate. With massive balance of payments deficits in prospect, they opted in 1983 for direct import controls in preference to a currency devaluation. They introduced a system of *ex ante* Central Bank controls over visible imports and introduced a plethora of tariffs, taxes and subsidies, which created many opportunities for rent seekers. When these measures proved insufficient, the Trinidad and Tobago dollar was devalued and a dual exchange rate regime adopted. The exchange rate moved from TT$2.40 = US$1.00 to TT$3.60 = US$1.00, except for imports of food, drugs and other 'basic' items which traded at the old rate.

With the collapse of oil prices in 1986 to less than US$10 per barrel, there was a precipitous decline in the level of foreign exchange reserves. For two more years the authorities persisted with quantitative import restrictions, though of a tamer variety. By 1988 the government realized that an approach to the IMF was inevitable, and struck pre-emptively by further devaluing the currency to a unified rate of TT$4.25 = US$1.00. Under the IMF stand-by programme of 1989, Trinidad and Tobago was required to dismantle its import controls.

In 1993 the government decided to abolish controls on both current and capital transactions, and to allow the value of the T&T dollar to be determined within the context of an inter-bank market with authorized foreign exchange dealers as the major players. The rate of the original 'float' was TT$5.35 = US1.00, but the Trinidad and Tobago dollar has since fluctuated around TT$6 = US$1.00. The narrow range of currency fluctuation betrays the fact that the float is not really *free* but *managed*. In fact, the Central Bank, the Ministry of Finance and the major commercial banks cooperate in a programme for the maintenance of orderly market conditions, which includes the rationing of foreign exchange sales, and the sharing of foreign exchange purchases among authorized dealers. The Central Bank has also made several interventions to stabilize the exchange rate. The IMF has described the Trinidad and Tobago exchange rate regime as a de facto peg; it certainly is not floating freely, nor is it pegged! Maybe the IMF's description is merely a tribute to the success of the Trinidad and Tobago authorities in *managing* currency stability.

The performance of the Trinidad and Tobago economy since 1993 suggests that the series of devaluations, followed by the adoption of a managed float, have borne fruit. Export manufacturing, in particular, has flourished, benefiting from cheap electricity generated from abundant supplies of gas, and from the cuts in real wages resulting from successive currency devaluations. Whereas real GDP grew annually at a rate of negative three per cent from 1985 to 1992, the average rate of growth since then has been three per cent.

The Role of the Cambio

A cambio may be described as a 'mom and pop' dealership in foreign currency, operating outside the regulatory framework of the formal commercial banking system. Whereas cambios in developed economies play the marginal role of money changing for the convenience of tourists, they have featured more prominently in the financial systems of those CARICOM countries whose foreign exchange markets have slipped into chronic disequilibrium. Historically, cambios have not existed in those CARICOM countries with fixed exchange rate regimes; its introduction in Belize is a very recent phenomenon.

Clearly, cambios have emerged because they provide a needed service. They serve individuals who wish to trade the relatively small amounts of foreign exchange that come into their possession, or who wish to obtain relatively small sums of foreign exchange to meet purchases and family obligations overseas, but find it intimidating or inconvenient to deal with commercial banks. On the macroeconomic level, they may consolidate numerous small quantities of foreign exchange that may then be utilized for more socially useful purposes. However, cambios have never brought in the quantities of foreign exchange anticipated, and have not significantly alleviated the foreign exchange constraint that mires the economies of LDCs in a low-production mode.

At the same time, neo-liberal economists have tended to regard the cambio rate as the 'true' market rate for the aggregate economy. A fall in the cambio rate therefore leads to a corresponding, and usually disproportionate, decline in asset values throughout the economy, triggering an upward spiral in prices, higher nominal wages and, as shown above, worsening the disequilibrium in the foreign exchange markets. As a result, the entire economy is held hostage to the cambio system; put another way, the tail wags the dog.

It is a fallacy to equate markets of the cambio system with the orderly financial markets of developed countries, which process information across the entire economy and so appropriately determine the national exchange rate. The distinction between an orderly market and a disorderly market is critical. Professor Paul Davidson points out that 'an orderly market means that changes in market prices can be expected to be small and appropriate, given the news of the day.'[4] The cambio systems of CARICOM do not meet these requirements of orderliness, and so cannot form the basis of a sound national foreign exchange rate policy.

This brings us to Professor Davidson's next point:

A market maker is defined as someone who publicly announces a willingness to act as a residual buyer or seller to assure orderliness if an abrupt disruptive change occurs on either the demand or supply side of the market. The market maker, following the pre-announced rules of that market, guarantees that the next market price will not differ chaotically from the last transaction price despite the disruption.[5]

The implications of the above analysis are that:

➢ The cambio system should be integrated into a system of orderly national financial markets.

> The Central Bank, as suggested above, is the institution most suitable for the role of market maker. However, as the example of Trinidad and Tobago has demonstrated, other informal arrangements can be made to accomplish similar results. Note that the market maker does not necessarily maintain a fixed price, but only orderly conditions.

Lessons from the CARICOM Experience

> Countries that maintained currency stability achieved the highest rates of economic growth.

> Fiscal discipline proved to be the most important factor in the maintenance of currency stability and sustained economic growth.

> Timely and credible currency devaluation proved to be the best policy in the event of a sharp fall in national income that was patently irreversible in the medium term.

> Multiple exchange rates created more problems than they solved.

> Even the most draconian measures failed to stem the flight of foreign exchange once public confidence in the domestic currency is lost; elaborate bureaucratic import control measures proved equally counter-productive.

> Once foreign exchange markets succumbed to chronic disequilibrium, even deep and repeated currency devaluations failed to shift resources from the domestic to the external sector.

> In no country did the cambio system significantly increase the supply of foreign exchange; cambios usually made matters worse by reducing public confidence in the domestic currency.

> The problems of exchange rate management were exacerbated in both Guyana and Jamaica by the absence of a minimal social and political consensus.

➤ The costs of currency under-devaluation appear to be as high, and may even be higher, than those of currency over-valuation. There is no doubt that the depreciation of both the Guyanese and the Jamaican dollar has been greater than warranted by their effective domestic purchasing power.

➤ In the case of those states (Guyana, Jamaica, and Trinidad and Tobago) dependent on price sensitive commodity exports, a managed exchange rate regime worked best. If a sharp decline in GDP or a sharp rise in the real wage rate so indicated, a currency devaluation should be swift and deep enough to be credible — as the experience of Trinidad and Tobago has taught us.

Theory of Exchange Rate Regime Choice

The various types of exchange rate regimes may be viewed as existing on a continuum with the 'free-float' at one end and the fixed rate, for example, peg, currency board or dollarization, at the other. (Diagram I gives a graphical representation of this continuum.) The most important factor in the choice of an exchange rate regime is the quality of its financial sector.

Diagram 1: Continuum of Exchange Rate Regimes

EXCHANGE RATE REGIME	FREE FLOAT		MANAGED FLOAT		FIXED RATE	
					PEG	CURRENCY BOARD
					DOLLARIZATION	
COUNTRY TYPE	LARGE	MEDIUM	LARGE / MEDIUM	MEDIUM / SMALL	SMALL	MINI-STATE
QUALITY OF FINANCIAL MARKET	HIGHLY DEVELOPED		EMERGING		EMBRYONIC	INSIGNIFICANT
COUNTRY EXAMPLES	USA EU	UK CANADA SWEDEN	ARGENTINA BRAZIL MEXICO INDIA CHINA	HONG KONG SINGAPORE TAIWAN TRINIDAD & TOBAGO	BARBADOS NETHERLANDS ANTILLES THE BAHAMAS	BERMUDA CAYMAN ISLANDS

Successful floating exchange regimes are usually those of countries with large developed economies, like the US, or a group of developed economies, like the European Union, or even relatively small economies with highly sophisticated financial markets like the UK, Sweden or Canada. Even large countries lacking deep and wide financial markets, such as Argentina and Brazil, have failed to operate successful floating exchange rate regimes, while the floating of the Russian rouble led to financial, economic, social and political chaos. China, with a large and rapidly growing economy, has hesitated to float its currency, and has only recently allowed the renminbi to be convertible outside of China.

Successful 'fixers' are usually mini-states with highly open economies, and are therefore price-takers. They are mainly involved in the export of tourism and financial services and frequently operate currency board regimes, for example, Cayman Islands and Bermuda. Dollarization is also a feasible option for such small economies, but the currency board solution is clearly superior in that it preserves the seignorage revenues lost in dollarization without any increased monetary stability.

Some small CARICOM services-exporting countries with central banks, like Barbados, Belize, The Bahamas and OECS, have operated successful fixed-rate regimes for over 25 years, but usually in the context of a disciplined fiscal policy and, in the case of Barbados, with benefit of an incomes policy made possible by social homogeneity and political consensus.

The current Argentine crisis has demonstrated that relatively large countries with significant commodity and/or manufacturing exports are not well served by a pegged exchange rate. When the currencies of trading partners depreciated, the 'hard' peg of the Argentine peso to the US dollar ruled out domestic cost adjustments through devaluation, and the rigid convertible peg to the US dollar broke down, leading to the collapse of the financial system. Furthermore, the integrity of the currency board regime had been fatally compromised by heavy foreign borrowing by the Argentine central government and the issue of debt by the provinces.

The reasons why similar currency board systems had worked so well in British and French colonies escaped academics who prescribed a currency board or dollarization regime for Argentina: it was because colonial governments could neither contract foreign debt (unless approved by the colonial power) nor issue bonds on the local financial markets. Argentina's plight would have been even greater had its currency been dollarized, as some American economists recommended. In that case, the Argentine monetary authorities could not have imposed capital controls to staunch the flight of capital, as they did when the financial crisis struck, since the public would have been holding US dollars, which it could have exported at will. Interestingly enough, the Washington international financial institutions have never expressly endorsed dollarization, preferring instead the free floating exchange rate regime, which had already failed Argentina and would also fail Brazil.

The current Brazilian crisis further demonstrates that even an economy as large and broad-based as Brazil's cannot successfully operate a freely floating exchange rate regime if its financial markets lack the requisite breadth and depth to absorb severe shocks from the global economy. (The financial markets of both Brazil and Argentina are puny when compared to those of the US.) Even neo-liberal economists now accept that it was the fragility of their capital markets that led to the financial collapse of 'Asian tigers', such as Malaysia, Thailand and South Korea, in the face of global financial turbulence.

Floating is even more hazardous for small countries with small and underdeveloped financial markets. External shocks requiring downward exchange rate adjustments can easily lead to overshooting and to unwarranted currency depreciation, and consequent depression of capital values. It is surprising that neo-liberal economists, who are highly vocal about the evils of an overvalued currency, are silent on the even greater disasters of massive under-devaluations. In fact, even the US does not conduct a perfectly free float. However, because of its highly developed financial markets, monetary authorities are able to use market-oriented policy instruments to moderate and smooth out currency fluctuations. For example, the Federal Reserve Board can raise interest rates to attract foreign capital inflows to reverse an undesired depreciation of the dollar — as little as ½ per cent increase might do the job! In extreme cases the monetary authorities of the US, EU and Japan, through concerted open market operations, may sometimes bring about the desired exchange rate outcome.

The options open to the monetary authorities of advanced industrial countries are not available to those of Argentina or Brazil, whose fragile financial markets do not qualify them to play in the 'big league'. Countries with poorly developed financial markets must therefore resort to non-market techniques of intervention to cope with severe shocks from the global economy. That is why Chile has instituted reserve requirements on short-term capital inflows to protect its financial markets. Professor Gerry Helleiner has strongly urged that the IMF should: 'recognize capital account controls, direct and indirect, as legitimate macroeconomic policy instruments in most developing countries to deal with volatile capital flows.'[6]

He adds that the full liberalization of financial markets should be phased. Even Professor Ronald McKinnon, the originator of the term 'financial repression' and prophet of 'financial liberalization', now concedes: 'Free foreign convertibility on capital account is usually the last stage in the optimal order of economic liberalization.'[7]

Moreover, neo-liberal economists who castigated Malaysia for imposing capital controls to defend its foreign exchange holdings, and Hong Kong for intervening heavily in its equity markets to defeat foreign speculators, now grudgingly concede that those countries did the right thing. Hong Kong, Singapore and Taiwan, which practised some measure of exchange rate management, best weathered the Asian Crisis of the 1990s. Also noteworthy is that they all maintain very large holdings of foreign exchange as a buffer against shocks from the global environment. In June 2002, Taiwan, Hong Kong and Singapore held foreign exchange reserves of US$155 billion, $112 billion, and $80 billion respectively, compared to US$10, 42, and 15 billion for Argentina, Brazil, and Chile respectively.[8] The CARICOM experience has also demonstrated the importance of holding adequate levels of foreign exchange.

Chronic Market Disequilibrium

Exchange rate overshooting becomes extreme when foreign exchange markets enter the stage of chronic disequilibrium. Chronic disequilibrium describes the situation, such as in Guyana and Jamaica, where the demand for foreign exchange so far outstrips its supply that foreign exchange markets fail to clear, and are unlikely to do so in the foreseeable future. In such situations, as the writer has demonstrated, repeated currency devaluations not only fail to restore market equilibrium, but worsen the situation.[9]

Chart 4 represents classical market conditions. Note that a currency devaluation, represented by an upward movement in the price of foreign currency from P1 to P2, brings supply and demand into equilibrium so that the disequilibrium defined by Q1, S1, S2, Q2, (shaded area) disappears.

Chart 5 represents a foreign exchange market in a state of chronic disequilibrium. The supply function is realistically shown as a perfectly inelastic supply curve, so that an upward movement in price from P1 to P2 (which reflects a devaluation) does not elicit an increase in the supply of foreign exchange. Note that as P1 moves higher to P2 (that is, a devaluation occurs) market equilibrium is not achieved, but disequilibrium grows worse as the shaded area Q2, S2, D2, Q2 exceeds the shaded area Q1, S1, D1, Q1. In conditions of chronic disequilibrium then, the equilibrium exchange rate becomes indeterminate, so that the adoption of a free float will most likely lead to further currency depreciation, without any significant economic benefit but with strong inflationary pressures, as the cases of Jamaica and Guyana have shown.

Chart 4
Automatic Market Adjustment for Foreign Exchange

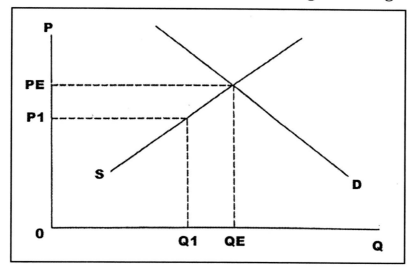

Chart 5
Conditions of Chronic Disequilibrium

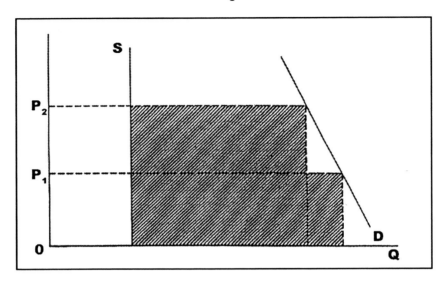

Chart 6
Policy Requirements in Conditions of Chronic Disequilibrium

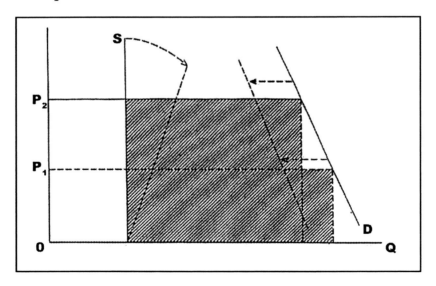

The inelasticity of the supply curve in Charts 5 and 6 indicates the extreme scarcity of foreign exchange; for developing countries, which must import the vast proportion of their capital and intermediate goods, a chronic shortage of foreign exchange imposes a severe constraint on production, leading to economic stagnation. For these reasons, then, currency depreciations worsen the situation: firstly, market dysfunction hinders a devaluation from shifting resources away from the domestic to the external sector; secondly, the low levels of productivity typical of LDCs minimize the availability of real resources for transfer, so that the increased export earnings predicted in textbook economics do not materialize; and thirdly, a devaluation is of little assistance to local producers if they cannot increase output to exploit the advantage of higher export prices.

To preserve some semblance of exchange rate stability in the short run, policy makers must therefore seek second best solutions by direct market intervention and rationing, even as they pursue medium to long-term strategies.

Structural economic change, as Chart 6 demonstrates, could produce a parametric shift of the demand curve to the left, possibly through foreign debt reduction and more economic usage of foreign exchange, and the parametric shift of the supply curve to the right through improved productivity; at the same time, confidence building measures could accelerate response to a higher price by rotating the supply curve to the right. In the meantime, the monetary authorities must manage the day-to-day changes in exchange rate variables as best they can; that responsibility cannot be left to the 'free market' in the circumstances of LDCs whose financial markets are so weak. The authorities of countries must be prepared to intervene decisively in their financial markets when it is necessary to protect the stability of the overall economic system.

Summing Up

The most important factor in the choice of an exchange rate regime is the quality of a country's financial markets. Highly developed financial markets are a necessary condition for the operation of a free-floating regime, and large size certainly helps. On the other hand, large size is not a sufficient condition for successful floating, while extremely small economies, such as those within CARICOM, are unlikely ever to develop financial markets of the width and breadth necessary to support a floating exchange rate regime.

Neo-liberal economists, in a strange failure to recognize the various stages of market development, and through their neglect of the institutional features of markets, have not focussed on an important macroeconomic function of financial markets — that of cushioning the economy against the effects of turbulence in the global financial market. That is why international financial crises have such negligible effects on the US and the EU, and such devastating effects on LDCs. Similarly, the economies of countries with highly developed real markets adjust more elegantly to volatility in the prices of internationally traded commodities than do LDCs; whereas the western industrial economies returned to balance of payments surplus within two or three years of the tripling of oil prices in 1974, the majority of LDCs remain mired in debt to this day.

Lacking highly developed financial markets, underdeveloped, and especially small, countries must insure against turbulence in the global financial market by maintaining high levels of foreign exchange reserves. The opportunity cost of holding reserves must be regarded as the premium paid for insurance against any economic fall-out from global financial crises and from volatility in international commodity markets. This explains the massive holdings of foreign exchange reserves held by Hong Kong, Taiwan and Singapore, which all doubt their capacity to float and so practise some degree of exchange rate management. On the other hand, countries with highly developed financial markets, such as the US and the UK, hold quite low levels of foreign exchange reserves.

Even very large economies like Brazil and Argentina may lack highly developed financial markets, and are therefore not promising candidates for the operation of successful floating regimes. This explains the reluctance of China to float its currency, and why it maintains extremely high levels of foreign exchange reserves.

Small countries like Barbados, Trinidad and Tobago, and Jamaica simply do not possess the capacity to develop financial markets with the width and breadth necessary for cushioning their economies against global financial crises, and are therefore poor candidates for the operation of a free floating exchange rate regime. It is only the blindness induced by ideology that has led neo-liberal economists to push them in that direction. Those small countries have done best which have pegged their currencies to a strong currency, held high levels of foreign exchange reserves, and pursued sound fiscal policies.

The choice of an exchange rate regime is most problematic for relatively large countries like Brazil and Argentina, whose lack of developed financial markets rules out floating exchange rate regimes, but whose relatively large commodity and manufacturing sectors require some degree of exchange rate flexibility if they are to compete in the global marketplace. They are too financially underdeveloped to float, but their real economies are too large for them to peg. They have no choice but to compromise by operating a managed float.

Originally prepared for XXXIV Annual Monetary Studies Conference (2002) Bank of Guyana, November 12–15, 2002

Notes

1. This section depends heavily on, *The Financial Evolution of the Caribbean Community, (1970–1996)* eds., Laurence Clarke and Donna Danns (St. Augustine, Trinidad: Caribbean Centre for Monetary Studies, University of the West Indies, 1997).

2. GDP statistics in this paper are calculated on a purchasing power parity basis.

3. Pauline Batchelor, et al., *The Financial Evolution of the Caribbean Community (1970–1976)*, 316.

4. Paul Davidson, *Post Keynesian Macroeconomic Theory* (Brookfield, Vermont: Edward Elgan Publishing Co, 1884), 49.

5. Ibid., 49.

6. Gerry K. Helleiner, *Private Capital Flows and Development: The Role of National and International Policies* (Guyana: Commonwealth Secretariat, 1988), 30.

7. Ronald I. McKinnon, *The Order of Economic Liberalization: Financial Control in the Transition to a Market Economy* (Baltimore: The Johns Hopkins University Press, 1991), 10.

8. *Economist*, August 31–September 6, 2002.

9. Courtney N. Blackman, *Central Banking in Theory and Practice: A Small State Perspective* (St. Augustine, Trinidad: Caribbean Centre for Monetary Studies, 1998). Cf. Chapter 6, 'Structural Adjustment in Conditions of Disequilibrium', 113–129.

SECTION III

'Washington Consensus': Contending with the 'Right'

10

THE FREE MARKET IN THE CONTEXT OF GLOBALIZATION

MYTH, MAGIC OR MENACE?

I have chosen to speak on the topic, 'The Free Market in the Context of Globalization: Myth, Magic or Menace'. Let us look first of all at globalization. There are two sides to globalization: the first is substantive; the second is ideological. On the substantive side, globalization may be defined as the information revolution, already apparent in the 1980s but which gathered increasing momentum in the 1990s. It is marked by the explosion in the usage of computers for the storage and processing of large volumes of information, and by new technologies in the field of telecommunications that make possible the virtually instantaneous transmission of information and capital worldwide. One result has been the 'death of distance', the title of Frances Cairncross' brilliant lecture on a similar occasion in 1998. It is now possible for multinational corporations to integrate the production and marketing of goods and services without regard to national boundaries.

The substantive process of globalization, driven essentially by these technological innovations, is irreversible. We must therefore treat it as a fact of life, and learn to adjust to it. Indeed, over the last three years, Prime Minister Arthur has taken several measures designed to reposition the Barbadian economy for the challenges of globalization. Tonight, I propose to treat the ideological aspects. An ideology is a system of belief about how the world ought to work. Modern scholars use the term 'paradigm' interchangeably with 'ideology'; so will I.

Let us first of all place the ideological aspects of globalization in historical perspective. For most of the Cold War the two opposing economic paradigms were Keynesianism in the west and Marxism-Leninism in the east. The latter espoused a command economy in which the vast majority of economic decisions were taken by a central planning authority. Keynesians, in the west, while leaving the vast majority of economic decisions to the private sector, argued the need for regulation of national spending and investment through fiscal and monetary policy so as to maintain full employment.

Keynesian policies began to lose their effectiveness in the 1980s, and as the command economies of the eastern bloc palpably began to fail, President Ronald Reagan in the United States and Prime Minister Margaret Thatcher in the United Kingdom launched a vigorous counter-revolution for a return to the pre-Keynesian laissez-faire paradigm, which held that the workings of the 'free market' would optimize the national welfare. Proponents of laissez-faire support the principle of 'minimalist' government — that that government is best which governs least, and that as few restrictions as possible should be placed on economic activities.

With the comprehensive collapse of the Soviet Union in 1989, the field of battle was left to the modern version of the laissez-faire paradigm, known as 'neo-liberalism', or 'market fundamentalism', with its mantra of the 'free market'. The collapse of the socialist bloc was seen as confirmation of the 'truth' of neo-liberalism, and neo-liberal economists soon began to occupy the top posts at leading American universities and the US Treasury, while there was a changing of the guard at the IMF from Keynesianism to 'market fundamentalism'. The new dispensation, reflecting 'free market' principles, came to be known as the 'Washington Consensus'.

The 'Washington Consensus' is a programme designed to reorganize the global economy along neo-liberal lines. Two months ago the Bush administration, in its policy statement, 'The National Security Strategy of the USA', reaffirmed its intention 'to ignite a new era of global economic growth through free markets and free trade.' I will focus on five elements of the 'Washington Consensus':

◆ Currency devaluation
◆ Financial liberalization – that is, removal of interest rate ceilings, the abolition of exchange controls, and the floating of currencies
◆ Financial globalization – that is, unfettered inward and outward capital flows
◆ Deregulation and privatization of government enterprises
◆ Free trade – that is, removal of restrictions on imports and exports

The designated vehicles for the implementation of the 'Washington Consensus' are the IMF and World Bank, whose policies are determined by the Group of Seven, comprising the UK, France, Germany, Italy, Canada, Japan, and especially the United States.

John Maynard Keynes, the greatest economist of the twentieth century, observed that:

[T]he ideas of economists and political philosophers, both when they are right and when they are wrong, are more powerful than is commonly understood. Indeed, the world is ruled by little else.[1]

In an ironic twist of fate, I spent the late 70s and early 80s resisting the left wing doctrines of Marxism-Leninism and the New World economists. Now I find myself defending against the doctrines of the Right.

The purpose of this exercise is to carry out a critical examination of the 'free market' ideology which underpins the agenda of the 'Washington Consensus' so that Barbados, and by extension CARICOM, may formulate an intelligent response.

Under the caption 'Myth', I expose the mythical elements of the 'free market' doctrine. Under 'Magic', I seek to demystify the ideology of the 'free market'. In so doing, I explain those features of the market which contribute to the superior productivity of the capitalist system; I also shine a light on the darker side of market operations. Under 'Menace', I recall the misfortunes which the programme of the 'Washington Consensus' has already inflicted, and will continue to inflict, if uncritical acceptance persists. I will wrap up with some personal reflections on our existing situation in Barbados.

Myth

What is a market? A market is a physical place or set of circumstances, in which goods and services are bought and sold. Is the free market a myth? Mostly! As a matter of fact, the expression 'free market' is not even a term of art, and is not found in economics textbooks. We find definitions of perfect and imperfect markets, of monopoly, oligopoly and monopsony, but nowhere is there mention of the 'free market'. I cringe every time I hear a trained economist refer to the 'free market'.

Indeed, neo-liberal and even neo-classical economists no longer distinguish between categories of markets, treating all markets as 'efficient'. This has led them to prescribe one-size-fits-all policies without taking into account the differences between the sophisticated markets of developed countries and the poorly developed, and sometimes non-existent, markets of LDCs. It is surprising that they should treat the market as a homogeneous institution, since markets are central to the study of economics. This is in marked contrast to the more worldly-wise Eskimo. Since snow is the most common feature of his environment, he has studied its characteristics exhaustively. I understand that Eskimos can identify more than 20 different kinds of snow: soft snow, wet snow, dry snow, et cetera.

Sociologically, the very expression 'free market' is a contradiction in terms. The substantive market, as opposed to the 'free market' of myth, is an institution which operates within the context of rules agreed upon among the participants, or laws and regulations enacted by government. What is more, disputes arising out of any market transaction can be referred to a court of law. Government and the market are therefore inextricable.

Indeed, even markets where illegal goods and services are traded are subject to rules and regulations. You may have noticed in gangster movies that drug traffickers taste the heroin before buying it to see if it is up to standard, and they even demarcate markets among themselves. The penalties for transgression of rules are even more certain and final in the underworld than in established courts of law.

It is not surprising then that the world's most efficient market, the New York Stock Exchange, is also the most highly and meticulously regulated, with the Securities and Exchange Commission acting as watchdog over its operations. Sharp surges or declines in market prices trigger curbs on trading — following the destruction of the World Trade Center on September 11, 2001, the Stock Exchange was closed for four days — and infractions such as 'insider trading' draw enormous fines and long prison sentences. That is why I have invented the aphorism: 'If it's free, it's not a market; and if it's a market, it's not free.'

Neo-liberal economists would also have us believe that developing countries can achieve optimal economic growth rates without government intervention. Just leave it to the 'free market', they tell us. In so doing, they are guilty of retrospective myth-making. Our own Nobel laureate Sir Arthur Lewis, who knew more about economic development than any living neo-liberal economist, observed in his celebrated work, *Theory of Economic Growth:*

> No country has made economic progress without positive stimulus
> from intelligent governments, least of all England, the foundations
> of whose greatness as an industrial power were laid by a series of
> intelligent rulers, from Edward III onwards; or the United States,
> whose governments, state and federal, have always played a large
> part in shaping economic activity.... Sensible people do not get
> involved in arguments about whether economic progress is due to
> government activity or to individual initiative; they know that it is
> due to both, and they concern themselves only with asking what is
> the proper contribution of each.[2]

With regard to government subsidies, against which neo-liberal economists warn developing countries so sternly, 'free market' myth-making is brazenly hypocritical. About 40 per cent of farm income in the US derives from government subsidies; the figure is over 50 per cent for the European Union, and over 60 per cent for Japan. The Bush administration recently extended US$750 billion in subsidies over ten years to agriculture. These subsidies go mainly to corporate farms and are called incentives; subsidies to the poor are called 'hand-outs', and are cut at every opportunity for the moral benefit of the recipients.

Finally, there is the myth of 'free trade'. If 'free trade' was in fact free, why would the regulations establishing the WTO and NAFTA fill hundreds of pages? Certainly, we should call such agreements 'managed trade agreements'! In fact, nations have historically embraced free trade only when they enjoyed a dominant position in world trade. Britain pushed for 'free trade' in the late nineteenth century, switching to imperial preferences in the twentieth century when Germany caught up with her. The American economy grew behind high tariffs in the nineteenth century, and the US is a relatively recent convert to free trade since it became the world's most powerful economy, displaying a marked propensity to backslide when foreign competition becomes too threatening.

Magic

Is the 'free market' magical? Half and half! It was President Reagan who coined the expression, 'magic of the free market', but it was Adam Smith, the founder of the discipline of economics, who first attributed a metaphysical quality to the 'free market'. He explained in *The Wealth of Nations,* published in 1776, how buyers and sellers, as they selfishly seek the best deals in the marketplace, unwittingly promote the efficient production and allocation of goods and services in the economy without the active intervention of outside agents. He saw an 'invisible hand' at work in this process, which he considered to be certainly beneficent, and suspiciously divine — clear proof that out of evil cometh good.[3]

In fact, Smith had identified what systems theorists call a self-organizing process. The self-organizing process in which most of you participate daily is the traffic roundabout. Once upon a time in Barbados, policemen were posted on platforms to direct traffic at busy intersections; they would later be replaced by traffic lights. The roundabout promotes a much more rapid and continuous flow of traffic than either the traffic policemen or the traffic lights, and without any outside intervention, as long as drivers follow the simple rule of giving way to vehicles approaching on their right.

To fully appreciate the marvellous features of markets, just think about the vast number of products in your own household: shoes, teacups, needles and pins, and so on. Even though you may have purchased them all at Cave Shepherd, you were really participating in a global shoe market when you bought shoes, a porcelain market when you bought tea-cups, and so forth, each time selecting the product which pleased you most at a price that you were prepared to pay. Millions of people participate in markets worldwide just as you do, and yet there is no centralized authority anywhere that decides how many shoes are to be produced, or to whom they should be sold. It all comes out in the wash of a multiplicity of self-organizing markets.

Contrast that with the command system of the Soviet Union prior to its collapse. Almost all goods and services were produced by state-owned enterprises as directed by the Central Planning Agency — the Gosplan. The Gosplan decided the quantities which thousands of enterprises should produce and at what price, and apportioned the working capital and materials for their production. This exercise involved a vast number of decisions and required a veritable army of bureaucrats. The command system was characterized by a horrendous mismatch between the quantity and variety of goods demanded and supplied, as evidenced by severe shortages and long queues. Moreover, the absence of private profits or productivity-based rewards made for very low quality goods and services to which, as a visitor to Moscow in 1979, I can attest. No wonder the system eventually collapsed!

But the almost magical efficiency of Adam Smith's free market also had its dark side. The first flaw in the 'free market' system is that only those who have money can participate, so that the poor and disadvantaged do not share in its bounty. This has given rise to the outrageous inequalities conspicuous within highly capitalistic economies like the US and among countries worldwide, with the rich getting richer and the poor getting poorer. In 1997 the top one per cent of income earners in the US received 15.8 per cent of total income, up from 9.3 per cent in 1981, while the top one per cent of all US households owned 40.1 per cent of total household wealth, up from 24.8 per cent in 1981. Worldwide, real per capita incomes for the richest one-third of countries rose by an annual 1.9 per cent between 1970 and 1995, whereas the middle third went up by only 0.7 per cent, and the bottom third showed no increase at all.

The second problem is that a free market would not deliver public goods, for example, health care, education, housing, and standard utilities, in an acceptable manner. The free market could deliver health care acceptably only if poor people did not get ill, and if the diseases that are most costly to cure affected only the rich. And suppose water was sold through a free market and poor people could not afford to buy it at the going price!

But the most serious flaw in the 'free market' paradigm is its exclusive predication on the selfish and competitive nature of human beings. Men and women are also capable of magnificent altruism and sacrifice. Moreover, human beings are social animals, and for any society to prosper its members must cooperate in a multiplicity of ways. Mutual trust is therefore essential to successful social cooperation. In a recent book entitled, *Trust*, Francis Fukuyama identified social cohesion as a critical factor in the creation of prosperity.[4] For many years I have myself argued that social cohesion, especially manifested in racial and religious tolerance, was the most important factor in any explanation of the prosperity of Barbados, a feature much admired by foreigners. Indeed, it is our most precious asset, and we should do nothing to diminish it.

Karl Marx, the author of *Das Kapital*, or *Capital*, and the prophet of socialism, severely criticized the inequalities and other blatant evils of capitalism, but he conceded that the market system was the most dynamic generator of economic growth so far in history. In replacing the market system with the command system, Marxist-Leninists clearly threw the baby out with the bath water. No non-market economy has ever flourished since the Industrial Revolution. Communism collapsed in Eastern Europe, the cooperative Kibbutzim in Israel are not doing very well, and within CARICOM, socialist experiments in Guyana and Grenada failed in spectacular fashion. The Scandinavians, especially the Swedes, were smart enough to retain the market system for the production of goods and services, taxing profits and personal income to ensure that all their citizens enjoy a decent standard of living.

Menace

Is the 'free market' a menace? Decidedly so; to the extent that countries, especially LDCs and small states are forced by the desperate need for foreign exchange to implement flawed IMF/ World Bank 'free market' policies and suffer the negative consequences thereof.

It was the debt crisis of 1982 that transformed the IMF from a low-keyed extender of balance of payments support into a purveyor of 'free market' based programmes and conditionalities. Following the oil shocks of the 1970s when OPEC increased prices threefold in 1974 and fourfold in 1978, non-oil producing LDCs borrowed heavily in the Euro markets to meet imports of this essential product. When their commercial credits dried up, they turned to the IMF. The World Bank would also insist that countries obtain the IMF imprimatur of good housekeeping to qualify for its own development loans.

The situation created by the debt crisis clearly required joint action by the governments of the developed countries and the international creditor banks to ease the burden on the highly indebted LDCs through loan restructuring, moratoria on repayments, and debt forgiveness. The example of the Marshall Plan, through which the US had contributed to European economic recovery after World War II, was an available model. However, no comprehensive programme was put in place. It was not until 1997 that an IMF programme was established to assist highly indebted poor countries (HIPC), and even then, only after years of 'satisfactory economic conduct' — a classic case of too little too late.

There are five areas where 'free market' based programmes have created or threatened the greatest havoc, especially for small countries, including some within CARICOM:

- ♦ Currency devaluation
- ♦ Financial liberalization

- ◆ Financial globalization
- ◆ Deregulation and privatization
- ◆ Free trade

I will deal with each separately.

Devaluation

The most common feature of IMF structural adjustment programmes is the currency devaluation. The currency devaluation seeks to correct a balance of payments disequilibrium by reducing the price of a country's exports and raising the cost of its imports. Theoretically, this leads to a decline in imports and a rise in exports, so that the balance in foreign payments is restored. This theory holds true, say, for Japan, for whom even a modest devaluation would lead to a disproportionately large increase in exports. But the foreign exchange and producer markets in LDCs are nothing as efficient as those of Japan; furthermore, LDCs seeking to borrow foreign exchange from the IMF would obviously lack the foreign exchange to purchase capital, equipment, raw materials, and even food for workers with which to produce goods and services for export.

In 1985 I demonstrated through the use of charts that in the case of countries like Jamaica and Guyana, with severe and chronic foreign exchange shortages, and whose foreign exchange markets were in chronic disequilibrium, a currency devaluation would not only fail to expand exports, but would make their existing situation even worse.[5] Since that time the Jamaican dollar has depreciated from about J$5.00 = US$1.00 to J$50.00 = US$1.00, and the Guyanese from about G$10.00 = US$1.00 to almost G$200.00 = US$1.00; their exports have contracted, and they are much poorer than they were in 1985.

It has always puzzled me that modern economists can rattle off several reasons why currency overvaluation is harmful, but never

217

stop to consider the downside of currency undervaluation. I have no doubt that devaluation was overdone in both Guyana and Jamaica, and that its citizens were impoverished to a greater extent than needed. Throughout my term as Governor, there was hardly a period when economists from Washington did not consider the Barbados dollar overvalued. I told one of them once, 'The more overvalued my dollar, the better my economy does!'

Financial Liberalization

Another IMF programme that has caused great pain for LDCs is the liberalization of the financial sector, based on the work of Professor McKinnon of Stanford University, whose theories the IMF and World Bank swallowed hook, line and sinker in the mid-1980s.[6] Central banks were required to remove ceilings on interest rates and abolish exchange controls. The need for high and positive real interest rates, that is, interest rates higher than the rate of inflation, was especially stressed. These policies were expected to lead to increased savings, to investment, and finally, to economic growth. McKinnon forgot that a rise in domestic savings was not the same thing as an increase in foreign exchange. In Guyana, for example, the commercial banks in the late 1980s and early 1990s were turning away domestic deposits, but domestic bank deposits do not necessarily translate into the foreign exchange needed for the production of goods and services for export.

The first outcomes of financial liberalization were not auspicious. As early as 1989 the World Bank, in its annual *World Development Report*, reported that financial liberalization had encountered serious difficulties in Argentina, Chile and Uruguay. By 1991, in his book, *The Order of Economic Liberalization*, McKinnon stressed that financial liberalization in developing countries should proceed step–by-step, and only after a number of conditions had been satisfied.[7] By then, however, the damage had already been done!

Within CARICOM, Jamaica's programme of financial liberalization, launched with high expectations in the early 1990s, quickly turned sour. The freeing-up of interest rates drove deposit rates to over 30 per cent per annum and commercial loan rates to over 60 per cent per annum, while financial deregulation led to a proliferation of financial institutions. The result was an initial boom in the financial sector, high rates of inflation and sharp currency depreciations, while real production stagnated. The Jamaican financial system eventually collapsed in the mid-1990s. Every single indigenous bank failed, representing 60 per cent of total bank deposits, as well as the two largest life insurance companies.

Financial Globalization

Financial globalization has probably injured LDCs more than any other IMF programme. It was based on the theory that the opening up of capital markets to unfettered flows of both direct and portfolio investment would optimise the allocation of capital resources to the benefit of all countries. The IMF therefore pressured, or certainly encouraged, LDCs to float their currencies and abolish all controls on capital flows in and out of their financial markets. Here again, the IMF economists failed to make a distinction between the highly developed financial markets of London, New York or Tokyo, and the small and unsophisticated markets of the LDCs, even those as large as Argentina and Brazil, which were too narrow and shallow to absorb the shocks of massive inflows and outflows of capital.

A series of financial crises ensued. Each one began with heavy inflows of capital that generated strong economic activity; investor sentiment would suddenly shift, and the process would reverse itself as foreign and domestic investors ran for cover, usually into the US dollar. The effects on the economies of affected countries were devastating: banks collapsed, currencies were sharply devalued, inflation soared, and companies failed and had to lay off workers; foreign debt could not be repaid, and countries were forced to submit to IMF programmes with painful conditionalities. Only those countries escaped which, like Singapore, Taiwan, Hong Kong and China, had maintained some degree of capital control and exchange rate management.

In 1995 I had the honour of representing Prime Minister and Minister of Finance, the Rt. Hon. Owen Arthur, at a hemispheric finance ministerial conference hosted by Secretary of the US Treasury, Robert Rubin, in New Orleans. I told the ministers of finance present that it was the process of financial liberalization itself (financial globalization had not yet been invented), that had caused Mexico's so-called Tequila Crisis, and that they could confidently expect other crises to follow. Following the Asian Crisis, I again represented the Prime Minister at the 1997 follow-up meeting in Santiago; I said, 'I told you so', and predicted further crises, which actually occurred in Brazil in 1998. At a third meeting in 2000, I repeated my routine; the Argentinean economy is now in ruins.

Deregulation and Privatization

In respect of deregulation and privatization, the UK and US, where 'free market' doctrines are most ardently propounded, also suffered grievously. Poetic justice, no doubt! In Britain, the privatised railways are a national disaster; nor did the deregulated telecoms flourish for very long. In the US, costs at privatised hospitals spiral out of control while the quality of health care declines; and the deregulation of both the savings and loans associations and the airline industry led to widespread bankruptcy with tremendous destruction of capital and loss of jobs.

But it was in Russia, following the collapse of the USSR, that the consequences of 'free market' policies exacted the greatest toll. Neo-liberal advisers insisted that Russia should move from a command economy to a market system in one fell swoop. Older and wiser heads, like Professor Kenneth Galbraith, recommended that Russia proceed step by step, as the Chinese have so successfully done, beginning with the privatization of 'mom and pop' establishments, and tackling the major industries later; but the neo-liberals insisted on the 'cold turkey' solution. In the ensuing chaos, a Russian mafia emerged to loot the state, and the citizens of the once great super power were reduced to abject poverty.

Fortunately for the LDCs, the dogma of deregulation and privatization largely coincided with economic necessity, not least within CARICOM. Over the decades pervasively incompetent, and frequently corrupt, management of state enterprises had racked up huge losses and destroyed massive volumes of capital. LDC governments must now learn how to keep the privatised industries, especially natural monopolies, under social control.

Free Trade

It is along the road to free trade that the most dangerous land mines await us. Economics text books teach that free trade, even between unequal partners, will bring benefits to both, and that over time wages in both countries will tend to converge. However, commonsense tells us that strong firms in strong economies will out-compete weak firms in weak economies. Nor has it escaped me that after 100 years of free trade between the US and Puerto Rico, with much grant aid thrown in, the per capita income of Puerto Rico is lower than that of Barbados.

The first mine to explode was the banana issue, set off by the complaint of the US at the World Trade Organization (WTO), at the request of Chiquita, which had made generous political contributions to both Democratic and Republican parties. The explosion wrecked the economy of Dominica, and inflicted considerable damage on other CARICOM banana growers. This had occurred in spite of a clause in the WTO agreement to the effect that, 'particular attention should be given to avoiding disruptive effects on the trade of less developed contracting parties.'

It also suggests that CARICOM representatives did not read the fine print at the WTO negotiations carefully enough. The Europeans, Japanese and Americans went to great pains to ensure that their highly protected agricultural sectors were secure from dispute challenges.

Actually, 'free trade' negotiations have more to do with politics than with trade, and in that equation political clout, financial power, and technical expertise are the most important factors. And here the major powers hold a distinct advantage. We could once count on their generosity; today they demand non-reciprocal agreements. Only the bulldog-like perseverance of Prime Minister Arthur, through the agency of the Commonwealth Secretariat, could move the World Bank to produce a document establishing that small states were more vulnerable to external shocks than large countries — a proposition intuitively obvious to a ten-year-old child. It has taken seven years for the US trade negotiator to concede the principle of 'differential treatment' for small states within the FTAA.

After my first few meetings in 1995 as Barbados's representative at the FTAA negotiations, I realized that no CARICOM state possessed the technical capacity to negotiate a FTAA. Some small states found it financially burdensome to attend meetings in far-away South American cities. Even with the pooling of regional resources the Regional Negotiating Machinery still requires support for its operations from foreign donors, some of whom will surely be pitted against CARICOM at disputes settlement proceedings sometime in the future.

In wrapping up, let me first make clear that my contention is with the 'free market' based policies of the 'Washington Consensus', and not an attack on the IMF or World Bank. I certainly do not share the view of former Secretary of the Treasury, George Schultz, that the IMF should be abolished, though I think its governance should be democratized. And I regard the World Bank as an indispensable institution, although the suggestion that its operations be decentralized appeals to me. The Washington head office might limit its operations to the study of macro issues, such as the environment, education and the mobilization of financial resources, leaving project implementation to the regional development banks that possess more intimate knowledge of country problems.

The Washington international financial institutions and the WTO have rightly come under tremendous international public pressure in recent years. The IMF and World Bank have certainly softened their 'free market' stance, and the WTO now professes greater concern for developing countries. But there is not yet a clear indication that the pendulum of 'free market' ideology has reversed its swing. Thomas Kuhn, in his seminal work, *The Structure of Scientific Revolutions*, teaches us that even the most defective paradigms, once entrenched, are most difficult to dislodge.[8] You may recall how much difficulty Galileo had convincing the Roman Catholic Church that it was the earth that revolved around the sun, and not the sun around the earth.

We on this island have been most fortunate that, in the best pragmatic Bajan tradition, our political directorate has over the years been able to separate reality from ideology, and has approached our problems from a Bridgetown, not a Washington, perspective. They have not devalued; they have not embraced high positive real interest rates; they have not removed all capital controls; they have not floated the currency. Moreover, they have succeeded in convincing the general public that fiscal discipline and wage restraint are the price to be paid for currency stability. At the same time they have placed sturdy planks under the welfare of the disadvantaged, so that poverty levels are lower in Barbados than in any other developing country. They should therefore, in military parlance, carry on smartly, recalling the dictum of the late Professor Okun: 'the market needs a place, and the market needs to be kept in its place.'[9]

Our greatest challenge will be in the area of trade negotiations — WTO, FTAA, and Lomé. Here, we simply cannot go it alone.

Hopefully, we shall soon have our Common Single Market and Economy in place. In approaching trade negotiations, we should heed the advice of Professor Dari Rodrik of Harvard:

> Developing countries have to engage the world economy on their own terms, not on terms set by global markets and institutions.[10]

We must define our objectives clearly, and fight hard to protect our regional interests. Then, we must place our fullest support behind the Regional Negotiating Machinery.

The challenge ahead will test our public servants to the limit; that is why we must move swiftly on public sector reform. And to optimise our scarce public resources, we must overhaul the governance of our statutory corporations, remembering that, like oil and water, politics and operations do not mix.

Delivered at the Twenty-seventh Sir Winston Scott Memorial Lecture, Frank Collymore Hall, Bridgetown, Barbados, November 25, 2002

Notes

1. John M. Keynes, *The General Theory of Employment, Interest and Money* (New York: Harcourt, Brace and World, Inc, 1964), 383.

2. W. Arthur Lewis, *The Theory of Economic Growth* (New York: Harper & Row, 1970), 376.

3. Adam Smith, *The Wealth of Nations* (New York: The Modern Library, 2000), 485.

4. Francis Fukuyama, *Trust: The Social Virtues and the Creation of Prosperity* (New York: The Free Press, Simon & Schuster, 1996).

5. Courtney N. Blackman, *Central Banking in Theory and Practice: A Small State Perspective* (St. Augustine, Trinidad and Tobago: Caribbean Centre for Monetary Studies, 1998), 113–130.

6. Ronald I. McKinnon, *Money and Capital in Economic Development* (Washington, DC: The Brookings Institution, 1973).

7. ———, *The Order of Economic Liberalization* (Baltimore: The Johns Hopkins University Press, 1991), 1–10.

8. Thomas S. Kuhn, *The Structure of Scientific Revolutions* (Second Edition) (Chicago: University of Chicago Press, 1970), 76.

9. As quoted by Robert Kuttner in, *Everything for Sale: The Virtues and Limits of Markets* (New York: Alfred A. Knopf), 39.

10. Dani Rodrik, *The New Global Economy and Developing Countries: Making Openness Work* (Baltimore: The John Hopkins Press), 5.

II

FINANCE, INVESTMENT AND ECONOMIC DEVELOPMENT

Towards An Investment-Friendly Financial Environment

This paper examines the inter-relationship between finance and investment with the view to formulating an appropriate policy-mix for the promotion of economic development in LDCs such as those of CARICOM. The theoretical framework we employ is in sharp disagreement with the McKinnon-Shaw thesis which attributes the ills of LDCs to 'financial repression', and prescribes the comprehensive deregulation of financial markets as a precondition, indeed the requirement, of economic growth.

Since the McKinnon-Shaw thesis has underpinned the structural adjustment programmes imposed by the IMF, World Bank and IDB on several LDCs, including some CARICOM states, it cannot be left unchallenged. We agree with the judgement of Nobel Laureate J.E. Stiglitz that:

> [M]uch of the rationale for liberalising financial markets is based neither on a sound economic understanding of how these markets work nor on the potential scope for government intervention. Often, too, it lacks an understanding of the historical events and political forces that have led governments to assume their present role. Instead, it is based on an ideological commitment to an idealised conception of markets that is grounded neither in fact nor in economic theory.[1]

Our first task is to lay bare the dynamics of investment, savings and finance in relation to economic growth. Secondly, we critique the McKinnon-Shaw thesis. Thirdly, we develop a policy framework based on the dynamics of investment, savings and finance in developing countries. Finally, we identify ten minimal elements of an investment-friendly financial environment.

Investment, Savings and Economic Growth

If there is one thing known about economic development it is that investment must increase relative to consumption as a proportion of the national income. Investment, in the words of John Maynard Keynes, is the engine of growth. Investment is made possible through savings. According to Sir Arthur Lewis, no industrial revolution can be understood 'until it can be explained why savings increased relative to the national income.'[2] Economic development, then, is about accelerating the rate of savings and investment, that is, of capital formation.

The equality of savings and investment is a fundamental proposition of Keynes's General Theory;[3] indeed, he had great difficulty explaining this equality. The Swedish School came to his assistance with the *ex ante* and *ex post* analytical device: whereas savings and investment may diverge *ex ante* (since savers were not necessarily the same as investors), equality between the two variables would be restored *ex post*. If part of *ex ante* savings remained uninvested, there would be a corresponding decrease in income, leading in turn to reduced savings and restoration of equality between savings and investment *ex post*. Similarly, should investment exceed savings *ex ante*, the resulting increase in income would raise savings proportionately, thus restoring the equilibrium between savings and investment *ex post*. Keynes is effectively saying that not only are savings and investment equal, but they are really two aspects of the same phenomenon. It is therefore as true to say that investment is a function of savings as to say that savings is a function of investment. The two phenomena cannot be divorced from each other. Our study, therefore, simultaneously seeks to discover the appropriate climate for both savings and investment.

It was Sir Arthur Lewis who contrasted the savings/investment problems of developing economies and of advanced capitalist economies, the latter of which were the concern of Keynes. Whereas developed countries enjoy unlimited supplies of capital, Lewis showed, LDCs possess unlimited supplies of labour.

The operative constraint on economic growth in advanced economies is the availability of labour. Because of the residue of productive capacity accumulated during successive waves of investment over several decades and even centuries, and since they produce capital goods, advanced economies enjoy unlimited supplies of capital. The economies of the 1930s, with which Keynes was concerned, were operating at extremely low levels of capital capacity; the problem was therefore one of stimulating effective demand so as to put both capital and labour back to work, and it could confidently be anticipated that full employment of labour would be achieved before maximum capital capacity was utilised and inflation entered the picture.

However, the operative constraint on economic growth in LDCs is capital. Should the central bank turn on the money spigot, production capacity would be used up long before full employment was reached; further expansion of the money supply would therefore lead to inflation and, since the marginal propensity to import is usually high for LDCs, to the collapse of the balance of payments.

The Lewis prescription is beautifully simple in conception. Observing considerable disguised unemployment in the traditional sector (that the marginal product of labour was zero or less), he suggested that capital imports might be combined with the superfluous labour of the traditional sector, thus enlarging the modern capitalist sector and expanding aggregate income. Lewis, the economic historian, also noted that even rich urbanising societies, like Australia and Canada, had traditionally imported massive amounts of capital to meet the requirements of social capital investment.[4]

Direct foreign investment was for Lewis the preferred type of capital import, since the foreign investor brought with him not merely liquid capital but technology, management and, above all, access to markets. Direct foreign investment is certainly superior to foreign loan capital in that business failures do not become liabilities of nationals nor of the national government. Europeans lost vast sums in failed American investment, but these did not enter the US national foreign debt accounts.

Lewis also anticipated that local entrepreneurs would learn the 'tricks of the trade', and would in time develop the capacity to establish enterprises which would progressively reduce the initial dependence on foreign capital. In short, they would learn the art of investment even as they absorbed the capitalist ethic of savings. Lewis is reported to have said that it was in South Korea that he witnessed the full realization of his theory. There indigenous enterprises, established with the assistance of foreign capital, now challenge the multinationals on almost equal terms.

Finance and Development

It is to be noted that both Keynes and Lewis focussed on real savings and real investment rather than financial savings or nominal investment. Keynes specifically rejected the classical proposition that savings and investment were brought into equilibrium through the interest rate mechanism: investment, he contended, depended largely on the 'animal spirits' and expectations of investors, while the readiness of savers to lend depended on their liquidity preference. Savings and investment were equilibrated, he showed, through changes in aggregate income. Keynes therefore favoured a low interest rate regime that promoted investment. Similarly, finance is excluded from

Lewis's basic two-sector model. Even Milton Friedman, the arch monetarist, agrees with Keynes and Lewis:

> what happens to output depends on real factors: the enterprise, ingenuity and industry of the people; the extent of thrift; the structure of industry and government; the relations among nations; and so on.[5]

Financial considerations are introduced into the investment/ growth argument when the ambitions of investors exceed the capacity of their own equity and retained earnings, and as they are forced to borrow from other economic units and households with surplus earnings. The investment decision, then, as Professor Hyman Minsky aptly puts it, is 'a decision both to acquire tangible assets and to emit financial liabilities.[6]

As an economy develops, the gestation period of investment projects tends to lengthen and the payback period to become more extended. Surplus lending units must therefore be persuaded to hold the liabilities of deficit spending units over longer and longer maturities. More and more, then, intermediation between savers and investors is accomplished through institutions comprising the financial markets.

Professors J.G. Gurley and E.S. Shaw[7] have shown that just as corresponding waves of real investment leave a residue of capital in the form of productive capacity, corresponding waves of financing decisions similarly leave a residue of debt. This residue of debt makes an imposition on the economy's financial capacity to sustain the liquidity of that debt. That is, savers must be persuaded to hold debt for very long periods of time — up to 30 years in the case of corporate bonds, and indefinitely, in the case of equity. Their incentive to do so is greatly increased if, in the event of some contingency, their loan assets can be readily liquidated without significant loss of value. To sustain the liquidity of debt of increasingly extended maturities, financial markets must be both wide and deep. We should note, however, that the development of financial markets is glacially slow.

Since a portion of the residue of debt in a capital importing economy will be foreign, it goes without saying that enough of the national product must be exported to service this foreign debt and to reduce future dependence on foreign capital. An export-oriented strategy is therefore the only game in town for LDCs like those of CARICOM.

Critique of the McKinnon-Shaw Thesis

In his influential work of 1973, *Money and Capital in Economic Development*,[8] McKinnon invented the term 'financial repression'. He describes his thesis as follows:

> When governments tax and otherwise distort their domestic capital markets, the economy is said to be financially "repressed". Usury restrictions on interest rates, heavy reserve requirements on bank deposits and compulsory credit allocations interact with ongoing price inflation to reduce the attractiveness of holding claims on the domestic banking system. In such a repressed financial system, real deposit rates of interest on monetary assets are often negative and are difficult to predict when inflation is high and unstable. Thus, the demand for money — broadly defined to include savings and term deposits as well as checking accounts and currency — falls as a proportion of GNP.
>
> But these monetary assets naturally dominate the financial portfolios of small savers in less developed countries. Thus, back in 1973, Edward Shaw and I hypothesized that repressing the monetary system fragments the domestic capital market with highly adverse consequences for the quality of real capital accumulation.[9]

McKinnon therefore prescribes the following:

> Remedying financial repression is implicit in its definition. We suggest keeping positive and more uniformly high real rates of

interest within comparable categories of bank deposits and loans by eliminating undue reserve requirements, interest ceilings and mandated credit allocations on the one hand, while stabilising the price level through appropriate macroeconomic measures on the other. Then, savers and investors would better "see" the true scarcity price of capital and thus reduce the great dispersion in the profitability of investing in different sectors of the economy.[10]

Acceptance of the McKinnon-Shaw paradigm has led several developing countries, including some within CARICOM, to institute financial reforms involving the removal of ceilings on interest rates, the deliberate promotion of positive and high real interest rates, the removal of exchange controls on capital movements and the floating of the national currency. The basic premise of financial liberalization is that market determined outcomes would optimise the rate of savings, investment and economic growth in developing countries.

Epistemology

It is remarkable that so simple a theory of a phenomenon as complex as economic development should exert so pervasive an influence as the McKinnon-Shaw paradigm of 'financial repression'. Indeed, it collapses quite rapidly before epistemological assaults from Professor Stiglitz[11] and Dr Mary Zephirin (Central Bank of Barbados).[12] They contend that the implication of the McKinnon-Shaw thesis that the free market outcome is *Pareto optimal*, holds only under rigorous conditions of market 'perfection'. In fact, the initial conditions that McKinnon and Shaw seek to alter are themselves a manifestation of severe market imperfection. It is therefore quite possible, Stiglitz and Zephirin show, that government intervention could produce sub-optimal outcomes more favourable than the McKinnon-Shaw 'free-market' solution. Indeed, the issue is not whether government intervenes into the market, but whether or not it intervenes intelligently.

According to Gibson and Tsakaldos,

> The South Korean case illustrates that government credit allocation schemes need not lead to a decline in the quality of investment and can be important in promoting capital accumulation and growth in the early stages of development.[13]

When the first outcomes of 'financial liberalisation' turned sour, McKinnon invoked the intervention of government to enforce prudential regulation and to promote macroeconomic stability. McKinnon cannot have his cake and eat it too. He cannot initially insist upon the withdrawal of government from the market and later invoke government intervention in the instances of market failure.

Exchange Rate Regime

The exchange rate regulates the relationship between imports and exports, and takes on increasing importance as the ratio of foreign trade to national income rises. In particular, it determines the price of capital imports, the critical input into the production processes of LDCs, who would therefore wish it to be both inexpensive and stable in price.

Since the Keynesian model is a closed system, there was no serious discussion in the *General Theory* of an appropriate exchange rate regime. Keynes's concern was that commitment to a fixed exchange rate should not elevate the real interest rate to a level inconsistent with full employment. He noted the wisdom of Mercantilists:

> [T]heir intense preoccupation with keeping down the rate of interest by means of usury laws ... by maintaining the domestic stock of money and by discouraging rises in the wage-unit; and in

their readiness in the last resort to restore the stock of money by devaluation, if it had become plainly deficient through an unavoidable foreign drain, a rise in the wage-unit, or any other cause.[14]

Neo-classical economists welcomed the collapse of The Bretton Woods System in 1971 and the transition to a floating rate regime. They were confident that the 'free market' would promote exchange rate stability and that, in any event, exchange rate risks could be effectively hedged in the forward markets. The turbulence in global currency markets in recent decades is testimony to neo-classical miscalculation.

Exchange rate volatility is most destabilizing for LDCs. In Lewis's basic two-sector model, conceived in the early 1950s, money is neutral and fixed exchange rates are assumed. However, in his 1978 publication, *The Evolution of the International Order*, Lewis considers free floating exchange rates 'a nuisance for countries with no organised forward markets'.[15] (Indeed, it is also a nuisance for countries with sophisticated forward markets). Lewis was therefore wary about the use of the exchange rate by LDCs as a means of balance of payments adjustment over the trade cycle. 'Besides,' he noted, 'devaluation is dangerous medicine for an economy whose imports are large relative to national income.' (As are all CARICOM member states.) 'Nowadays,' he continues, 'such an economy is likely to find itself on a treadmill, where devaluation raises money incomes and prices, so setting off further devaluation *ad infinitum*.' However, he did indicate that devaluation might be necessary when the cost structure was in severe disequilibrium: 'When one says of our economy that its money costs are too high in relation to world prices for it to be able to provide full employment, this is the classical definition of an "overvalued currency".'[16]

In Chapter 8 I demonstrated that for economies in chronic balance of payments disequilibrium, that is, where the demand for foreign exchange could not be satisfied in the foreseeable future, the equilibrium exchange rate is indeterminate, and would not necessarily be achieved through currency devaluations. In these circumstances, I argued, policy measures should be directed primarily towards a parametric shift to the right of the supply curve for foreign exchange (for example, increased export earnings) and a parametric shift to the left in the demand curve for foreign exchange (for example, external debt forgiveness). Various confidence-building measures might also impart greater elasticity in both the supply of, and the demand for, foreign exchange, prompting a movement towards equilibrium. But parametric shifts are, almost by definition, difficult and time-consuming (see charts 7, 8, and 9). The experiences of Guyana and Jamaica have confirmed this thesis.

Chart 7
Automatic Market Adjustment

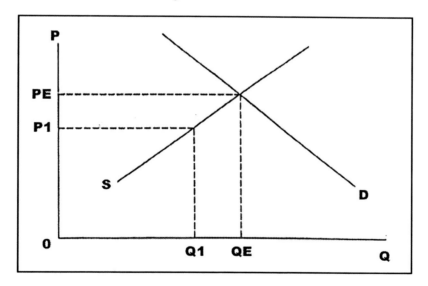

Chart 8
Conditions of Chronic Disequilibrium

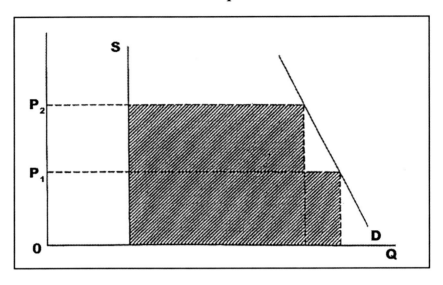

Chart 9
Policy Requirements in Conditions of Chronic Disequilibrium

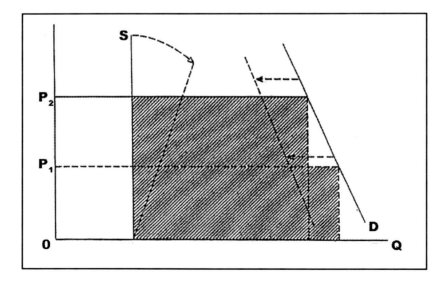

Since the exchange rate is such an important price for the LDCs, we cannot leave it to the vagaries of the marketplace, even though our options will be limited by the degree of turbulence in the international financial markets. However, we must do everything we can to maximize our options. Most obviously, we must try to maintain internal price stability. For LDCs, this means essentially that we should keep government deficits under control and restrain the excessive rise in money incomes. In the absence of a large war chest of foreign exchange reserves for central bank market intervention, some rationing of existing reserves, and regulation of destabilising capital outflows and inflows, may also be necessary.

None of the above arguments rules out currency depreciation if real wage rates become hopelessly uncompetitive or the price of a major export commodity falls precipitously (for example, oil prices for Trinidad and Tobago in the 1980s). However, such devaluations should be swift and deep enough to be credible rather than piecemeal and drawn out. Repeated currency depreciations through the 'free market' are debilitating, requiring workers to surrender more and more of their product for a decreasing volume of imports. Experience has shown, both in CARICOM and elsewhere, that saving and investment flourish best in an environment of relative price and exchange rate stability.

Role of Interest Rates

McKinnon's most obsessive concern is with positive and high real interest rates. The logic of his argument is (1), that households do not save unless real interest rates are positive; (2), that higher saving leads automatically to increased investment; and (3), that increased investment leads to economic development.

The persistence of the first proposition is remarkable, since the relationship between the rate of interest and the volume of savings is clearly an empirical issue: sometimes people increase savings when real interest rates are positive; sometimes they increase savings when real interest rates are negative. Deena Khatkate observes:

> The evidence for developed and developing countries alike is not quite conclusive in regard to the interest elasticity of savings. For the United States, income and wealth are found to have a more predominant influence on personal savings than interest rates. For less developed countries, even allowing for the dubious nature of statistics, the evidence points toward the same kinds of doubt about the interest elasticity of savings.[17]

Secondly, if the rate of interest on business loans significantly exceeds the marginal revenue of the enterprise, investment will not take place except in hyper-inflationary conditions where product prices can confidently be expected to increase. And since the rate of interest is itself a cost of production, rising real interest rates act as a drag on production, especially in the case of small businesses which depend heavily on commercial bank loans.

Thirdly, it is *real* savings, as we have seen, not financial savings, which promote growth. If there are no surpluses being generated in the real economy, there can be no real savings to invest no matter how high the real rate of interest. Moreover, as we demonstrate above, the causal relationship between savings and investment flows, not only from the former to the latter, but also from the latter to the former.

Fourthly, it must be recognized that operational losses, both in the public and private sectors, are tantamount to the destruction of capital. Just as productive investment promoted economic growth, so will chronic operational losses plunge an economy into a downward spiral of decline.

Financial Market Efficiency

It is also naïve of McKinnon to think that the mere removal of interest rate ceilings and other forms of 'financial repression' automatically results in competitive and effective markets. In this respect, he is typical of neo-classical economists who neglect the institutional features of markets — a transgression which greatly irritates Nobel laureates R.H. Coase and James Buchanan.

Buchanan observes:

> A market is not competitive by assumption or by construction. A market becomes competitive, and competitive rules come to be established as institutions emerge to place limits on individual behaviour patterns. It is this becoming process, brought about by the continuous pressure of human behaviour in exchange, that is the central part of our discipline, if we have one, not the dry rot of postulated perfection. [18]

Coase is even more caustic in his condemnation of the divorce of theory from the real world:

> The consumer is not a human being, but a set of preferences.... Exchange takes place without any specifications of its institutional setting. We have consumers without humanity, firms without organisation, and even exchange without markets. [19]

McKinnon was on the right track when he observed that the financial markets of developing countries were fragmented, that is, that they are imperfect. Indeed, if their markets were not imperfect, these countries would be developed! But financial markets do not become perfect because they are deregulated, but as they expand, and as governments and participants devise and discover rules and practices which make them function better. As they become more competitive, they will allocate resources with increasing efficiency. That is why the New York Stock

Exchange, the world's most efficient market, is also the most highly regulated.

Capital Flows

Finally, in prescribing the complete deregulation of capital flows and the floating of exchange rates, McKinnon shows insensitivity to the crucial importance of foreign exchange in the productive processes of LDC economies typified by openness. Since LDCs must import a preponderance of their capital and intermediate goods, only savings which are readily convertible into foreign exchange are generally usable for investment purposes. *In the case of LDCs, therefore, savings are virtually the same thing as foreign exchange.* This misunderstanding has also led financial liberalizers to greatly underestimate the current burden of external debt borne by LDCs. Historically, developing countries have been net importers of capital; for two decades now the highly indebted LDCs have been net exporters of capital. Yet the international community is puzzled by their failure to grow!

The McKinnon-Shaw Theory in Practice

As early as 1989 the World Bank commented that in the 'far-reaching programme of financial reforms carried out by Argentina, Chile and Uruguay in the mid-1970s each programme encountered serious problems, partly because of the way in which financial deregulation was handled and partly because of problems in the real sector.'[20] In its study, *The East-Asian Miracle,* the World Bank also conceded that 'financial sector interventions — specifically repression of interest rates and contest-based direction of credit — may have contributed to rapid growth in such economies as Japan, Korea, Taiwan and China.'[21]

McKinnon himself, the father of 'financial liberalization', now recognizes that 'our knowledge of how best to achieve financial liberalisation remains seriously incomplete'.[22] However, this has not moved him to re-examine the premises of his original theory, but to reconsider 'the order in which the monetary system is stabilised in comparison to the pace of deregulation'. He has also learned that 'fiscal control should precede financial liberalisation', and that 'free foreign exchange convertibility on capital account is usually the last stage in the optimal order of economic liberalisation'. The IMF itself has also recently conceded that capital controls may be necessary in certain circumstances.[23] The McKinnon programme is now hedged around by so many caveats and contingencies that there is not very much left of the original theoretical structure.

Elements of an Investment-Friendly Financial Environment

The above theoretical analysis and the lessons of recent financial liberalization allow us to outline an investment friendly macroeconomic policy mix.

Market Orientation

Although rejecting the McKinnon-Shaw laissez-faire doctrines, we declare a bias towards the allocation of resources through the market. The market is a social device for the inexpensive allocation of resources that reduces the burden on a society's information systems and decision-making mechanisms. But the market is not infallible. Wherever the market allocates resources in a socially acceptable manner, we will use it; but we reserve the right to intervene where the outcomes of 'free market' allocation are socially unacceptable. This will frequently be the case in LDCs, especially in small countries, where markets are usually monopolistic or oligopolistic. For example, the commercial banking system of any CARICOM state will, for the foreseeable future, be oligopolistic, and so would that of an integrated CARICOM. CARICOM authorities cannot therefore leave the determination of interest rates to a 'free market' comprising a few commercial banks that exercise overwhelming market power. Clearly, central banks must exercise countervailing power.

Financial Market Deepening

We accept the need for the deepening of financial markets as economic development proceeds. However, this process is slow and cannot be expected to create a decisive expansion of savings from indigenous sources in the short run. For some time to come CARICOM must rely heavily on capital imports. In the meantime, measures must be put in place for the continuous improvement of financial markets. Not least of all will be the strengthening of prudential regulation of financial institutions.

Direct Foreign Investment

Direct foreign investment should be especially encouraged because of the by-products of technology, management and market access. Indeed, even advanced countries, like the UK, the US and Canada, actively promote foreign direct investment. Local entrepreneurs may also obtain the benefits of foreign capital through joint ventures, franchising, production under subcontracts, and through marketing alliances. Hopefully, in the process they will learn the 'tricks of the trade', as Lewis puts it.

Credit Allocation

Because of the imperfection of financial markets, the allocation of scarce credit among various sectors of the economy cannot be left solely to market forces. Government must, through fiscal policy primarily, but also through selective credit arrangements if necessary, ensure that crucial industries are not starved of scarce capital resources. In particular, small businesses must have access to soft loans, accompanied by technical support to the greatest extent possible. This practice is followed even in advanced economies so as to create a nursery of future entrepreneurs.

Interest Rate Regime

We should especially eschew the dogma of high and positive real interest rates. Interest rates should be high enough to deter capital flight, but not necessarily to attract 'hot' money that may be withdrawn on the slightest provocation. High real interest rates cannot stimulate real savings unless surpluses are generated in the real sector. At the same time, high interest rates add to the cost of production, suppressing output and fuelling inflation. Monetary authorities must pragmatically balance the return to savers against the cost to investors. Most damaging of all, savings rates above a certain level render investment in the real sector irrational, and promote a situation, as occurred in Jamaica in the early 1990s, when the financial sector boomed while the real sector stagnated.

Exchange Rate Regime

We must reconcile ourselves to the fact that only internationally traded currencies can realistically be floated on international currency markets. Indeed, we cannot even be sanguine of the stability of even major currencies like sterling or the Euro. To be traded on international markets, currencies must either be backed by relatively stable traded currencies like the US dollar, be perceived to be exchangeable for goods and services in widespread demand, or be regarded as commodities in themselves, as is the US dollar. CARICOM currencies are not held by foreigners as stores of value, and frequently not even used as units of account by CARICOM nationals; strictly speaking they are not 'floatable'. For example, the Jamaican dollar does not 'float' against the US dollar; in fact, the US dollar is a commodity bought and sold on the Jamaican financial market.

The best hope of achieving the stability of CARICOM currencies is for their central banks to hold high levels of foreign exchange reserves for defending a given exchange rate or band of rates, as do Singapore and Taiwan, which currently hold reserves of US$74 billion and US$113 billion, respectively. Their holdings are much greater than those of the UK, whose sterling more resembles a commodity. Ironically, large reserves holdings are especially needed when strategic devaluations are required.

Even though exchange controls may be progressively liberalized, they should be maintained on major capital outflows, and excessive capital inflows should be sterilised. Sudden shocks to the balance of payments are more likely to come from global capital movements than from foreign trade, and in a liberalised foreign exchange regime, any domestic funds or available credit can be used to purchase foreign exchange for effecting capital flight. Whereas we can see the build-up of imports coming from afar and take preventive measures, massive capital outflows can occur in the twinkling of an eye. For this reason, the conventional measure of foreign exchange reserve adequacy — three months import cover — has been obsolete for some time now.

Fiscal vs. Monetary Policy

Since financial markets in CARICOM will remain narrow and shallow for the foreseeable future, they will not provide a medium for the effective operation of monetary policy, and governments must rely heavily on fiscal policy for the execution of macroeconomic policy. Governments should avoid inflationary deficit spending, and must generate the surpluses needed to finance infrastructure and to support, though not necessarily own, productive investment.

Elements of an Investment-friendly Financial Environment

- ➢ A stable or gently rising price level.
- ➢ An interest rate regime with savings rates below 10 per cent and loan rates under 20 per cent.
- ➢ A financial sector which expands in tandem with the real sector and becomes progressively deeper.
- ➢ Progressive liberalization of exchange controls, with maximum assurance that original capital, dividends and retained earnings will be remitted with a minimum of red tape.
- ➢ Arrangements for sterilizing excessive inflows of hot money and for moderating massive and untimely capital outflows.
- ➢ Either anchorage of the currency to a major internationally traded currency or to a basket of currencies together with the maintenance of high levels of foreign exchange reserves; or the operation of a managed float that modifies market overshooting and horrendous currency undervaluation. (It is remarkable that neo-liberal economists, who are so traumatized by overvalued exchange rates, have nothing to say about grossly undervalued currencies.)
- ➢ Primary reliance on fiscal, rather than monetary, measures in the conduct of macroeconomic policy.
- ➢ Central banking arrangements with maximum independence from government so as to minimise the likelihood of money creation for the financing of runaway fiscal deficits.
- ➢ Regulatory arrangements which facilitate direct foreign investment.
- ➢ Special arrangements for the financing and technical support of small and start-up businesses.

Prepared for the XXXIII Annual Monetary Studies Conference, November 19–23, 2001, Belize City, Belize

Notes

1. J.E. Stiglitz, 'The Role of the State in Financial markets', *Proceedings of the World Bank Annual Conference on Development Economics* (IBRD, 1994), 19–56.

2. Sir W. Arthur Lewis, 'Economic Development with Unlimited Supplies of Labour', *The Economics of Underdevelopment*, eds., A.N. Agarwala and S.P. Singh (New York: O.U.P.), 416.

3. John M. Keynes, *The General Theory of Employment, Interest and Money*, 1936, Reprint (New York: Harcourt, Brace & World, Inc, 1964), 39.

4. Sir W. Arthur Lewis, *The Evolution of the International Economic Order* (Princeton, NJ: Princeton University Press, 1978), 39–44.

5. Milton Friedman, *Money Mischief: Episodes in Monetary History* (New York: Harcourt, Brace & Company), 48.

6. Hyman Minsky, 'Money Market and Savings Intermediation', *Issues in Banking and Monetary Analysis*, eds., G. Pontecorvo, R. Shay, and A. Hart (New York: Rinehart and Winston, Inc), 43.

7. John G. Gurley and Edwards S. Shaw, 'Financial Aspects of Economic Development', *American Economic Review* (September 1955): 523.

8. Ronald McKinnon, *Money and Capital in Economic Development* (Washington: The Brookings Institution, 1973).

9. ———, *Financial Liberalisation and Economic Development* (San Francisco: International Center for Economic Growth, Occasional Paper 6), 1–2.

10. Ibid., 2.

11. J.E. Stiglitz, 'The Role of the State in Financial markets'.

12. Mary Zephrin, 'Financial Liberalisation: A Theoretical Perspective', *Money Affairs*, Centre for Latin American Monetary Studies, vol. VI, no. 2 (July–December, 1993): 1–26.

13. Heather D. Gibson, and Euclid Tsakalotos, 'The Scope and Limits of Financial Liberalisation in Developing Countries', *The Journal of Development Studies* 30, no. 3 (April 1994): 611.

14. Keynes, *The General Theory of Employment*, 340.

15. W. Arthur Lewis, *The Evolution of the International Economic Order*, 53.

16. Ibid., 54.

17. Deena Khatkate, 'Analytic Basis of the Working of Monetary Policy in Less Developed Countries', in *Money and Monetary Policy in Less Developed Countries*, eds., W.J. Coats Jr. and D.R. Khatkate (Oxnard: Pergammon Press, 1980), 134.

18. James Buchanan, *What Should Economists Do?* (Indianapolis: Liberty Press, 1979), 29.

19. R.H. Coase, *The Firm, the Market and the Law* (Chicago: The University of Chicago Press, 1990), 3.

20. The World Bank, *World Development Report 1989* (New York: Oxford University Press).

21. The World Bank, *The East Asian Miracle* (New York: Oxford University Press, 1993), 358.

22. Ronald McKinnon, *The Order of Economic Liberalisation* (Baltimore: The Johns Hopkins University Press, 1991), 3–10.

23. International Monetary Fund, *International Capital Markets: Development, Prospects and Policy Issues* (Washington, 1995), 95–108.

12

SENSE AND NONSENSE IN AGRICULTURAL CREDIT

INTEREST RATE POLICIES IN JAMAICA

Introduction

Almost 11 years ago, actually on March 14th 1980 I addressed residents of my old hall — the 'Gentlemen of Chancellor' — at the Mona campus of the UWI. I delivered a vehement attack on the Marxian and New World schools, which propounded the state-centred orthodoxy of the day. You can imagine the consternation when I declared that the self-inflicted economic disasters of the 1970s 'had their roots in the social science faculties of this university'.[1] Those remarks branded me for many years as a right wing reactionary and bourgeois economist. Fortunately, the comprehensive collapse of those two paradigms throughout most of the world has ended my notoriety.

When I learned that, on the insistence of the IDB and World Bank, the interest rate structural adjustment loans to the agricultural sector were tied to the Jamaican treasury bill rate, currently at 30 per cent per annum, I thought it was time to take issue with the 'free market' school which now holds sway over the international economy. I have therefore entitled my address, 'Sense and Nonsense in Agricultural Credit: Interest Rate Policies in Jamaica'.

SENSE AND NONSENSE IN AGRICULTURAL CREDIT

The 'Free Market' Counter Revolution

After the failure of the neo-Keynesians to diagnose and successfully treat the stagflation of the 1980s, the 'free market' model was restored to the central position in economics from which John Maynard Keynes had temporarily dislodged it. 'Free market' doctrines quickly engulfed the economics departments of First World universities, and permeated international financial institutions (IFIs) like the IMF, the World Bank and IDB. The 'free market' model now underpins structural adjustment programmes throughout the Third World, and is imposed with little consideration for the particular circumstances of countries involved. The two main articles of faith are the efficacy of devaluation in balance of payments adjustment, and the critical importance of high and positive real interest rates for economic growth.

I have on many occasions over the last 15 years fulminated against the proactive use of devaluation as a policy instrument. In my view currency devaluation is analogous to amputation in surgery: sometimes necessary but never a blessing. I was therefore relieved to read in the *Economist* of November 24, 1990, that a study of 83 LDCs by Ricardo Faini of Johns Hopkins University and Jaime de Melo of the World Bank, of all places, casts great doubt on the efficacy of devaluations in improving the trade balances of primary producers. The *Economist*, itself an inveterate supporter of currency devaluations, was forced to conclude:

> Though one-off devaluations may sometimes be necessary, the costs, in terms of inflation, great macroeconomic uncertainty and less investment, may be greater than are often thought. And the benefits, at least for primary producers, do not seem as strong as devaluationists have often claimed.[2]

The Caribbean experience fully confirms the judgment of the *Economist*: 'Those countries have fared best which have avoided devaluation.'

The case for high and positive real interest rates has its origins in separate publications in 1973 by Ronald McKinnon[3] and Edward Shaw,[4] two American academics. The logic of their thesis runs something like this. It begins with the assumption that the equilibrium real interest rate is always positive; that is, higher than the rate of inflation. If, for example, the real savings rate; that is, the nominal rate less the rate of inflation, becomes negative, savers will reduce their level of savings and buy goods for hoarding instead; the lower rate of savings will, in turn, reduce funds for investment, and the lower investment rate will lead to a reduced rate of economic growth.

Two policy implications of this theory are — removal of all restrictions on interest rates, which will then find their equilibrium market rate, presumably at positive real levels and discontinuation of credit ceilings and selective allocation of resources to critical productive sectors.

The trouble with structural adjustment programmes based on the Shaw-McKinnon thesis is that they work only under conditions of perfect competition; that is, in markets with numerous buyers and sellers, homogeneous products, perfect information, and so on. However, the markets of LDCs are, by definition, generally imperfect. If they were perfectly competitive, the countries would not be underdeveloped. It is not surprising then that structural adjustment programmes predicated on financial liberalization and high positive real rates of interest have failed.

The 'Free Market' Paradigm Exposed

In small economies like Barbados, the financial system is usually dominated by three or four commercial banks. Facing this oligopoly, the Central Bank can hardly leave the determination of interest rates to the market. Similarly, in small open economies that are dependent on two or three export commodities for foreign exchange earnings, the monetary authorities must ensure an adequate flow of credit, at acceptable rates, to these critical industries. In these circumstances, imposition of ceilings on commercial bank credit to importers of consumer durables, and extension of preferential rates of interest to key exporters and domestic producers of essential foodstuffs, constitute highly responsible economic management.

Neither the association between interest rate levels and the rate of savings, nor between real positive interest rates and economic growth, as predicted by Shaw and McKinnon, has held true in Barbados. Dr Roland Craigwell, an economist at the Central Bank of Barbados, found that 'changes in interest rates in Barbados had only a minor impact on the accumulation of financial assets. Other factors, [he concluded] such as disposable income, appeared to have been more important.'[5] Moreover, real interest rates were negative in Barbados throughout the period 1976–1980 when we achieved our highest rates of growth in the post-World War II period, while they were positive during 1983–1986 when the economy stagnated.

The Jamaican experience, as set out in Dr Headley Brown's splendid paper to this seminar, does not contradict the Barbadian case. Extraordinarily high and severely positive real rates certainly helped to improve the external balance and reduce inflation, but can hardly be said to have contributed significantly to economic growth. Foreign exchange is the operational constraint on Jamaican economic growth, and high positive real interest rates are ineffective in attracting foreign savings, given the lack of confidence in the Jamaican dollar. However, the experiences of both Barbados and Jamaica point to the critical importance of fiscal policy in the maintenance of internal and external balance.

But the most serious flaw in the McKinnon–Shaw thesis is the identification of financial savings with real savings. Real savings derive from the excess of output over the consumption of goods and services. Monetary authorities must therefore be concerned, first of all, with what is happening in the real sector, and do all they can to maintain the economic health of important industries. If there is no surplus production in the real sector, there can be no real financial savings. For this reason, the real rate of interest in economies with collapsed financial markets, as in Guyana, is quite irrelevant.

There are signs that disillusionment with the efficacy of the Shaw-McKinnon thesis is building. The World Bank, commenting in its 1989 *World Development Report* on the far-reaching programmes of financial reforms carried out by Argentina, Chile and Uruguay in the mid-1970s, reported that 'each programme encountered serious difficulties, partly because of the way in which financial deregulation was handled and partly because of problems in the real sector.' Although reporting that Turkey was 'on the right track', the report concedes that 'macroeconomic changes ... hit corporate profits and left businesses struggling to adjust', while 'financial problems in the corporate sector caused distress in the banking system.'[6]

The report purports to have learned a number of lessons from these experiments in financial liberalization, especially that 'direct intervention in finance must be replaced by an adequate, if less invasive, system of laws and regulations.' In short, the more you deregulate the financial system, the more you must supervise it. It is just a matter of time before a study is written showing that structural adjustment programmes based on the McKinnon–Shaw thesis may have done more harm than good.[7]

Rationale of European Agricultural Policy

The insistence on the full market rate on adjustment loans to agriculture reflects further inroads by the 'free market' ideology. In a recent study of the OECS, the World Bank advised:

Agricultural diversification should result from the exploitation of natural market opportunities, both local and foreign, rather than protectionist policies which generate high cost crops aimed at import substitution.[8]

But no developed nation in the world conducts its agricultural policy on the basis of 'exploitation of natural market opportunities, both local and foreign'. In fact, they regard the domestic market as the 'natural opportunity' for native farmers. Japanese farmers obtain prices for their rice production which are several times the international market level. The annual average subsidy per farmer in the US exceeds US$15,000. In the EEC, subsidies to the farm sector have reached what even European economists describe as obscene levels, with the rich farmers benefiting even more than the poor. Yet the Jamaican government is required to on-lend to farmers at interest rates of up to 30 per cent per annum.

Edward Nevins, in his book, *The Economics of Europe*, explains the rationale of EEC support of agriculture as stemming from the universal short-term and long-term problems of agriculture. There are three main short-term problems:[9]

> ➢ Output is subject to random shocks due to natural forces outside the control of producers: climate changes, plant and animal diseases, and so forth.
> ➢ There is a rather long and inescapable lag between product decisions — when crops are planted or animals bred — and the distribution of corresponding output to the market.
> ➢ The demand for most foodstuffs has a low price elasticity (that is, food consumption does not increase significantly relative to a fall in price).

The above factors make it extremely difficult for the farmer to respond effectively to price movements in his markets. Having planted coffee in January, he cannot switch production in March because the price of bananas has doubled in one month, and then move into yams in June when the price of bananas falls sharply. Having planted coffee, he must wait years for his crop! Furthermore, both the human and physical resources of the farmer are highly specialized, and are not readily transferable to other occupations. Indeed, farming is not simply a job, it is a way of life, and farmers must feel confident that the nation will support them through thick and thin.

The long-term problem of farmers, Nevins explains, is that the demand for foodstuffs is relatively inelastic in respect to changes in income. 'That is to say, as incomes rise, the demand for foodstuffs is unlikely to rise as rapidly, if for no other reason than that the capacity of the human stomach is limited.'[10]

Interestingly, the Common Agricultural Policy (CAP) has absorbed more money and commitment than any other activity of the EEC. There were five main objectives:

> ➤ Increase in productivity of the agricultural sector;
> ➤ An increase in the real income of farmers and a closing of the income gap between farmers and other citizens;
> ➤ A stabilization of markets;
> ➤ Guaranteeing regular supplies;
> ➤ Reasonable prices to consumers.

The cost of CAP to West Europeans has been horrendous. By 1986 the cost of subsidies to farmers had risen to ECU23 billion, or 70 per cent of the entire community budget, and involved tremendous wastage and over-supply — all this in spite of the fact that farmers constitute less than five per cent of the Common Market workforce. Obviously, the Europeans value their farming community. Jamaica, with its chronic shortage of foreign exchange, should be even more appreciative of its farmers.

SENSE AND NONSENSE IN AGRICULTURAL CREDIT

Lessons for the Caribbean

The real issue is not whether we should subsidize our farmers, but how. I have always been puzzled by how virtuous it is to make large payments to rich farmers in developed countries, and how damaging to the economy it is to assist poor farmers in the LDCs. One argument of the World Bank is that subsidies, if absolutely necessary, should be made through explicit payments from the Treasury to the recipients rather than through subsidized interest rates. Clearly, subsidized interest payments to the rich farmers in developed countries are unnecessary since their governments guarantee that crop prices will cover their cost of production and, in the US, even pays them for not growing crops on their land.

The situation is different in LDCs where governments lack the ability to make cash payments up front. In these circumstances, the subsidized interest rate loan makes a lot of sense. For one thing, the capital fund from which the loans are made can be rolled over and used again and again. More importantly, subsidized loans are more politically feasible than direct payments. This was a particularly difficult problem in Barbados where the sugar plantations have been historically owned by white citizens who are held up to ransom every two years by the trade unions, and wages extracted which bear no relation to the price of sugar. Government has therefore been forced to guarantee sugar industry bonds which everyone knows cannot be repaid out of sugar earnings. The Central Bank has also discounted loans to the industry through the Barbados National Bank against the receipt of export earnings at low rates of interest, thus reducing production costs.

I noticed in your last annual report that the JADF moved swiftly to make soft loans with moratoria to farmers affected by hurricane Gilbert. How else could they have resumed cultivation? Unlike theorists in universities and bureaucrats in Washington, political decision makers must do whatever it takes to keep the ship of state afloat. I encourage the JADF to use its utmost creativity in support of the farming community, including the use of loans at subsidized interest rates, if that is the most sensible thing to do.

Conclusion

Permit me a few Parthian shots as I take my leave: Firstly, though conceding that high real interest rates may have been necessary to restore internal and external balance, I believe that there has been a strong administrative element at work in the Jamaican situation, reflecting pressure from IFIs to institute positive and high real interest rates. The Jamaican monetary authorities should exploit every available opportunity to ratchet downward the structure of interest rates. In the long run excessively high real interest rates exercise a considerable drag on economic growth, placing great pressure on business enterprises, especially small operators and farmers. Since the rates of return required to recover the rates of interest prevailing in Jamaica are obtainable only in inflationary conditions, a prolonged period of such high interest rates could very well trigger an hyper-inflationary spiral of the Latin American variety.

Secondly, the internal and external balance of the Jamaican economy would more reliably be achieved in the context of a regional monetary framework. Had a CARICOM monetary union been in place, the orgy of money creation of the late 1970s would not have taken place, and Jamaicans and Guyanese would have been spared much of the economic pain they have suffered since then.

Thirdly, I urge that the international financial institutions formulate their financial liberalization programmes with the caution and humility of the pragmatist, rather than with the certitude and arrogance of the ideologue.

Finally, the rich creditor nations should recognize that structural adjustment programmes alone will not restore heavily indebted countries, such as Jamaica, to a sustainable growth path unless significant new money is forthcoming, and unless the heavy burden of past debt is lifted from their shoulders. In other words, they should treat the LDCs in the same way as they are anxiously waiting to treat their long lost brothers from Eastern Europe.

Luncheon address delivered at a Seminar on Interest Rate Policies, Kingston, Jamaica, February 14, 1991

Notes

1. Courtney N. Blackman, *The Practice of Persuasion* (Bridgetown: Cedar Press, 1982), 2.

2. *Economist*, November 24, 1990, p.71.

3. Roland I. McKinnon, *Money and Capital in Economic Development* (Washington, DC: The Brookings Institution, 1973).

4. Edward S. Shaw, *Financial Deepening in Economic Development* (New York: Oxford University Press, 1973).

5. Roland Craigwell, 'Interest Rate Policies, Financial and Economic Growth in Barbados, 1973–1986', *Money Affairs* (January–June 1990): 72.

6. 'Toward More Liberal and Open Financial Systems', *World Development Report 1989* (The World Bank, 1989): 122–32.

7. Some months after this address was delivered, Professor Ronald I. McKinnon published *The Order of Economic Liberalization: Financial Control in the Transition to a Market Economy* (Baltimore: The Johns Hopkins University Press, 1991). In it he warns against headlong deregulation, such as his earlier works had inspired IMF/World Bank economists to impose on LDCs, including Jamaica. McKinnon now warns that financial deregulation should proceed in a step-by-step progression and on a case-by-case basis:

How fiscal, monetary, and foreign exchange policies are sequenced is of critical importance. Government cannot, and perhaps should not, undertake all liberalizing measures simultaneously. Instead, there is an 'optimal' order of economic liberalization, which may vary for different liberalizing economies depending on their initial conditions. (p.4)

8. The World Bank, *The Long Term Economic Prospects of the OECS Countries,* 1990, 52.

9. Edward Nevins, *The Economics of Europe* (New York: St. Martin's Press, 1990), Chaps. 14 & 15.

10. Ibid., 148. It is estimated that in Britain a ten per cent increase in income will lead to a rise of 18 per cent in the demand for services but an increase of only 4.5 per cent for food.

13

DOLLARIZATION

THE PROS AND CONS FOR CARIBBEAN STATES

I must commend the Commissioner for her diligent approach to the determination of an appropriate currency regime for St. Maarten. This is the kind of decision it is important to get right the first time; the costs of a wrong decision could be disastrous. Since the collapse of the Bretton Woods fixed exchange rate international monetary system, we have been reminded time and again that a sound currency is a prerequisite for sustained economic growth.

I am even more impressed that the Commissioner has involved Civil Society in the consultations leading up to this most important decision. Again and again events around the world have demonstrated that economic policies embarked upon without the involvement of those affected are unlikely to succeed. I am equally impressed that so many of you have turned out this evening to participate in this consultative exercise.

I have been greatly assisted in my assignment by the excellent booklet *Central Banking and Currency in the Country of St. Maarten*, prepared by the Work Group for Constitutional Affairs. In eleven brief pages the study has touched on the key issues, treating them in a most balanced and sophisticated manner. I have no fundamental disagreement with the report.

Over the years economists with impressive credentials have descended from the North to prescribe some new economic remedy for the developing countries of the South. Currency devaluation was for many years the standard prescription; then came privatization; then financial liberalization and floating exchange rates; and then the opening up of domestic financial markets to unrestricted international capital flows. Those Caribbean countries, like my own Barbados, have fared best which have resisted the uncritical adoption of those recommendations. Dollarization is the most recent in the series, and my assignment this evening is to examine its pros and cons so as to help you to make a judgment as to whether this newest prescription is best for Caribbean states, and especially for St. Maarten.

What Is Dollarization?

By 'dollarizaton' we mean the adoption of the US dollar as legal tender in the settlement of domestic transactions. Dollarization would mean the extinction of Caribbean currencies, and the end of Caribbean central banks as we know them. There have been only two dollarizcd national economies during the last century — Liberia and Panama — both with peculiar and highly dependent relationships with the US; they are not distinguished by their economic, social and political records. Puerto Rico and the US Virgin Islands are dollarized territories, but that has not made them more prosperous than St. Maarten.

Note that by 'dollarization' we are *not* speaking of so-called 'partial dollarization', especially in tourism-oriented economies like The Bahamas, where US dollars may be in widespread use in daily transactions but the national currency remains sole legal tender; nor of instances where residents may legally hold foreign currency deposits at domestic banks, as in Jamaica, and Trinidad and Tobago.

How It All Began

The recent dollarization movement has curious origins. Early in 1999, President Carlos Menem ordered Argentina's Central Bank to study the feasibility of dollarization. Weary of repeated currency depreciations, Menem had, as far back as 1991, effectively transformed the Central Bank of Argentina into a currency board by making the peso convertible into the US dollar at par. A currency board issues currency notes against counterpart holdings of foreign exchange securities. Unlike a central bank, it cannot create new money. Fearful of contagion from the financial crisis in neighbouring Brazil, Menem sought a way of warding off currency devaluation forever. The de facto currency board served Argentina well for almost a decade, but chronic fiscal deficits have led to a massive currency depreciation and to the collapse of the Argentine economy. Argentina has now returned to more flexible central banking arrangements.

Over in Ecuador, President Jamil Mahuad assumed office in 1998 under the most difficult circumstances. The Ecuadorean economy was reeling from the devastating climatic effects of El Niño, and of plunging oil prices. Like a drowning man grasping at the proverbial straw, President Mahuad announced his intention to replace Ecuador's 'sucre' with the US dollar. Before he could implement that decision, he was toppled from office in a military coup; his civilian successor, Gustavo Noboa, went through with dollarization in 2000. In that same year El Salvador, economically depressed after many years of civil strife, followed the example of Ecuador and replaced the 'colon' with the US dollar. It is still too early to assess the consequences of dollarization in Ecuador and El Salvador.

By the time of the IMF–World Bank meetings in Prague in the fall of 2000, Professor Rudi Dornbusch of MIT and other leading First World economists were declaring 'dollarization' to be the only salvation for developing countries. In June 2001, Dr

Timothy Kearney of Bear Stearns told a workshop in Barbados that 'the trend started by El Salvador and Ecuador is going to continue.' Citigroup chairman John Reed recommended dollarization for Mexico; there was even talk of dollarization for Canada and, in the vision of Zanny Beddoes, the *Economist* correspondent in Washington DC, the dollar should rule 'from Alaska to Argentina'.

The International Monetary Fund View

An IMF brochure, *Full Dollarization: The Pros and Cons*, has summed up the main advantages and disadvantages as follows:

Advantages:

> ➢ Dollarization avoids currency and balance of payments crises. Without a domestic currency there is no possibility of a sharp depreciation, or of sudden capital outflows motivated by fears of devaluation.
> ➢ A closer integration with both the global and US economies would follow from lower transaction costs and an assured stability of prices in dollar terms.
> ➢ By definitively rejecting the possibility of inflationary finance through dollarization, countries might also strengthen their financial institutions and create positive sentiment toward investment, both domestic and international.

Disadvantages:

> ➢ Countries are likely to be reluctant to abandon their own currencies, symbols of their nationhood, particularly in favour of those of other nations. As a practical matter, political resistance is nearly certain, and likely to be strong.
> ➢ From an economic point of view, the right to issue a country's currency provides it government with seigniorage

revenues, which show up as central bank profits and are transferred to the government. They would be lost to dollarizing countries and gained by the United States unless it agreed to share them.

> A dollarizing country would relinquish any possibility of having an autonomous monetary and exchange rate policy, including the use of central bank credit to provide liquidity support to its banking systems in emergencies.

However, the IMF sits adroitly on the fence:

What is the balance of costs and benefits of full dollarization? The answer may seem frustratingly two-handed. This is inevitable, given the complexity of the issue and the current state of knowledge about it. The potential benefits of lower interest rates and the cost of foregone seigniorage revenues can at least be estimated. But many of the most important considerations, such as the value of keeping an exit option and lender of last resort protections, are virtually unquantifiable.[1]

What Is Seigniorage?

It is impossible to follow the debate on dollarization intelligently without an understanding of the ancient concept of seigniorage. To do so we must take a journey back into the history of money.

The earliest varieties of money were commodities — such as salt. Sugar and tobacco both served as money during early Caribbean history. Indeed, some primitive forms of money were live: to this day cattle is used as money in parts of Africa. A Masai warrior's opinion of my wealth position fell sharply when he learned that I had no cows — and only one wife! Even from biblical times gold and silver were used as money because of their indestructibility, high value/weight ratios, scarcity, and divisibility — it is especially difficult to divide cattle to make small purchases.

An important feature of gold and silver coins was that face value was equal to intrinsic value.

In medieval times the prerogative of coinage belonged to the King. Subjects who wished to have raw gold or silver transformed into coinage would go to one of the royal mints located throughout the kingdom and have new coins struck. For this service they would pay a fee to the King. This fee was called 'seigniorage', and was an important source of income for the Crown. Profits deriving from the monopoly of currency issue have since come to be known as 'seigniorage'.

Irresponsible kings would encourage their mints to issue coins with a face value greater than their intrinsic value, surreptitiously increasing the seigniorage. This was known as 'debasing the currency' and, when the truth got out, led inevitably to inflation — with its usual devastating economic effects. Henry I of England was one king who took a sound currency seriously.

Around Christmas 1124 he ordered all his 'moneyers' (that is, heads of mints) to attend an inquest into the coinage. Ninety-four of a total of 150 moneyers were castrated and had their right hands severed for the poor quality of their coins.[2]

An important economic development was the widespread use of paper money in Britain in the early eighteenth century. (The Chinese had in fact used paper money two thousand years before!) Adam Smith, the founder of Economics, observed at the time:

> The substitution of paper in the room of gold and silver money, replaces a very expensive instrument of commerce with one much less costly (so that) the whole circulation may thus be conducted with a fifth part only of the gold and silver which would otherwise have been required.[3]

From that time the major national currencies became hybrids of commodity money and paper money: a proportion of total currency outstanding was held in gold and/or silver on reserve at the Central Bank, while bank notes mostly circulated. It was not until 1973 that the requirement to maintain gold as backing for outstanding paper money was lifted in the US, and the entire issue of US dollars became fiat money, that is, determined by law. The use of paper money substantially increased the potential for seigniorage, since the expense of printing currency notes is a very small fraction of what it costs to issue gold and silver coins.

By issuing currency notes — which are essentially promissory notes that bear no interest — the Central Bank acquires assets that do pay interest, such as foreign currency deposits, government securities, and loans to domestic commercial banks. The income from such interest-bearing assets, along with the non-interest bearing reserves of commercial banks which it holds, constitute the seigniorage of the modern central bank. The annual flow of seigniorage is measured by the increase in base money; that is, currency outstanding plus bank reserves, or more crudely by central bank profits.

Whereas Caribbean central banks earn seigniorage only from domestic currency circulation, the Federal Reserve System, the US central bank, earns seigniorage both at home and abroad, since US currency notes are used extensively in transactions throughout the world. Of the US$500 billion in currency notes outstanding, an estimated US$300 billion circulate outside the US — about half in the former USSR. About US$15 billion in new notes are exported annually to meet this buoyant demand, more than the total non-military US foreign aid. US currency notes held by foreigners represent a non-interest bearing loan to the US of indefinite maturity. The export of 'greenbacks' is a highly profitable business for the US Federal Reserve. The foreigner must put up the equivalent value in a hard currency for a US $100 note, the favourite denomination abroad, which costs pennies to print!

The American Perspective

Not surprisingly, Americans are generally not opposed to dollarization in other countries, but there is no unanimity on how it should be handled. Hearings of the Senate Banking Committee have suggested 'exciting potential benefits for the US', such as increased US investment in the dollarized countries, increased trade with them, and consequently more jobs for American workers. Former senator, Connie Mack, a Republican from Florida and chairman of the Senate Banking Committee, once sponsored a bill to encourage the process, with provisions for sharing some of the seigniorage with the dollarized countries under rigorous conditions.

Professor Barro of Harvard University would like to see the dollar 'reign from Seattle to Santiago', and proposed that the US provide the initial stock of US\$16 billion currency notes free of cost to Argentina; he would even have put in place arrangements to have the US Federal Reserve assist in bailing out Argentinean banks in case of financial crisis. But the US Treasury insists on keeping all the seigniorage, and Federal Reserve Board chairman, Alan Greenspan, would neither guarantee the bail out of dollarized financial systems nor share US monetary decision-making authority with foreign countries.

Implications of Dollarization for the Netherlands Antilles

The cost of dollarization to the Netherlands Antilles (as presently constituted) in terms of seigniorage lost would be tremendous. First, government would lose in perpetuity the net profits from central bank operations — about US\$33 million in 2000. But that is not all. To implement dollarization, the Netherlands Antilles would have to purchase an original stock of US currency in the value of total Netherlands Antilles currency in circulation, which at year end 2000 exceeded NAf229 million, or US$128 million. This expense would have to be met by running down the Central Bank's foreign exchange reserves (roughly US$270 million at the end of 2000), or from foreign US dollar loans.

Moreover, increases in currency circulation, which can be expected to rise as the economy expands, would have to be met with additional purchases of US dollar notes annually, probably five per cent per annum, or approximately US$6.5 million, a far cry from the US$200,000 or so that it now costs to purchase new Netherlands Antilles currency notes each year.

Finally, the US$128 million currency notes in circulation would no longer earn interest as did the foreign exchange reserves used to purchase them, and would, in effect, represent a perpetual loan from the Netherlands Antilles to the US at a zero rate of interest. Even at the modest rate of return of five per cent per annum, the Netherlands Antilles would be losing about US$6.5 million annually.

We may summarize the financial cost of dollarization to the Netherlands Antilles as follows:

Original cost:	US$ 128 million
Purchase of stock of US currency notes	
Annual cost:	45 million
Loss of Central Bank profits:	33 million
Purchase of additional US currency notes:	6 million
Loss of interest on US$ notes in circulation:	6 million

US$128 million down and an annual tribute of US$45 million to the USA thereafter is reminiscent of one definition of marriage: 'All your money down and the rest of your life to pay.'

The Balance Sheet of Dollarization

The advantages of dollarization set out in the IMF brochure are imprecise and of low visibility. The chief advantage put forward is that 'the interest premium owing to devaluation risk would disappear.' However, since the foreign debt of Caribbean states is normally denominated in US dollars, the issue of a devaluation risk premium does not arise. But the interest penalty for country risk on foreign loans would *not* disappear with dollarization. Country risk derives from the probability of default from several causes, such as natural disaster, political or social instability, the international business cycle, or poor economic management.

The second presumed advantage of the benefits of a closer integration with both the global and US economies is highly doubtful. Indications are that unfettered financial globalization widens the gap between rich and poor countries.

The third alleged advantage is that, by removing the option of inflationary financing, dollarization 'might also strengthen their financial institutions and create positive sentiment towards investment, both domestic and international'. However, the numerous and incalculable factors affecting investment decisions make that proposition highly doubtful.

Whereas the advantages that proponents of dollarization hold out are vague and mostly speculative, the disadvantages are clear cut and concrete. The loss from surrender of seigniorage, as we have seen, is especially severe and is realizable up front. Dollarization would also involve the surrender of monetary policy to the Federal Reserve Board, and a consequent loss of flexibility in national economic management. How can we be sure that US monetary policy will always be in our interest? In the case of independent Caribbean states, the disappearance of the national currency would constitute a humiliating loss of sovereignty. And sovereignty is the most precious possession of a state — especially of a small state.

The loss of the central banking functions of lender of last resort in times of banking crises, and its role of banker to government and technical and policy adviser to the Minister of Finance, would detract considerably from the quality of nation economic management. To sum up, dollarization would distribute its advantages to the US, and its disadvantages to the Caribbean states.

Dollarization, then, is a policy of despair, appropriate only for countries that have lost all confidence in their capacity to conduct their own affairs. Even so, a currency board would deliver very much the same results as dollarization — without the loss of seigniorage. However, the Argentinean experience has shown that even currency board regimes are not proof against prolonged and irresponsible fiscal policy. But then no currency regime is, including dollarization! Indeed, it would have been even more costly for the Argentines to disengage from dollarization than from the currency board system. The optimal currency regime remains a well-managed central bank operating in the context of responsible fiscal policy. In economic management, as in any other human enterprise, there is no substitute for discipline — especially fiscal discipline.

Finally, economic development has historically involved the transfer of capital and other resources from the developed to the developing economies, as was the case with UK investments in North America, Australia, New Zealand and South Africa. The transfer of scarce resources from the world's poorest countries to the world's richest country, as dollarization would involve, has usually been associated with colonial exploitation, not with economic development!

Presented to the Second Public Consultation Session: Money and Banking Series St. Maarten, NA., March 21, 2002

Notes

1. Andrew Berg, and Edwards Borensztein, 'Full Dollarization: Pros & Cons', IMF Publications, *International Monetary Fund Economic Issues*, no. 24 (2000): 16.
2. Nicholas Mayhew, *Sterling: The History of a Currency* (Penguin Books, 1999), 10.
3. Adam Smith, as quoted by Nicholas Mayhew, *Sterling*, 123.

SECTION IV

Critical Caribbean Issues

14

THE AGONY OF THE EIGHT REVISITED

Sir Arthur Lewis was, throughout the 60s and the 70s, a living example of the biblical quotation, 'A prophet is not without honour save in his own country.' His recommendations for economic development were dismissed as 'industrialization by invitation', and he himself was derided as an 'Afro-Saxon, conservative neo-classical economist'. In the best Caribbean traditions, we discovered his intellectual qualities when the people 'from away' honoured him with the Nobel Prize. But it is still wonderful that, within his lifetime, we are honouring him for his tremendous contributions to the social sciences.

As an economist, I have been most enlightened by Lewis's celebrated paper, 'Economic Development with Unlimited Supplies of Labour',[1] a classic in the literature of development economics. As a policy maker, I have been most influenced by *The Principles of Economic Planning*,[2] which stripped the market of its mystique and revealed it as merely a social device for inexpensively allocating resources, and therefore to be preferred unless there are compelling reasons to do otherwise.

Today, however, I have chosen as my point of departure Lewis's obscure tract, *The Agony of the Eight*, which describes his gallant attempt in 1960 to persuade the 'Little Eight' to federate.[3] The 'Little Eight' included Antigua and Barbuda, Barbados, Dominica,

Grenada, St. Kitts and Nevis, Saint Lucia, St. Vincent, and Montserrat. Immediately prior to retirement from public service, I was the object of the malevolent attention of the ruling Barbados Democratic Labour Party. Compared to other governments in the region, the hostility of a Barbadian administration may appear almost benign. Yet, I can confirm, it is most unpleasant for any individual citizen to be subjected to the wrath of the state. I recalled the following passage from *The Agony of the Eight*:

> [T]he maintenance of good government requires a federal structure. In a small island of 50,000 or 100,000 people, dominated by a single political party, it is very difficult to prevent political abuse. Everybody depends on the government for something, however small, so most are reluctant to offend it. *The civil servants live in fear, the police avoid unpleasantness; the trade unions are tied to the party; the newspaper depends on government advertisements; and so on. This is true even if the political leaders are absolutely honest.* In cases where they are also corrupt, and playing with the public funds, the situation becomes intolerable. The only safeguard against this is federation. If the government in island C misbehaves, it will be criticised openly by the citizens of island E. The federal government must be responsible for law and order, and for redress of financial or other abuses. (Emphasis added)[4]

My paper focuses on those features of Caribbean societies which militate against freedom, justice and democracy. Like Sir Arthur's paper, it starts with the observation of the existential problems facing citizens in society, eschewing those grandiose and over arching theories which bring intellectual delight to Caribbean academics but do not advance, but frequently obstruct, our progress towards a better society.

I have identified three factors which militate against freedom and democracy in the Anglophone Caribbean: *A heritage of authoritarianism; the primacy of politics;* and *a predilection for centralized government.* These mutually reinforcing pathologies are exacerbated by the small size of our territories. My proposals for reversing an inherent bias in our societies towards authoritarianism involve action on three fronts: (i) the intellectual, (ii) the national and (iii) the regional. Firstly, we need to retreat from utopianism in our studies of political economy, and to concentrate on making what we have work better. Secondly, we need to tame the state and make it supportive rather than oppressive of the citizen. Thirdly, we need to return to Sir Arthur's premise, outlined above, and redouble our efforts at the economic and political integration of CARICOM.

The Heritage of Authoritarianism

Authoritarianism is an important aspect of our colonial heritage. Professor Clive Thomas admits that authoritarian trends in Guyana possess 'a distinctive national character'; he rightly insists that its genealogy is not unique, but shares commonalities with the rest of the Caribbean: 'The State which I have labelled as authoritarian ... has roots in the Caribbean past. Guyana is only the Caribbean's best prototype.'[5] This year Barbados celebrated 350 years of parliamentary practice, but this is not the same thing as parliamentary democracy. For over 200 years slavery, the most extreme manifestation of authoritarianism, thrived in our region. Even the plantocracy itself struggled continuously over this period against the domination of King or Parliament in Britain; eventually only Barbados would enter the twentieth century with its representative form of government intact, crown colony government prevailing in other territories.

The powers of the colonial governor were comprehensive and backed by a supreme imperial authority. He could override any colonial Act and impose any decree. The governor also directed a highly centralized bureaucracy untrammeled by the conventions which restrained the Crown in Britain. At independence, the governmental apparatus of the colonial government was handed over virtually lock, stock and barrel to the local political elites and, as Professor Thomas astutely observes, 'The supreme power previously exercised by the colonial state (has) devolved on the chief executive of the post-colonial state rather than to the population at large.'[6]

Christopher Clapham agrees with Thomas:

> The administrative structure established to run the colonial territory was necessarily both centralized and authoritarian. Authority came from overseas. . . . Many of the assumptions and values have been abandoned. But the structure itself is recognizably the same.[7]

Clapham further contends that many colonial attitudes persist:

> From the rulers, a sense of superiority over those whom they ruled, a sense of power emanating from above, rather than growing from below; for the ruled, a sense of the state as an alien imposition, to be accepted, certainly, and to be feared, cajoled and where possible exploited, but existing on a plane above the people whom it governed, and beyond any chance of control.[8]

At the same time the informal conventions of the unwritten British constitution, which protect against arbitrary government, did not travel well across the Atlantic. Without the formal checks and balances of a US-type constitution, the rights of opposition parties, the independence of the civil service, the electoral process, press freedom, et cetera are most vulnerable at the hands of charismatic and long-serving prime ministers, who become more imperious as their tenure of office proceeds. Furthermore, the 'top-down' management style of the colonial governors became the model of post-colonial prime ministers. As a result, the perception of government as a distant and alien authority, persists in the public mind, and is manifested in the pervasive abuse of government property excused by the retort, 'It belong to de government.'

It was unfortunate for civil rights in the region that independence came during a time of great emphasis on economic development. This has inclined governments towards intervention into every aspect of the citizen's life. To quote Thomas again, 'The expansion of state property and the development of state-controlled mechanisms of economic regulation are a result of the development orientation of the State.'[9] As a consequence, we have seen the development in the Caribbean of what Paul Johnson calls the 'omnicompetent state'.[10] Guyana, with 80 per cent of the formal economy owned or controlled by government, is an extreme example of omnicompetence.

The small size of Caribbean states provides a fertile soil for the seeds of authoritarianism which were planted in our colonial past. Limited geographical area and small populations lead logically to monolithic administrative structures. There is no room for devolution of significant responsibilities and authority on regional assemblies. (Large size, on the other hand, imposes its own diversity and decentralization.) The result is a ridiculous and extraordinary centralization of governmental decision making. For example, the average number of notes considered by the Trinidad and Tobago Cabinet at its weekly meetings exceeded 4,000 over the decade 1974–1984, reaching as high as 5,176 in 1981.[11] The comparable figure for Barbados, I understand, is about 1,000 and rising! In 1942, at the height of the Second World War, and with the nation's survival at stake, less than 100 notes were submitted to the British Cabinet! The Dolly Report expressed the following concern for over-centralization in Trinidad and Tobago:

> There is a high degree of centralization of authority, particularly since 1966; in the office of permanent secretaries and in such bodies as the Public Service Commission, the statutory authorities, Service Commission and the Central Tenders Board. Cabinet, following the tradition of the previous Executive Council, continues to deal, not primarily with broad policy formulation, but also with a large number of matters of detail.[12]

In Barbados the head teacher of a secondary school in St. Lucy must obtain permission from the Ministry of Education in Bridgetown before he can suspend classes in the face of present danger. But above all, small size exposes the citizen to the direct pressure of political action, an issue which we will explore further in the next section.

The Primacy of Politics

'We live in a world of politics,' a minister of government once said to me. 'We live in many worlds,' I vainly protested. Of course, in the Caribbean context he was perfectly right. Politics permeates every tissue of our society. The ultimate example is Guyana, where the ruling political party has been declared paramount over the state.

In Latin America, the military won independence from Spain and Portugal and never passed it on to the civilians; in the Caribbean it was the politicians who received power from Britain, and they, too, have been most reluctant to share it with the population at large. The good news is that Caribbean politicians, generally speaking, have not created a military strong enough to seize total political power. It is much easier to wrest political power from politicians than from soldiers!

Three factors have contributed most to what I have termed the 'primacy of politics'. The first is the high incidence of charismatic leadership typical of newly independent countries; the second stems from what Christopher Clapham terms 'neo-patrimonialism';[13] the third is the low level of incomes obtaining in the region. Again, all three of these influences are heightened by the small size of our societies.

The righteousness of the struggle against colonialism created a drama-filled environment which was custom-built for the charismatic leader. The classic image of Caribbean charisma is the figure of Alexander Bustamante bearing his breast before the colonial forces and pleading: 'Shoot me, but spare my people!' Each territory boasts at least one messianic leader; some have produced several. Charismatic leaders are indispensable in critical times, as during the struggle for independence. Invariably, these 'fathers of the nation' become liabilities if they tarry too long in power. The fault is not so much in themselves as in their followers, who perceive them as the embodiment of the nation. Citizens who disagree with the leader are perceived, not merely as political opponents, but as traitors to the nation. If the opposition parties are too weak, the post-independence regime rapidly degenerates into a one-party system. If a multi-party system emerges, party rivalries soon evolve into political tribalism.

Tribal political parties cannot conceive of defeat at the polls since such an eventuality would bring the treasonous opposition to power and precipitate national disaster; the opposition must be kept out of power at all costs — preferably within the available constitutional means. This may include control of the media, election budgets, changes in the electoral boundaries, or even in the constitution when the required majority is available. Sometimes, the bending or even breaking of the constitution may be necessary to win the election.

The second ingredient of the primacy of politics is neo-patrimonialism. Patrimonialism, in Weberian terms, describes a situation in which authority is ascribed to a person rather than to an office-holder. Whereas in advanced democracies the expression 'minister' is a metaphor that identifies the person ultimately responsible for a set of administrative outcomes, in the Caribbean that responsibility is ascribed to the minister personally, who assumes omnicompetent characteristics, and feels fully justified to intervene into administrative details at every level and in any discipline. Furthermore, as Clapham explains;

> In a system held together by a patrimonial logic, those lower down the political hierarchy are not subordinates, in the sense of officials with defined powers and functions of their own, but rather vassals or retainers whose position depends on the leader to whom they owe allegiance.[14]

Neo-patrimonialism manifests itself most notably in tribal politics, and is most observable on those occasions in the Caribbean when incumbent administrations are negligent enough, as Forbes Burnham said of Errol Barrow's 1976 defeat, to lose elections. On such occasions, not only must ministers and active politicians go, but even career public servants who served during the tenure of the outgoing administration as the constitution required.

Professional managers of public enterprises are summarily removed or hounded out of office through public attacks, frequently from the sanctuary of the floor of Parliament. Permanent Secretaries, theoretically protected by the constitution, are sent on leave and their public careers destroyed.

The governing boards and general managers of statutory corporations are also dismissed, with damaging consequences for organizational morale and continuity. Even more absurd, the governing board of each secondary school in Barbados is replaced with each change of administration, as if political considerations have any place in the management of schools. Even the priest who says prayers in Parliament is removed with a change of government.

The third operating factor is the fact that the fortunes of a significant number of people are dependent on politics. This phenomenon is not absent in rich democracies like the UK, US and Canada, but it is also true in these societies that most of those who seek the highest offices in the land do so at a financial loss. The prize is political power, and departure from office does not threaten financial disaster. In poor societies, political office is frequently a means of enrichment.

Dr Patrick Emmanuel comments on this issue as follows: 'given the underdeveloped state of these economies and the consequent scarcity of opportunities for stable, lucrative employment, politics and government have become a principal source of high income.'[15] The effects of charismatic politics and neo-patrimonialism are reinforced by the personal nature of most relationships. Emmanuel also comments on the impact of size on charismatic politics in the Leewards and Windwards: 'In small societies 'personalism' is a major force in determining social relationships and hence political behaviour. In the world of politics the most intense expressions of 'personalism' are conceptualised in terms of charismatic leaders.'[16] This 'personalism' also makes it difficult for people in small societies to distinguish between the office and the office holder whom they frequently know quite intimately. The net result of this politicization and personalization of public transactions is to inhibit the development of 'rational-legal' authority on which the organization and the legitimacy of the modern state rest. As Clapham concisely puts it: 'The basis of that authority is that individuals in public positions, possessing power over their fellow citizens, exercise that power in accordance with a legally defined structure towards a publicly acknowledged goal.'[17]

Predilection for Centralization

The inherent tendencies towards centralization in Caribbean government noted above were reinforced by the dominant ideologies of the 1960s and 1970s. Two paradigms dominated the social sciences during these decades: the Marxian and the 'dependency' models. The Marxian programme involves the comprehensive nationalization of the factors of production, including foreign financial, agricultural and mining interests, and the introduction of central planning.

The 'dependency' school proposed 'delinking' Caribbean economies from the metropoles, and the adoption of policies of self-reliance involving the 'ownership and control' of indigenous resources and occupation of the 'commanding heights' of the economy. Both these programmes implied the increased involvement of the state in the economy, either as the owner and operator of nationalized enterprises, or in the detailed direction of the economy, or in the enforcement of far reaching economic regulations, including the restriction and exclusion of imports.

C.Y. Thomas, the dean of Caribbean Marxist scholars, has consistently espoused nationalization and central planning. However, he admits that such socialist policies enhance the authoritarian potential of the state:

As events have shown, nationalisation in Guyana aided the expansion of the state bureaucratically, ideologically and militarily and in so doing, increased the capacity of the ruling PNC to assert its various forms of authoritarian control over civil society.[18]

I share Professor Thomas's alarm at the trends towards authoritarianism in the region and the high value which he places on parliamentary democracy. However, I am confused by his insistence that 'the struggle for political democracy is vital to the struggle for socialism. One cannot exist without the other.'[19] In fact, the outcome of democratic practice is indeterminate; we cannot be sure that parliamentary democracy will lead us to socialism — it never has! The establishment of Marxist socialist states has always involved coercion or subversion. That is the lesson of Grenada.

Although diametrically opposed to Dr Trevor Munroe's ideological position, I accept the logic of his critique of Thomas's attachment to bourgeois rights:

Concretely, Thomas's concept of socialist or popular democracy complementing bourgeois democracy rather than negating it dialectically — taking what is good in it and discarding the rest — would, consistently applied, oppose the censorship imposed by the Sandinistas on *La Prensa*; reject the closure of *Torchlight* under Grenada's Popular Revolution; denounce the disbandment in 1960 of the political organizations in supporting the Batista tyranny in Cuba.... Measures such as these violate "the democratic phase" into which the struggles against authoritarianism must lead.[20]

Professor Thomas must decide whether he is a liberal democrat like me or a Marxian socialist like Dr Munroe.

Agenda for Reform

If my picture of Caribbean society appears bleak, it is because I have concentrated on the symptoms of pathology in the body politic rather than on the indicators of good health. When compared with Africa, Latin America, Eastern Europe and most of Asia, the Anglophone Caribbean, with the exception of the 'sick man' Guyana, is in great shape.

As far as the observance of civil rights and the provision of basic needs are concerned, it is among the more fortunate regions on earth. Indeed, there are distinct signs that its immune system, bolstered by the antibodies produced during two hundred years of the supreme authoritarianism of slavery, has successfully repelled the totalitarian viruses of the left. However, it needs to be strengthened against the more insidious bacteria of authoritarianism systemic to our societies.

What follows is not so much a grand strategy for dealing with the problems I have touched on above, as a partial agenda of practical measures for enhancing civil rights in our region.

Building on the Heritage

The most pressing need is for Caribbean social scientists to retreat from utopianism and to concern themselves more with empirical issues. We have a fatal attraction for cosmic and overarching paradigms which involve the radical restructuring of our societies. Professor Thomas wants to move us through parliamentary democracy to socialism; Dr Trevor Munroe wants to move us to socialism after the overthrow, violent if necessary, of parliamentary democracy; Dr George Beckford insists on the destruction of the plantation system 'if the people of the plantation society are to secure economic, social and political advancement';[21] Dr Louis Lindsay demands 'the complete destruction of Westminster politics and Westminster politicians and their replacement by a new breed of leaders'[22] — an outcome almost accomplished in Grenada. I submit that the political system which we have developed in the Caribbean (Guyana again excepted), though not perfect, is admirable in many respects. Our region is almost unique in the Third World: reasonably free and fair elections are regularly held and governments routinely removed from office via the ballot box.

The number of bona fide political prisoners in our jails, as well as the number of 'disappeared ones', is minimal if not non-existent. Newspapers are freely published and citizens travel freely without let or hindrance. Besides, there is really no other alternative than to start from where we are, since the arrow of time moves in only one direction. We cannot wipe slavery, the plantation system, or the Westminster model from our past. We must do our best with the cards that history has dealt us. One objective should be to do better today than we did yesterday, and better tomorrow than we did today. Let us spend less time remonstrating about the world economic order or the international capitalist conspiracy, about which we can do little, and expend greater effort on specific and practical steps to improve our societies.

Restraining the State

On the national front we must seek means of taming the state, that is, of reducing its intrusions in our private lives, of limiting its ability to injure us, and of increasing the scope for the 'bottom-up' management of national affairs.

Here our agenda is a long one. Following are some of the most important items:

- Liberation of the media, especially television, from the tyranny of the administration in power;
- Professionalization of the civil service and the de-politicization of public enterprises;

- ◆ The decentralization of decision making in public administration — starting with the Cabinet and the ministries — and the privatization of public enterprises unless required by strategic considerations;
- ◆ The facilitation of civilian redress against damage by the State;
- ◆ More independent electoral commissions;
- ◆ Improved financial accountability in the public sector;
- ◆ The restriction of the term of office of prime ministers to ten years, as suggested by Prime Minister Arthur Robinson of Trinidad and Tobago, deserves consideration.

A Federal Solution

As Lewis suggested, a federated structure would considerably improve our prospects of developing a 'rational-legal' context for the conduct of our political affairs:

- ■ It would diffuse charismatic influences in politics.
- ■ The authority of insular politicians would be limited.
- ■ The wide dispersal of the region's population would make for more impersonal relationships and greater disinterestedness among public officials.

There is one special remaining task on the regional front — the liberation of the University of the West Indies from the embrace of politics. We must begin to build an endowment to reduce and eventually eliminate the virtually complete dependence of the University on financing from governments. This is a long-term proposition; that is why we should start immediately.

Conclusion

The timing for the implementation of our agenda is excellent. The calamity of Guyana and the catastrophe of Grenada have done much to cure the region of 'ideological pluralism'. The Marxian paradigm appears to have run its historical course and Dr Norman Girvan, in a brilliant critique of Professor Thomas, has admitted to the errors of the radical 'dependence' school.[23] On the international front, Mr Gorbachev is imposing democratic change — from above — in the best Russian tradition. In China, the demand for democracy wells up from beneath. Here in the region, Mr Michael Manley has substituted the business suit for the messianic 'rod of correction'; in Trinidad and Tobago, Mr Robinson is privatizing, and in Guyana, President Desmond Hoyte struggles to escape from his ideological strait-jacket.

We must strike while the iron is hot! It is time for us to adopt the Lewis technique of rooting our operational models in historical experience and directing them towards the achievement of realistic objectives. In particular, we should address once again the proposition which Sir Arthur posed almost 30 years ago — that freedom and democracy would more profitably be pursued in the context of a federated West Indies.

Presented at the XIVth Annual Conference of the Caribbean Studies Association Barbados, in honour of Sir Arthur Lewis, May 23–26, 1989

Notes

1. G. Arthur Lewis, 'Economic Development with Unlimited Supplies of Labour', *The Economics of Development*, eds., A.N. Agarawala, and S.P. Singh (New York: O.U.P., 1963).

2. ———, *The Principles of Economic Planning* (London: Allen & Unwin, 1969).

3. ———, *The Agony of the Eight* (Bridgetown: Advocate Commercial Printery, 1960), 16–17.

4. Ibid., 16–17.

5. Clive Y. Thomas, 'The Authoritarian State in Caribbean Societies', in *The State in Caribbean Society*, ed., Omar Davies (Mona, Jamaica: University of the West Indies, 1986), 62.

6. ———, *The Rise of the Authoritarian State in Peripheral Societies* (New York: Monthly Review Press, 1984), 92.

7. Christopher Clapham, *Third World Politics: An Introduction* (Madison: University of Wisconsin Press, 1985), 19.

8. Ibid., 19.

9. Clive Y. Thomas, *The Rise of the Authoritarian State in Peripheral Societies*, 89.

10. Paul Johnson, *Modern Times: The World From the Twenties to the Eighties* (New York: Harper & Row, 1983).

11. Gordon Draper, 'The Quest for Appropriate Public Service', *Trinidad and Tobago, the Independence Experience, 1962–1987*, eds., Selwyn Ryan and Gloria Gordon (St. Augustine, Trinidad: Institute of Social and Economic Research, 1988), 238.

12. As quoted by Draper, ibid., 236.

13. Christopher Clapham, *Third World Politics*, 44.

14. Ibid., 48.

15. Patrick Emmanuel, 'Independence and Viability: Elements of Analysis', in *Size, Self-Determination and International Relations: The Caribbean*, ed., Vaughan A. Lewis (Mona, Jamaica: Institute of Social and Economic Research, University of the West Indies, 1976), 8.

16. Ibid., 7.

17. Christopher Clapham, *Third World Politics*, 44.

18. Clive Y. Thomas, *The Poor and the Powerless: Economic Policy and Change in the Caribbean* (New York: Monthly Review Press, 1988), 255.

19. ———, *The Rise of the Authoritarian State in Peripheral Societies*, 99.

20. Trevor Munroe, 'Comments on Thomas', in *The State in Caribbean Society*, 86.

21. George Beckford, *Persistent Poverty* (New York: Oxford University Press, 1972), 215.

22. Louis Lindsay, 'Colonialism and the Myth of Resource Insufficiency in Jamaica', in *Size, Self-Determination and International Relations: The Caribbean*, 65.

23. Norman Girvan, 'C.Y. Thomas and the Poor and the Powerless: The Limitations of Conventional Radicalism', *Social and Economic Studies* 37, no. 4 (December 1988): 253–274.

15

WAGE/PRICE GUIDELINES FOR INCREASING INTERNATIONAL COMPETITIVENESS IN THE CARIBBEAN

The invitation from the Caribbean Development Bank to speak about wage-price policies came to me as a great surprise. Wage-price policy is a transparent euphemism for wage restraint and while Governor of the Central Bank of Barbados, my calls for wage restraint were always met with hostility. A union leader once described my recommendations on the subject as 'unwarranted, untimely and malicious'. Indeed, my own staff frequently advised me against mentioning the word *wage restraint*: some disagreed with me; others feared for my job security — with good reason, as it turned out.[1] Today, not only have I been invited to speak about wage restraint, I am being paid to do so

It occurred to me as I prepared this paper that my spectacular lack of success in selling wage restraint might rest in its negative connotation. I was reminded of the tale of the two monks. Seeing a brother smoking in the room designated for meditation, one monk reminded him of the rule against such a practice. The smoker explained that he had received permission from the abbot. The monk hurried away only to return later with the news that his own request had been refused. 'What did you ask?' the smoker enquired. 'I asked whether I could smoke during meditation.' 'That was your mistake,' replied the smoker, 'I asked whether I could meditate while smoking.'

I have decided that the term 'incomes policy' might strike a more positive tone without doing violence to the spirit of the topic on 'Wage-price policies for increasing international competitiveness in the Caribbean.' Wage restraint is the centrepiece of incomes policy and price control its occasional companion. Furthermore, the substitution of incomes policy for wage-price policy provides greater pedagogical opportunities in that it permits the integration of wage-price policy into the framework of overall macroeconomic management

Failure to treat wage rates as a controllable policy variable, and hence to recommend an incomes policy, has been a costly error on the part of Caribbean economists. Professor Eric St Cyr, for example, regards wages as endogenously determined by domestic prices and the price of exports.[2] In fact, wage rates in the Caribbean have for a generation been administered by trade unions, governments and, more recently, by the International Monetary Fund. Yet only recently have a few Caribbean economists assigned a role to wage restraint in macroeconomic management. In his recent book, *Small Island Economies*, Dr DeLisle Worrell dismisses incomes policy as unworkable.[3] Some economists at the Cave Hill campus of the University of the West Indies, in mistaken application of the Keynesian closed-system model, have applauded inflated wage awards as a means of stimulating aggregate demand. The Trinidad and Tobago experience has demonstrated conclusively that the consequence of Keynesian-type remedies in economies as open as ours is to destroy the balance of payments.

In fact, Sir Arthur Lewis recommended an incomes policy to Caribbean governments as early as 1964,[4] and again, in his brilliant presidential address at the annual general meeting of the Caribbean Development Bank in 1972. However, it was fashionable those days in the region to decry the future Nobel Prize winner as 'Afro-Saxon', 'neoclassical', and 'non-progressive'. We have paid dearly for our neglect of his work and advice.

Even without the stamp of academic approval, Caribbean governments have resorted to wage-restraint when nothing else seemed to work. While in opposition both the Barbados Labour Party and the Democratic Labour Party flayed the incumbent administration for breaking off negotiations with trade unions and legislating wages, only to do the same when next in power. The Guyana government foreshadowed the Thatcher wage restraint technique of trade union bashing; the Jamaican government has used frequent currency depreciations to cut real wages; the Chambers administration in Trinidad and Tobago imposed its famous 'one-two-three' wage settlement for the civil service — one per cent increase in the first, two per cent in the second, and three per cent in the third year. The succeeding Robinson administration went beyond wage restraint to cut civil service salaries by ten per cent — a vindication of my position on incomes policy which I would rather have foregone.

The argument of this paper is that an incomes policy is an essential tool in the kit-bag of serious macroeconomic managers in small open economies like ours in the Caribbean. Firstly, it supplements fiscal and monetary policy by restraining aggregate expenditure and, considering our high propensity to import, by restricting imports; secondly, by restricting the price of non-tradeables, it curbs domestic inflation; thirdly, by limiting the price of tradeables, it improves our international competitive position; finally, by containing the wage bill, it limits the rate of substitution of capital for labour.

Section I describes the international competitive environment in which CARICOM operates. Section II discusses the strategic framework in which an incomes policy might most beneficially be applied. In particular, we contrast the approach of small West European nations with that of CARICOM countries in dealing with similar problems of economic survival. Section III presents a macroeconomic model explaining the inter-relationships between an incomes policy and the other three policy instruments — fiscal, monetary, and exchange rate policies. Section IV enumerates ten measures related to the implementation of an incomes policy.

We close with recommendations for the institutionalization of an incomes policy.

The Competitive Environment of CARICOM

The economic environment of CARICOM has been marked in recent decades by increasing volatility, dynamism and competitiveness. From the safety of Commonwealth commodity preferences and the security of marketing arrangements with metropolitan mother companies, Caribbean producers are now more and more exposed to competition from other developing countries and simultaneously confronted by the protectionism of the developed countries. The last vestiges of imperial concern — the Lomé Convention and the CBI — promise more than they deliver.

In the immediate post World War II period, Caribbean commodities, such as sugar and bananas, enjoyed preferential markets in the UK and, to a lesser extent in Canada and the USA. Trinidad's oil, Guyana's sugar and bauxite, and later Jamaica's bauxite and alumina, were produced by British, Canadian or American multinationals and their access to world markets assured. At the same time, regional financial markets and, indeed, our monetary system were integral parts of the Sterling Area, and our balance of payments was protected by the limitations imposed by the currency board system. These protective arrangements began to disintegrate in the 1970s. There were three main solvents at work: political nationalism, economic nationalism, and the coming of the Information Age. Beginning in the early 1960s, Anglophone Caribbean islands moved in regular succession towards independence. Today only Anguilla, the Cayman Islands, the Turks and Caicos, Montserrat and the British Virgin Islands remain British colonies.

In the 1960s, the strident 'New World' economists provided the ideological stimulus for the delinking of our economies from 'dependence' on the metropoles. Their theories promoted nationalization of foreign enterprise and favoured autarchic economic strategies. As it turned out, formal colonialism has been replaced in some instances by the even more complete economic tutelage of international creditors.

Finally, the New Information Age, brought into being by fantastic developments in transportation, computers and telecommunications, has transformed the world into a global village. As a result, our economic fortunes are increasingly sensitive to events in remote parts of the world of whose existence and geography we had hitherto been only dimly aware.

With the global village has come the global marketplace and global workplace. Multinationals now purchase raw materials and components from the cheapest sources, assemble them in the most efficient production centres, and sell them into the most lucrative markets without any recognition of national borders, indulging in what we might call 'production arbitraging', to borrow a term from the world of finance. If they find that products can be produced more economically in the Philippines, they close their plant in Barbados, as did Intel Corporation. If shirts can be produced more cheaply in Thailand, then orders shift from Jamaica. Meanwhile, long-standing loyalties fade, preferential quotas shrink, and we move inexorably into a world where each nation or trading bloc fends for itself and the devil takes the hindmost. The devil has been having a field day!

Reflecting these revolutionary changes, our international economic and financial environment has become most problematic. For one thing, the terms of trade have turned sharply against commodity producers like CARICOM. At the same time, interest rates and exchange rates have fluctuated violently as vast volumes of capital move daily from one financial centre to another in search of the highest rate of return.

What is more, our competitors are not so much the old imperialist bogeymen as other developing countries in the Pacific basin and Latin America, who compete with us as suppliers of garments, electronic parts and other manufactured components to the markets of Western Europe and North America, and that also offer their sand, sun and sea to European, North American, and, increasingly, Japanese tourists. It should be clear by now that we are in a new ball game.

The chips used in this international poker game are political stability, quality of infrastructure and, especially, labour costs. It is in labour costs that our rivals hold the upper hand. Up to date comparative statistics of wage rates are difficult to obtain. I have included in tables 1-4 the most recent data available to the investment promotion agencies of Barbados and the OECS. The general impression gained from the data is that wage rates and productivity of the OECS are comparable to those in other Latin American countries, about the same level as those of Hong Kong and South Korea, but far above those of China, Thailand and Sri Lanka. Wage rates in Jamaica are slightly higher than in the OECS; rates in Barbados and The Bahamas are about twice as high, and comparable to those of Taiwan and Singapore. Rates in Trinidad and Tobago, which were the highest in CARICOM during the oil boom, are now somewhere between those of Jamaica and Barbados.

A fierce Latin American rival of CARICOM is Mexico which, in cooperation with the US government, has developed a series of industrial estates, called *maquiladora*, on its northern border with the US. A large number of American and Japanese firms have also established themselves on the US side of the border to facilitate production-sharing with the Mexicans. There is a continuous flow of components and materials south for further manufacture or assembly, and a return flow north of semi-finished or finished products. This phenomenon deserves careful study by CARICOM governments and manufacturers. As a tourist destination Mexico has the additional advantage of proximity to the US.

Undoubtedly, our most formidable opponents are the 'four tigers' of East Asia. Their greatest advantage is their exceptional wage productivity, reflecting a culturally inspired work ethic. Singapore and Taiwan, although no longer low-wage producers, employ capital and technology far superior to that employed in CARICOM. Most important, the success of these 'four dragons' derives in a large degree from their rigorous practice of wage-restraint. All of these countries, to some extent, have authoritarian governments and traditionally docile trade unions, a combination which adds up to a most effective incomes policy. This type of incomes policy, however, is not generally available to us in CARICOM, with our West European traditions of parliamentary democracy and trade unionism. That is why the experience of small west European states given below is of such interest.

Strategic Framework of Incomes Policy

Almost every economic report or paper on the Caribbean begins with a comment on the small size, limited resource base and openness of our economies. Citizens of European states like Holland, Belgium, Norway and Sweden also consider their economies small, of limited resource base and highly open. It is instructive to review their strategic response to this situation and compare it with ours in the Caribbean.

The central theme of the economic strategies of small West European states is flexible adjustment in the face of developments in the international economy which they are unable to control. Being small, they cannot, as the Japanese have so adroitly done, transfer the cost of adjustment to other nations through the adoption of protectionist measures. Instead, they have combined liberal trading policies with compensatory domestic policies. Professor Katzenstein describes this approach as follows:

> For the small European states, with their open economies and fear of retaliation by other governments, exporting the costs of change

through protectionist policies is not a viable political strategy. Protectionism would not only invite retaliation but also increase the costs of the intermediate inputs of products manufactured for export, thus undermining the international competitiveness of these small, open economies.[5]

Indeed, small west European states have been far more supportive of free trade practices than larger countries like the UK, France, Canada and the US, not to speak of Japan. Sweden and Denmark regard import competition as a useful check on domestic inflation and on monopolistic tendencies in their small domestic markets. Alice Bourneuf reports the Norwegian position on this issue thus: 'The solution is not to develop ... industries and protect them from more efficient foreign competition.'[6] Although favouring a liberal international economic order, small west European states have occasionally formed their own regional trading arrangements: Benelux, its Nordic version, and (in the 1950s) the European Free Trade Area.

In monetary matters, the small west European states have favoured the free convertibility of their currencies and have generally striven for currency stability. For example, Switzerland has pursued conservative monetary policies promoting an extremely strong currency; Austria has pegged to the strong deutschmark; the Benelux countries have huddled around the deutschmark under the umbrella of the European Monetary System that will probably unify west European currencies before the end of the century. Yet they have not hesitated to devalue if circumstances dictate, as did Sweden in the late 1970s.

The centrepiece of this compensatory strategy is the policy of restraint on wage increases imposed or agreed upon under a national economic strategy. Occasionally, price controls are coupled with wage restraint. Katzenstein observes: 'Economic openness has made the adoption of incomes policies an opportunity with which most of the small European states have experimented in the last two decades.'[7]

Three major considerations underpin the incomes policies of west European countries. First, they understand the futility, over the long run, of subsidising inefficient labour. Subsidies to domestic enterprises are calculated to bring their operations to the level of international competitiveness through restructuring, mergers, and assistance with research and development; they do not invite indefinite featherbedding. Secondly, they respect the imperative of the balance of payments — protected and inefficient labour does not promote balance of payments stability in the long-term. Thirdly, they recognize that the wage rate is a production variable that is domestically controllable. What is more, in small and cohesive societies with centrally organized trade unions, the negotiation of sensible wage rates is well within the ingenuity of politicians, businessmen and trade unionists who have the national interest at heart.

An important feature of the West European approach is the absence of dogma and ideological grandstanding which has promoted a climate of rationality and compromise. Katzenstein sums up:

> The strategy of the small European states is flexible, reactive, and incremental. It does not counter adverse change by shifting its costs to others abroad; it does not attempt to preempt change by ambitiously reordering the economy at home. Instead, the small European states continually improvise in living with change.[8]

This quotation echoes Lloyd Best's famous essay, 'Size and Survival' in which he suggests:

> Economic development is a problem of management — of timing, sequencing and manipulation in an unending effort to perceive or create, and in any case, to exploit a multiplicity of little openings and opportunities.[9]

The typical Caribbean approach to dealing with an uncertain and volatile environment has been almost the direct opposite to that described immediately above. Indeed, we have behaved more like big countries than like small countries. We have invited conflict with larger nations and multinationals by nationalizing foreign assets or unilaterally abrogating commercial agreements. Some of us have adopted autarchic strategies, seeking, in Clive Thomas's words, 'a convergence between production and consumption'.[10] Instead of trade liberalization we have put in place fierce exchange controls and import restrictions. Instead of minimizing intervention, our governments 'occupy the commanding heights of the economy', and sometimes virtually the entire economy.

Furthermore, instead of encouraging industrial efficiency, we have pampered inefficient public sector and private sector enterprises with quotas, import licenses, and other protectionist devices. Instead of economic and political cooperation, we have indulged ourselves in beggar-thy-neighbour devaluations and trade wars, and have pursued divergent economic and political strategies under the excuse of 'ideological pluralism'. To sum up, instead of nimbleness, we have promoted rigidity in our industrial and economic policies.

We have also paid inadequate attention to our balance of payments: In the case of both Guyana and Jamaica, a balance of payments crisis was triggered in the mid-1970s by policy decisions that wiped out foreign reserves in less than two years. In the case of Trinidad and Tobago, the Bobb Report had warned as early as 1978 that government expenditure patterns were unsustainable.[11] In Barbados, neither the steady decline in manufactured exports since 1984 nor the steady rise in external debt costs has deterred an inexorable rise in government expenditure.

Most notably, we have neglected to institutionalise an incomes policy as a technique of internal adjustment to developments in our external environment. We have preferred adjustments in real wages through traumatic devaluations that have thrown our economies into a state of chronic crisis, and condemned us to react rather than initiate and, in some cases, forced us to surrender control of our economies to international creditors.

Incomes Policy in Macroeconomic Management

There are four established objectives of macroeconomic policy: economic growth, full employment, price stability and balance of payments stability. In a famous theorem the Dutch economist and Nobel laureate, Jan Tinbergen, proved that the number of policy instruments must match the number of policy objectives being pursued. I would identify the minimum policy instruments required in the CARICOM situation as fiscal policy, monetary policy, incomes policy and exchange rate policy.

Fiscal policy is the policy instrument most closely associated with the objective of economic growth. If there is one thing we know about economic growth, it is that investment must increase relative to consumption as a proportion of GDP. Through their budgetary measures governments may regulate the allocation of income between national investment and consumption. As the major recipient of the national income, the government's own allocation to capital expenditures, relative to disbursements on wages, salaries and social services, will also be important.

Monetary policy is the instrument most closely associated with the objective of price stability. Ultimately price stability depends on the liquidity of consumers relative to the supply of goods and services. By controlling the availability of money and credit in the economy, the monetary authorities can regulate the rate of inflation. In the case of imperfect financial markets, differential interest rates may also be used to favour investment at the expense of consumption expenditures, and so promote economic growth.

Exchange rate policy is the tool that applies most specifically to balance of payments stability. If for some reason a disequilibrium develops between foreign payments and inflows, a change in the exchange rate may, in some circumstances, restore equilibrium. In the case of a deficit, a currency devaluation increases the cost of imports and reduces the price of exports. In the case of a balance of payments surplus, an upward revaluation of the currency produces the opposite effect.

Note that the three policy objectives of growth, price stability, and balance of payments equilibrium are interrelated. Economic growth promotes price stability by increasing availability of goods and services, thus easing the burden on monetary policy; it also increases the volume of exports by promoting equilibrium, or even surplus, in the balance of payments. (Surpluses, in moderation, are easier to deal with than deficits.) Balance of payments stability especially promotes a favourable climate for investment and growth, and thus reduces the burden on fiscal and monetary policy.

In a regime of floating exchange rates, currency adjustments take place continuously so that balance of payments equilibrium is automatically achieved. Increased expenditures on imports resulting from excessive wage increases quickly result in a fall in the value of the currency on the foreign exchange markets, bringing the balance of payments back into equilibrium. For small developing countries with thin foreign exchange markets, the operation of a floating exchange regime would be most hazardous. For this reason most of them peg their currency to a strong international currency or currency basket and make discrete changes in their exchange rate, should their currency move significantly out of equilibrium.

The CARICOM experience has also shown that frequent devaluations can be destabilizing and prejudicial to economic growth by creating a climate of uncertainty, and expectations of future devaluations. For this reason some CARICOM states, most notably The Bahamas, the OECS, and Barbados, have opted to hold the exchange rate variable steady, and rely on strict fiscal and monetary policies in order to maintain balance of payments equilibrium. The nature of their monetary arrangements best equips the OECS to conduct this policy: the inability of member states to use the Eastern Caribbean Central Bank to finance fiscal deficits imposes a salutary discipline on both monetary and fiscal policy in that sub-region.

Up until the 1960s, policies that promoted investment might also have been expected to stimulate employment. This became less true in the 1970s and 1980s. As Drucker explains, 'In the industrial economy itself, production has become uncoupled from employment.'[12] An additional policy instrument is therefore required to promote employment. That is where the incomes policy comes in. The restraint of wages slows the rate at which capital is substituted for labour in the production process. Moreover, by restraining wage increases, an incomes policy may prolong the viability of firms and give them time to adjust to economic change.

An incomes policy also complements the other three instruments. A lower rate of wage increase reduces the burden on fiscal and monetary policy by restraining disposable incomes. The slower growth in disposable incomes curbs inflationary pressures in the economy and restricts imports, thus assisting exchange rate policy. Post-Keynesian economists believe that, even in the highly developed market economies, an incomes policy is necessary to achieve price stability. As Alfred Eichner insisted:

> There is a maximum growth of wages which will still be non-inflationary, and it is this fact that requires that the more conventional fiscal and monetary policy instruments be supplemented by an incomes policy if inflation is to be brought under control.[13]

By dismissing an incomes policy, Dr Worrell throws the full burden of macroeconomic policy making on fiscal and monetary policy, since he agrees with pegged exchange rates for Caribbean states and also elects to hold the exchange rate variable steady. Effectively he is using two and one-half policy instruments to address four policy objectives. He deplores the chronically high levels of unemployment which plague the region but suggests no macroeconomic policy tool to deal with that policy objective.

Invoking the Tinbergen theorem, it would seem that the additional tool of an incomes policy is essential for dealing with the policy objective of full employment, especially when adjustment of real wages through a currency devaluation is ruled out. Without an incomes policy, the economy will adjust to wage increases in excess of productivity gains by shedding labour, even if aggregate demand and aggregate supply remain in equilibrium and foreign payments are in balance.

If the trend of excessive wage increases continues unchecked, domestic wage levels will eventually render exports uncompetitive and precipitate balance of payments disequilibrium. This imbalance may be adjusted through foreign borrowing for some time. However, when foreign exchange reserves run out, and national credit-worthiness is eroded, attempts to correct the balance of payments through tight monetary and fiscal policies will exacerbate, rather than alleviate, the employment problem, as the examples of Jamaica, Guyana, and Trinidad and Tobago have shown. Only a traumatic currency devaluation, or a series of devaluations, will restore the competitiveness of export tradeables.

The moral of the lesson is that in small open economies that elect to maintain stable exchange rates, the use of an incomes policy, formally or informally, is unavoidable. 'The question, then,' as Alfred Eichner argues even for developed economies, 'is not whether an incomes policy should be implemented but instead how such a policy can be made to work successfully.'[14]

An incomes policy is even more critical in promoting the international competitiveness of small open economies. Small size implies, first of all, narrow domestic markets and, as we have so painfully learned in the region, viable manufacturing enterprises cannot be sustained by our island markets and hardly by our regional market. Short of capital, as we are, and heavily dependent on imported raw materials and intermediate goods as inputs for our production systems, labour cost remains the only variable under our control; all other factors of production are available to our competitors on the same terms. It stands to reason, then, that wage increases in excess of productivity gains must inevitably lead to losses, and to the ultimate collapse of enterprises with the concomitant loss of jobs. The process is painfully well known in

Trinidad and Tobago, and Barbados where the decline in wage cost competitiveness has led to significant job losses. Similarly, a wage level that is too high will deter new investors as the sharp decline in new foreign business start-ups in Barbados also proves. Domestic firms are more prepared to trim labour costs and hold on as long as possible in defence of their original investment.

Excessive wage increases also depress profits and reduce the availability of funds for new investment, threatening the survival of the enterprise, the jobs of its staff, and the contributions of its export earnings to the balance of payments. A well conceived incomes policy would address this problem. A conversation with a trade unionist, which Peter Drucker recounts, vividly illustrates the need for wage restraint:

> It is our proudest boast, [the mass-production unionist said,] that the total wage package in our industry is some 30 per cent to 40 per cent higher than the average wage package in American manufacturing. But would there be record unemployment in our industry, approaching the levels of the Depression, if that 30 per cent to 40 per cent had been put into plant modernization instead of into wages and benefits? I know that all my colleagues in the union leadership ask themselves this question. But not one dares come out with it into the open — he wouldn't last ten minutes if he did.[15]

That is why we need government intervention into the wage-determination process.

Aspects of Incomes Policy

An incomes policy may be described as a continuing program, whether formal or informal, for the regulation of wages and salaries so as to reflect changes in productivity. It is a process of continuous dialogue and negotiations between government, business and labour unions, with government acting as honest broker, and final arbiter where consensus cannot be achieved. In this respect, to quote Christopher Saunders,

> Incomes policy cannot be regarded simply as an instrument of economic management, short term or long term, on the same plane as monetary policy. It is political in the widest sense.[16]

The incomes policy is a multi-faceted instrument, hence its versatility and effectiveness. I have identified ten measures which might be used at some time or other in the application of an incomes policy:

'Wage-cut or Voluntary Give-back'

Wage cuts are usually imposed by governments in extreme circumstances as a means of saving public sector jobs, as was the case recently in Trinidad and Tobago. Such a drastic measure can be expected to influence wage determination in the private sector. Both Curacao and Aruba have used employment cuts in civil service and public enterprise wages and salaries as a substitute for a currency devaluation, the effects of which they considered unpredictable and more damaging. American trade unions, especially in the steel, automotive and airline industries, have frequently agreed to enormous 'give-backs' in the form of reduced wages and benefits in order to ensure the survival of the enterprise.

Wage Freeze and Price Control

Wage freezes are frequently used as a shock treatment to halt spiralling inflation. They are usually imposed in tandem with price freezes. Price freezes are difficult to sustain over long periods except in time of national emergency. However, they can provide a welcome breathing space within which more comprehensive and sustainable policies can be put in place.

Wage Restraint

Wage restraint is based on the principle that wage and salary increases should be related to gains in productivity. Indeed, the traditional practice of linking wage and price increases has no basis in economic logic; the only means of curbing inflation is to ensure that wage and salary increases fall short of the rate of increase in prices. In periods of declining sales, wage restraint reduces the incentive of management to lay off workers in the short run, or to substitute capital for labour over the long-term.

Wage Inflation

The establishment of a statutory minimum wage technically falls under the rubric of incomes policy. In a rare move in the 1970s, the government of Singapore deliberately stimulated a rise in wages for the declared purpose of squeezing low-wage industries out of business. It had concluded that the use of Singaporean labour in low-tech jobs was uneconomical. This policy created difficulties during the 1981–1982 recession.

Differential Wage Increases

Under an incomes policy governments may deliberately promote wage and salary differentials in order to stimulate the supply of strategic skills. Here in the Caribbean, especially in Barbados, the practice of granting progressively lower percentage increases to senior staff has so compressed wage scales as to provide little incentive for senior officers to take on increased responsibility.

Trade-offs

Governments seek to trade cheap social services or income tax concessions that raise real incomes in return for reduced wage increases. This technique is quite common in Western Europe. The late Prime Minister Tom Adams tried this once in Barbados — without success.

Employee Share Ownership Plans (ESOPs)

ESOPs, a form of payment in kind, have become very popular in the US. They reduce cash payments to employees and improve the cash-flow of the enterprise. In effect, the employees trade off current earnings in return for job security, future earnings, and a share in the management of the enterprise.

Flexible Wages

It is the practice in many Japanese enterprises to pay a relatively low base wage, with an annual bonus variable with the profitability of the firm. This reduces the pressure on the enterprise to lay off workers in periods of declining profits.

Retreading

The retraining of workers enables them to earn higher wages from their improved skills. 'Retreaded' workers may be moved out of 'sunset' into 'sunrise' industries, with the cost being met entirely by government, or shared between government and private enterprise. Sweden is most famous for this practice.

Corporate Strengthening

Government subsidies are sometimes extended to failing enterprises to assist them in restructuring or merger programmes as a means of restoring their viability. The purpose of this measure is to protect jobs and increase the future earnings of workers.

Conclusion and Recommendations

The measures described in the last section are not likely to succeed if applied, as hitherto in CARICOM, in a piecemeal and haphazard fashion. An incomes policy is a comprehensive programme of indefinite duration in which the major participants in the wage determination process conduct ongoing study and review of labour markets, and consultation and negotiation about appropriate wage and salary levels in the economy. In short, an incomes policy must be institutionalized.

Incomes policy formation, essentially a political process, is quite practicable within most of CARICOM owing to the fact that both business and labour are already centrally organized. The failure of the British Labour Party to institute an incomes policy in the 1970s was mainly due to the extreme fragmentation of the British trade union movement.

The purpose of an incomes policy is not to set rates for every individual job, but to establish guidelines, ceilings and floors. The majority of salaries and wages, especially in small and family businesses, would be market determined. Sometimes, and only if absolutely necessary, minimum wages would be established.

The preconditions for the institutionalization and successful operation of an incomes policy are as follows:

> A consensus must emerge in the society at large that the wage rate is an important factor in the achievement of economic growth, price stability, balance of payments equilibrium, and full employment; and that it is critical to our international competitiveness. In this respect it would help greatly if Caribbean economists would accept that the wage rate is an administered price, which depends very much on the attitudes brought to the negotiating table by business, trade union and government officials. The wage rate does not emerge from the blind workings of the market.

Moreover, it is the only factor of production over which we may collectively exert considerable control.

➤ Governments must take the lead in the institutionalization of incomes policies. They must be continuously involved in the wage determination process; they cannot regard themselves as *dei ex machina* who intervene only after negotiations have become hopelessly deadlocked.

➤ The trade union movement should liberate itself from obsolete images of commerce and industry in which management and labour are perceived as natural opponents. This would enable us to move our industrial relations forward from confrontational zero-sum conflicts into the arena of positive-sum games.

➤ Business must similarly develop greater openness in its dealings with staff and trade unions. Participative management should be gradually developed, and staff encouraged to take a stake in the enterprise through ESOPs.

➤ Government, in close cooperation with labour and business, should promote greater flexibility in our labour markets, so that improved operation of market forces may progressively reduce the burden on incomes policies. For example, experiments with flexible wages might be initiated. Pension rights should be made more portable. Severance payment schemes should be reformed so as to facilitate mergers and restructuring of ailing businesses. Programmes should be developed for retraining workers with obsolete skills, and opportunities provided for low-paid workers to improve their skills and marketability. Finally, the flexibility of our labour markets would be greatly enhanced if we could eliminate the plethora of impediments to the free movement of skilled labour within CARICOM.

Table 1
Average Direct Labour Cost by Country

Country	Wage (US dollars per hour)	Fringes[a] (percent)	Total[b] (US dollars per hour)	Effective[c] (US dollars per hour)	Percentage of Barbados Rate
Barbados	1.61	35	2.17	2.53	100
Costa Rica	0.86	50	1.29	1.40	59
Dominican Republic	0.60	45	0.87	0.99	40
Mexico	0.75	37	1.03	1.44	47
Puerto Rico	5.76	41	7.66	8.79	353

a. Fringe as percentage of direct labour cost
b. Total includes only required fringes plus base pay
c. Total pay per actual hour worked

Source: Mentor Interviews, *Mentor International.*

Table 2
Comparison of Indirect Monthly Salaries (US$)

Job	Barbados	Costa Rica	Dominican Republic	Mexico	Puerto Rico
Product Manager	650	740	583	872	4,500
Quality Control Manager	n.a.	594	1,083	734	4,000
General Accountant	1,200	440	975	1,190	2,916
Analyst	n.a.	158	100	311	1,720
Computer Operator	550	250	n.a.	265	1,273
Secretary	550	300	866	265	1,600
Clerk	400	170	100	140	860

n.a. = Total pay per actual hour worked

Source: Mentor Interviews, *Mentor International.*

Table 3
Wage Rates of Selected Countries

Country	Wage Rate (US dollars per hour)
Antigua and Barbuda	1.25
Barbados	1.20–2.50
British Virgin Islands	1.30
China	.13
Costa Rica	1.20
Dominica	.70
Dominican Republic	.50
Grenada	.73
Hong Kong	.80
Malaysia	.50
Montserrat	1.00
St. Kitts and Nevis	1.00
St. Lucia	.75
St. Vincent and the Grenadines	.93
Sri Lanka	.20
Thailand	.30

Source : Eastern Caribbean Investment Promotion Service.

Table 4
Wage Rates in the Garment Industries of Selected Countries, 1986

Country	Wages (US dollars per hour)	Fringes[a]	Percentage of US Productivity
Antigua	1.25	28	60–65
Bahamas	2.10	25	65–70
Barbados	2.30	26	70–75[b]
Dominica	0.83	26	55–60
Grenada	0.75	22	60–65
Guyana	0.70	30	55–60
Jamaica	1.09	17	65–70
Montserrat	0.95	24	60–65
St. Kitts and Nevis	0.90	24	60–65
St. Lucia	0.95	27	60–65
St. Vincent	1.15	26	60–65
Trinidad and Tobago	1.66	37	70–75
Costa Rica	0.78	33	60–65
Dominican Republic	0.78	22	65–70
Guatemala	0.89	29	60–65
Honduras	0.83	46	60–65
Panama	1.58	40	70–75
Puerto Rico	4.28	25	85
Haiti	0.58	40	75

a. Fringe as percentage of direct labour cost
b. In US owned and managed companies in Barbados this ranges from 85 to 95 per cent

Source: Bobbin Consulting Corp, 1986.

Delivered at a seminar sponsored by the Caribbean Development Bank and the World Bank Economic Development Institute Barbados, May 22–24, 1989 and published in *Increasing the International Competitiveness of Exports from Caribbean Countries*, eds., Yin-Kann Wen and Jayshree Sengupta (Washington, DC: World Bank, 1991)

Notes

1. My position on incomes policy is more elaborately spelt out in Chapter 7, 'The Balance of Payments Crisis in the Caribbean: Which Way Out?'.

2. Eric St Cyr, 'Wages, Prices and Balance of Payments: Trinidad & Tobago, 1956–1976', *Social and Economic Studies* 30, no.4 (December 1981): 111–31.

3. DeLisle Worrell, *Small Island Economies: Structure and Performance in the English Speaking Caribbean since 1970* (New York: Praeger, 1987), 217–18.

4. Sir Arthur Lewis, *Daily Gleaner, Special Supplement,* September 1964.

5. Peter J. Katzenstein, *Small States in World Markets: Industrial Policy in Europe* (Ithaca & London: Cornell University Press, 1985), 44.

6. Alice Bourneuf, as quoted in *Small States in World Markets*, 40.

7. Peter J. Katzenstein, *Small States in World Markets*, 52.

8. Ibid., 79.

9. Lloyd Best, 'Size and Survival', *New World, Guyana Independence Issue* (1970).

10. Clive Y. Thomas, *Dependence and Transformation: The Economics of the Transition to Socialism* (New York: Monthly Review Press, 1974), 123.

11. Euric Bobb, (Chairman), 'The Report of the Committee to Review Government Expenditure' (submitted to the Trinidad and Tobago government, October 1978).

12. Peter F. Drucker, *The Frontiers of Management* (New York: Truman Talley Books, and E.P. Dutton), 21.

13. Alfred S. Eichner, *Towards a New Economics: Essays in Post Keynesian and Institutionalist Theory* (Armonk, New York: M.E. Sharpe Inc, 1985), 209.

14. Ibid., 210.

15. Peter F. Drucker, *The Frontiers of Management*, 208–9.

16. Christopher Saunders, as quoted in *Small States in World Markets*, 53.

16

CRITICAL ISSUES OF NATIONAL PRODUCTIVITY

When Governor Francis invited me to organize a seminar on 'productivity' some time ago, I detected a distinct passion in his voice. You may very well ask why a central bank governor should feel so strongly about productivity. The *Economist* explains it well: 'Productivity growth is probably the single most important indicator of an economy's health: it drives real incomes, inflation, interest rates, profits and share prices.'[1] In fact, Dr Alan Greenspan, Chairman of the US Federal Reserve System, has no doubt that it was the sharp rise in productivity, arising from revolutionary technologies in computers and telecommunications, which underpinned the longest economic upswing in US economic history (1992–2001). People spoke then of the 'Goldilocks economy', characterized by high economic growth, low unemployment, low inflation, and a strong currency. There is obviously an element of self-interest in the Governor's sponsorship of this seminar: a sharp surge in the productivity of the Bahamian economy would transform his presently strenuous job into a 'cake-walk'.

My presentation seeks to illuminate important issues related to productivity in the national economy. We begin with a basic definition of productivity. This is followed by a discussion of the dynamics of productivity. Thirdly, we focus on the grave responsibility of management for the continuous increase in productivity. Fourthly, we examine the critical role of trade unions in the drive for greater productivity. Fifthly, we explain government's special responsibility for creating an environment that nourishes productivity growth. Finally, we demonstrate the central importance of productivity as a factor in macroeconomic policy making.

What is Productivity?

'Productivity' is a slippery but indispensable concept in economic management, and is widely used by economists and managers. Professor Solomon Fabricant describes it as follows:

> Productivity refers to a comparison between the quantity of goods or services produced and the quantity of resources employed in turning out these goods or services. When the same resources that were employed in the past now produce more than they did before, we agree that productivity has increased.[2]

Productivity then is measured by changes over time in the ratio of two indices — output and input. Using this statistical technique, economists are able to track the efficiency of a production system over time or compare the efficiency of one production system with that of another. Diagram 2 shows a simple model of the production process. Note that if the quantity of inputs used is doubled and this results in twice the quantity of outputs, there would have been no change in productivity.

Economists have traditionally treated land, labour and capital as the basic factors of production. 'Land' subsumes natural resources such as mines, rivers, arable land and, in the case of the Caribbean, sun, sand and sea. In the preparation of national statistics 'labour' usually refers to hourly paid workers, the reason being that the hours worked by salary owners is less responsive to changes in output than that of wage-earners.

There are two main concepts used by economic statisticians in the measurement of productivity: labour productivity and total productivity. In the first of these concepts total output is compared with total man-hours spent in production, and is expressed as 'labour productivity'. In the second case, aggregate output is compared with total input, that is, with all the resources of production, each appropriately weighted, and is usually expressed as 'output per unit of labour and capital' or 'total productivity', or more pretentiously as 'total factor productivity'.

For specific policy-making purposes, such as the fixing of wage and inflation guideposts, government, business and labour may wish to have productivity data on various economic sectors or industries. The US Bureau of Labour Statistics, the world's most sophisticated producer of productivity statistics, publishes productivity and costs statistics for various elements of the US economy, such as quarterly and annual output per hour and unit costs for US business, non-farm business, and manufacturing business. These statistics not only inform national decision makers, but also enable individual enterprises to compare their productivity performance against the national average.

Economic statisticians are painfully aware that the productivity measurements they calculate are merely estimates, and are subject to error. Moreover, the concepts of labour and capital themselves are far from precise. Because of the work of Professor Theodore Schultz, for which he gained the Nobel Prize in 1979, economists have known for decades that considerable capital, in the form of education, training and experience, is embedded in labour, and have coined the term 'human capital'. Modern economists consider human capital the most productive form of capital. But statistics on productivity do provide us with a pretty good idea of trends and relative values so that we will certainly do better with than without them.

The Dynamics of Productivity

Let us revisit our basic production model in which inputs of land, labour and capital are introduced into the process and transformed into outputs of goods and services. Productivity gains then depend upon the choice and quality of inputs and the manner in which they are combined — the 'mix' or, more elegantly, the technology.

Choice and Quality of Inputs

Productivity gains may be obtained by improvements in the quality of inputs. In the case of land; that is, natural resources, ores of higher quality may be discovered, or one type of input replaced by another; for example, the replacement of steel by aluminium. In the case of labour, better educated or more skilful workers may become available, or workers may gain experience on the job or become more highly motivated. In the case of capital, more modern equipment may become available, rendering the old obsolete.

Technological Change

Prior to the Industrial Revolution (1650–1750), productivity gains were achieved through a myriad of incremental operational improvements, usually made by relatively uneducated individuals over long periods of time. It is difficult for us today to appreciate the productivity gains brought about in agriculture by progressive improvements in the design of the plough, or the adoption of the horse collar, which made it easier for the animals to pull heavier loads. Occasionally, seemingly simple discoveries, like that of the wheel thousands of years ago, have had far-reaching implications for economic growth over the centuries. Indeed, the failure of civilizations in the Americas to learn of the wheel until the arrival of the Spaniards in the sixteenth century must have exerted a tremendous drag on their economic growth.

It was the cumulative effect of numerous improvements in agriculture; (for example, new crops), in workshops; (for example, Arkwright's spinning jenny), and in commercial practice; (for example, double-entry accounting first used by the Venetians), that gave rise to the Industrial Revolution and to the market-based capitalist system. Such improvements were usually made by clever and persistent craftsmen; even a renowned scientist like Sir Isaac Newton, in the seventeenth century, depended more on native genius than on formally acquired knowledge.

The mini-industrial revolution of the late nineteenth century drew heavily on formal scientific knowledge; even so, some of the industrial breakthroughs that so dramatically raised productivity were the triumphs of 'gifted tinkers', like Thomas Edison, who invented the light bulb, and Alexander Graham Bell, who gave us the telephone, rather than of highly trained university graduates.

Beginning with the Manhattan Project, code name for the American development of the atomic bomb, and continuing with the recent revolutionary developments in computers, telecommunications and materials science, today's productivity gains are increasingly based on high-powered scientific research in corporate and university laboratories conducted by 'knowledge workers', as Peter Drucker, the 94-year-old doyen of management gurus, was first to term them. He warns that not only will productivity gains increasingly require the employment of knowledge workers, but also the application of knowledge to the work of manual workers. For there will still be abundant scope in the New Information Age for incremental improvements in the workplace.

Management and Productivity

'The developing countries are not underdeveloped,' argues Drucker, 'they are undermanaged.'[3] It is management that decides on the choice of production inputs and on the technology to be used in their processing. Drucker explains: 'The continuous improvement of productivity is one of management's most important jobs.'[4]

Of the economic inputs — land, labour and capital — labour is at once the most productive and the most problematic. Whereas natural resources are depletable and capital becomes obsolescent, the capital embedded in labour, that is, human capital, can be continuously upgraded and made more productive through training and life-long education. But the creativity of human beings, which makes possible continual innovations and improvements at the workplace, also renders them prickly and difficult to manage. That is why the handling of labour requires resort to the behavioural 'science' of management.

I have too frequently heard regional managers ascribe low productivity to the laziness of workers; the same workers do two or three jobs when they get to the United States. Another common excuse of failing top management is that middle management is weak. Why then isn't it upgraded or removed? Workers must be made to work, not harder and harder, but smarter and smarter; and only management can get them to do so — through direction, training, motivation, improved equipment, and an environment that stimulates and rewards the initiative required for continuous innovation. This is especially true for the 'knowledge worker', who is needed if management is to exploit the new technologies. As Drucker observes, the knowledge worker 'is not productive under the spur of fear; only self-motivation and self-direction can make him productive. He has to be achieving to produce at all.'[5]

But management is not only responsible for productivity within the production process, it must also anticipate and respond to adverse developments in the environment — inflation, currency depreciation, domestic and international unrest, not to speak of relations with trade unions.

Finally, without reliable measurements of productivity, management will be like a man driving in the dark. But for him, total productivity and labour productivity statistics, though essential, will not suffice. Management will also need to measure the productivity of capital, and the relationship between capital and labour costs; and, of course, farmers will be especially interested in the productivity of their arable land. For there is no one perfect productivity measurement.

Productivity and the Trade Union

The issue of national productivity presents the regional trade union movement with a most challenging paradox, the resolution of which will require a radical adjustment of its modus operandi and, indeed, a redefinition of its role in the economy and society at large. Some trade unions, both in The Bahamas and in Barbados, have already begun to move in this direction, but much remains to be done. Simply put, the dilemma is this: whereas the traditional goal of trade unions has been to secure higher wages and job security for their workers, enterprises in today's increasingly competitive global economy must be continuously raising labour productivity if they are to remain in business, and this will often involve shedding labour. Should trade unions press for unrealistic wage rates without the acceptance of lay-offs, firms will either go out of business or relocate elsewhere, with the loss of *all* jobs.

In the first 25 years or so following World War II, pressure by Caribbean trade unions for higher wages was justified by the grossly inequitable distribution of incomes and abominable working conditions in the colonies. Significant increases in wages and vast improvements in working and living conditions were made feasible by guaranteed foreign markets for regional commodities, and by generous development aid. Nor did trade unions hesitate to use the strike weapon to appropriate a greater proportion of the economic surplus. Trade unions were especially successful in raising wages and salaries in the public sector, since they had often served as the vanguard of independence movements, were often allied with political parties, and because many trade union officials sat in Parliament, many of them becoming prime ministers. Besides, governments were naturally reluctant to see essential public services interrupted and readily bowed to trade union demands.

This situation has changed considerably over the last three decades. Guaranteed markets and quotas are rapidly becoming a thing of the past, while new trade agreements are increasingly based on reciprocity, and foreign aid is rapidly drying up. Furthermore, the oil crises of the 1970s, and the consequent debt crisis, broke the backs of some CARICOM economies, especially Guyana and Jamaica, resulting in massive currency devaluations. The general economic weakness throughout the region has led to high rates of unemployment in the private sector, while acute fiscal stress has reduced the power of trade unions to obtain significant wage increases for public sector workers. Indeed, they have had to accept considerable lay-offs from the civil service and, in the case of Barbados, wage cuts as well.

It is of little consolation to Caribbean trade unionists that American workers have also been the victims of massive corporate 'down-sizing', especially in the airline industry where tens of thousands have been laid off, and the remainder forced to make deep wage concessions to management in a desperate attempt to keep companies afloat. Even so a number of large airlines have been forced to merge or close.

What are trade unions to do? First of all, the new realities of globalization require that they place the national interest above narrow trade union interests, and work together with business and government to promote a competitive national economy.

Secondly, they should recognize that the external competitiveness of the national economy requires continuous gains in labour productivity.

Thirdly, they should accept that external national competitiveness is inconsistent with unrealistic wage settlements.

Fourthly, they should cooperate with both government and business in raising national productivity.

Fifthly, they should press for national policies leading to the creation of new businesses, and programmes for retraining workers idled by rising productivity so that they may more easily find alternative jobs.

The Role of Government in Productivity Growth

Government plays a dual role in productivity growth. The first role derives from its ultimate responsibility for the performance of the national economy; we call this its macroeconomic role. Its second role stems from the fact that government employs a greater proportion of national resources than any other economic player — about a third of GDP in most CARICOM countries — and is usually the largest single employer in the country, providing jobs for more than 40 per cent of the workforce in some cases. This is its microeconomic role

Macroeconomic Role

Let us look at diagram 3, a more elaborate version of diagram 2. Diagram 3 shows two areas surrounding the production process: the inner area represents the domestic environment of the process, while the outer area represents the global environment. The *first macroeconomic task of government* is to enhance, as far as it can, the quality of the three basic inputs into the national production process — land, labour and capital — and hence the potential productivity of all economic units that make use of these inputs.

➢ Enhancement of land involves programmes of conservation of national resources, such as water, forests, ore deposits, and so forth, which provide the raw materials for various industries.

➢ Enhancement of labour involves policies for improving the welfare of the working population as a whole — personal security, public health, leisure facilities and human rights

➢ The enrichment of capital, the most complex input, is most challenging of all. It subsumes financial capital, human capital, and social capital.

➢ Enhancement of *financial capital* involves the regulation of the money and banking systems, the development of capital markets, and the injection of public funds in circumstances where crucial financing is not forthcoming from private sources.

➢ Enriching the productivity of *human capital* requires generous expenditures on education and health. Senior UWI officials are especially concerned that the region lags far behind the 'East Asian Tigers', like Taiwan, South Korea and Singapore, in the supply of tertiary graduates. The Caribbean private sector should emulate the practice of its American counterpart in providing systematic and sustained support for institutions of higher learning. With respect to health, it is obvious that healthy workers are more productive than unhealthy ones. The AIDS pandemic and the SARS epidemic have in recent years demonstrated what a devastating effect a health crisis can have on national, regional and, indeed, international economic productivity.

➢ *Social capital* is one of those national resources whose value is appreciated only when it has been destroyed, leading to economic collapse and social and political chaos. The tangible element of social capital, also known as social overhead capital, is the nation's physical infrastructure of public utility plants, highways, bridges, etc. which underpins the productive process. The intangible element of social capital connotes those characteristics which enable citizens to cooperate productively in both formal and informal situations — tolerance, civility and a sense of community which promotes social cohesion. Professor Havelock Brewster has attributed Barbados's superior economic performance over that of Jamaica to the smaller island's richer endowment of social capital. Political parties in the region should especially resist the temptation to play the ethnic card in election campaigns, and maintain a continuing dialogue with opposition parties and civil society.

The *second macroeconomic task of government* in the fostering of productivity growth lies in the regulation of the domestic environment of the production process. The maintenance of law and the suppression of crime are obvious imperatives. Jamaica and Guyana provide clear evidence of the tremendous economic cost of criminal activity.

A *third macroeconomic task* is the insulation of the productive sectors from adverse developments in the global economy. In this regard, currency stability, as the experience of The Bahamas and Barbados has clearly demonstrated, constitutes the most important defence against crises in global financial markets. Neo-liberal economists now grudgingly concede that a pegged exchange rate and liberally administered capital controls are highly appropriate policies for small developing countries with underdeveloped financial markets. We in The Bahamas and Barbados have known that for over a quarter of a century. That's why we have flourished.

As small countries, it is also critical that we in CARICOM pool our resources in negotiations with major powers, and forge common positions on international issues. We should put maximum support behind the Regional Negotiating Machinery. We certainly need to recognize that small countries need better diplomats than do big ones.

Microeconomic Role

The microeconomic role of government derives from its responsibility for the direction of the civil service bureaucracy and for the operations of state-owned corporations, both profit-oriented and not-for-profit. There is enormous scope throughout the region for increasing the productivity of the civil service which is presently associated with log-jams, delays, poor customer service and widespread wastage, and, at times, corruption. What is more, gains in civil service productivity would lead to disproportionately large gains in productivity throughout the national economy, since government provides so many essential services to households and firms; for example, water, transportation, education, health services and security. But late payment of government debts to business enterprises is perhaps the most egregious obstacle to productivity among small and medium-sized enterprises.

There has been much talk about civil service reform throughout the region, but little progress has been made. The *three most urgent measures* required are:

- A rigorous review of colonial regulations established for imperial control rather than the promotion of productivity.
- Decentralization of decision making so as to minimize log-jams and bottlenecks, and a recognition that timeliness in project implementation is itself a prolific source of productivity, for time is the scarcest and least substitutable resource of all.
- The enhancement of the considerable human capital embodied in our well educated and industrious civil servants through the employment of the new information and integrated systems technologies.

Improved governance of state-owned government enterprises is equally crucial. The failure to exclude political considerations from operational issues has cost the region billions of dollars since CARICOM states gained their independence. The failure of state-owned enterprises to submit audited financial accounts for years on end is scandalous. Most important of all, ministers of government in the region must come to recognize that operational autonomy is the sine qua non of effective management. The *role of ministers* is clear:

> to set goals and establish policy parameters; select managers on the basis of their capacity to carry out the required tasks; establish performance criteria; insist on timely reporting, especially of financial results; punish and remove, if necessary, managers who do not perform.

In short, management must be made accountable for results.

The establishment of performance criteria is admittedly difficult in public sector operations where inputs are costed by the market, but outputs are distributed to the general public at subsidized rates or even free of cost. Moreover, even in profit-oriented state-owned enterprises, national policy may legitimately preclude a strategy of profit maximization. But it is always possible in any particular operational situation to devise measures of performance that indicate whether we are doing better or worse than we did before.

Productivity and Macroeconomic Management

The factor of productivity is inevitably an important consideration in the formulation of macroeconomic policy. There are four well established objectives of macroeconomic policy: economic growth, full employment, price stability and balance of payments equilibrium.

Economic Growth

In a closed economic system economic growth could theoretically be achieved by simply introducing slack resources of land, labour and capital into production without any change in technology. However, when full employment of all resources was reached the economy would stagnate and then go into decline in the absence of surplus capital for investment. Productivity gains are therefore central to the generation of new capital for investment and growth in any economy.

Full Employment

In the increasingly competitive global economy, enterprises that cannot match the prices of foreign competitors must either raise their productivity or go out of business, adding to the unemployment rolls.

Price Stability

Inflation occurs when the demand for goods and services outstrips supply. The preferred antidote for inflation is an increase in productivity so as to restore the equilibrium between supply and demand with demand.

Balance of Payments Equilibrium

Highly open economies with low productivity are typically unable to pay for imports of essential goods and services, or to service foreign debt — leading to the collapse of their balance of payments — with dire economic consequences. This hypothesis has been amply confirmed by the chronic disequilibrium conditions prevailing in some member states of CARICOM.

Diagram 2
Production System

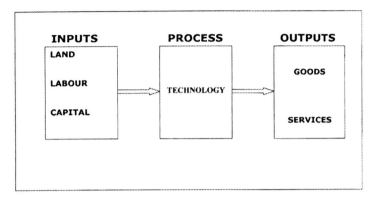

N.B. Value is realized outside the process. Within the process there are only costs!

Diagram 3
Environments of the Production System

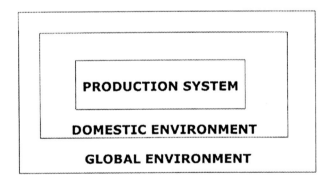

First presented at Productivity Seminar, Central Bank of The Bahamas, Nassau, The Bahamas May 19, 2003

Notes

1. *Economist,* 'Economics Focus – A Productivity Primer', November 6, 2004.

2. Solomon Fabricant, *A Primer on Productivity* (New York: Random House, 1969), 3–4.

3. Peter Drucker, *Management: Tasks, Responsibilities, Practices* (New York: Harper & Row, 1973), 14.

4. Ibid., 111.

5. Ibid., 176.

17

MANAGEMENT, EDUCATION AND NATIONAL POLICIES

The text of my address, to borrow an ecclesiastical term, is taken from Peter Drucker's definitive work, *Management: Tasks, Responsibilities, Practices*.[1] 'Economic and social development means above all management.' Economists in the 1950s identified the establishment of modern institutions as a prerequisite of economic development in the Third World. However, they paid very little attention to management in the process of institutional development. In our region, ideological fervour and political commitment were widely believed, during the 1960s and the 1970s, to be the wellsprings of economic development.

From the mid-1970s I had the temerity to suggest that management was the critical element in economic development. In a 1975 paper entitled 'The Economic Development of Small Countries: A Managerial Approach',[2] I spoke of the 'managerial imperative' in economic development. I suggested that economic development required the diffusion of sound management practices throughout the entire economy — in government, in business enterprises, in hospitals, in schools, in the church and even in our homes. I opposed nationalization, not on ideological grounds, but because it implied the creation of larger organizations whose complexity would overwhelm the meagre managerial resources of Caribbean states. The collapse of the Marxist and 'dependence' paradigms in the Caribbean has cleared the way for the acceptance of the 'managerial imperative' in economic development. Indeed, this management development programme in which we are engaged, is proof of a growing recognition of the crucial importance of management in development. I shall argue that regional economic development requires not merely the application of new managerial techniques, but the diffusion of a management culture throughout our societies.

We begin with an exploration of the roots of regional underdevelopment. Secondly, I shall discuss various aspects of management as they relate to economic development. Thirdly, I shall reflect upon the phenomenon of a management culture. Fourthly, I shall indicate the potential contribution of government to the promotion of a management culture. I conclude with recommendations on the institutional framework required for the development of a management culture.

Why We Are Underdeveloped

Why are Caribbean islands underdeveloped? I shall let Peter Drucker speak once again: 'There are no underdeveloped countries, only undermanaged ones.' Management is the means by which economic inputs, such as labour, capital and natural resources, can be converted into outputs whose value exceeds that of the original inputs. Here in the Caribbean we have managed our economic inputs so indifferently that the value of the outputs — our gross domestic product (GDP), — is now far less than the value of our original inputs. On a per capita basis, few countries other than Israel have absorbed more capital than the CARICOM Caribbean over the last two decades in the form of grants, loans and windfall earnings. Yet, we are collectively poorer today than we were in 1970, with a foreign debt of over US$5 billion for the region — about US$1,000 for each individual. We must seek explanations for our failures in the poor quality of our management at all levels of society.

Why did our management fail us so comprehensively in the 1970s and the 1980s? Admittedly, the 70s were difficult times. Speaking in 1979 at the University of the West Indies, I said: 'If you thought the 70s were rough, wait until you see the 80s!' In fact, the 80s turned out to be far worse than I had anticipated. Yet, there were some countries, notably the four tigers of the Pacific rim — Hong Kong, Singapore, Taiwan and South Korea — less endowed in natural, human and political resources than the Caribbean, which flourished in those years.

Our first misfortune, as I have hinted earlier, was in the selection of inappropriate paradigms of political economy — Marxism, and the 'dependence' thesis of the Caribbean New World School — both of which downplayed the role of management. Secondly, and more seriously, the management models which we did utilize proved totally inadequate to the needs of the times. We have inherited three basic management models: The family business model, the plantation model and the British civil service model — the bureaucratic model.

None of the above models fills the bill in turbulent times. Family management relies heavily on the ability of a single man, and frequently the enterprise does not survive him. The plantation model, with its flat hierarchical structure and an army of workers performing far below their intellectual capacities, is also limited and rigid, and succeeds only in an environment of preferential markets. The bureaucratic model, while performing repetitive tasks quite efficiently, is unsuited to a dynamic environment. For this reason creole Caribbean societies have done poorly in the development of effective corporate structures — the form of organization best suited to the perilous times in which we live. There are less than 50 indigenous corporations in the CARICOM Caribbean substantial enough to be listed on our three stock exchanges. Too many of our enterprises stumble at the threshold leading from small business to corporate enterprise.

Moreover, a strange mutation has appeared on our organizational scene — the corrupted bureaucracy. Statutory corporations were originally established to overcome the rigidity of the bureaucracy. Yet, they have been subjected to civil service type regulations and are extensively manned by former civil servants. Furthermore, positions far below the level of top management are subject to the approval of ministers who can at times be as capricious as plantation owners or single proprietors. It is no wonder then that the institutional landscape of the region is littered with the ruins of failed or dysfunctional public sector institutions.

Aspects of Management

Management is the art of achieving a common purpose through people and in the service of people. There are three aspects of management on which I shall focus: the scientific, the moral and the cultural.

The *scientific aspect* covers the managerial principles and techniques derived from the systematic study of organizations. These are readily accessible in textbooks and are being taught with increasing effectiveness in our university and in the training programmes of our institutes of management.

Because management is by, through, and for people, it is of necessity a humane activity. As such, it automatically assumes a *moral* dimension. Good managers then must be concerned about the ethics of their vocation: What are their responsibilities to clients and to their customers? What are the effects of their decisions on the overall economy, on society, on the environment? These are difficult and evolving problems which are never satisfactorily answered and yet require continuous study.

The practice of management also takes place in a *cultural context* which is conditioned by geographical, historical, religious, ethnic, political and other influences. The effective manager must be sensitive to, and make allowance for, these multifarious influences. He is therefore most dependent for his insights on several academic disciplines — economics, history, sociology, theology, anthropology, political science and, of course, moral philosophy. It is for this reason that the study of management is most appropriately located in the University.

Management and Culture

Whereas science is, ideally at least, value-free, and while morality is universal in its application, culture is time-and-space-specific. For this reason, cultural considerations will feature heavily in the design of any national policy on management education. This will be especially true in the Caribbean, where history and our social scientists have conspired to create a distinctly anti-management culture. Management, in the Caribbean mind, is generally identified with slavery, the plantation, the foreign corporation and with exploitation. The trade union, which spearheaded the drive for economic justice and political independence in the region, is the legitimate protagonist. Management is the dragon to be slain.

This is in marked contrast with the United States, which possesses an unmistakable management culture. Whereas American trade unions constitute a minor sub-culture, Caribbean trade unions dictate to governments. As President Calvin Coolidge put it, 'The business of America is business.' American managers and entrepreneurs are held in high repute: the autobiographies of Lee Iacocca and Donald Trump are best sellers. Indeed, a familiarity with management practices and the manifestation of managerial attitudes permeate American society. One of my students at Hofstra University excused his tardiness in completing an assignment with the explanation that his business was making so much money that he didn't have time to do his homework! In his book, *The Rommel Papers*,[3] the great German commander recognized the fighting qualities of the American GI. But what impressed him most was American managerial and logistical virtuosity.

By contrast, the Caribbean might be described as possessing a distinctly political culture. Politics permeates the very fabric of our societies. Journalists report faithfully the most platitudinous statements of politicians. At the same time managers, at even the highest levels, are not regarded as being capable of professional conduct, and are therefore expected to sabotage the programmes of incoming administrations. Indeed, management is viewed as so unimportant a factor that top executive positions in state-owned enterprises go unfilled for many years. Can you imagine the position of chief executive officer remaining vacant at IBM for even a week?

Cultural considerations will also determine the style in which management principles are applied and managerial techniques implemented. The Japanese have been especially successful at adapting western management science to their cultural context. They have replaced American individualism with Japanese consensus. We, too, need to guard against the uncritical acceptance of foreign management styles. The familial nature of small societies must be an important consideration for Caribbean managers.

Developing a Management Culture

The development of a management culture is not a pure accident. Even though the free enterprise ideology provided a favourable environment, the development of the American management culture reflects much deliberate effort. The private sector gives its unstinting support to the great business schools and, indeed, conducts a considerable amount of training itself. Federal and state governments also spend vast amounts on business development and training programmes. The Japanese, starting in the 1860s, deliberately promoted the importation of western management techniques and principles. Indeed, it was the American, Edward Deming, who implanted into the culture of Japanese management the passion for quality which US firms so assiduously copy today. Since the Second World War the West Europeans have established numerous American style business schools. The Russians and the Chinese have followed suit in recent years.

Similarly, we in the Caribbean will need to formulate policies which promote the evolution of a management culture in our region. Government, which plays so dominant a role in our societies, has an obvious responsibility in this exercise. We will need new legislation to encourage business activity and to stimulate entrepreneurship, and considerable sums must be allocated to establish new educational facilities. Hopefully, an expanding private sector will, in time, assume an increasing share of the financial costs of management and education.

But perhaps the greatest potential contribution of Caribbean governments to a management culture would be the adoption of modern management practices in the conduct of their own operations at all levels — in cabinet proceedings, in the legislature, in the civil service. For example, discontinuation of the widespread regional practice of sending the most unimportant matters to Cabinet would raise our GDP several percentage points a year. This means that matters of strategic importance receive far less attention than they deserve. Perhaps CARICOM governments might seek the advice of an experienced management consultant firm on the comprehensive reform of public sector operations.

The management of statutory corporations is especially critical. Unless ministers learn to differentiate between policy and operational issues, CARICOM tax-payers will continue to shoulder an increasing burden of subsidies to inefficient public sector enterprises. Ministers should understand that management is the art of locating knowledge and authority in the same place. At the same time, governments should be uncompromising in their insistence on the accountability of top management. I have often wondered how state-owned enterprises could be allowed to operate for years without the publication of annual financial reports. The presence of two ministers of government at this conference is a hopeful sign that Caribbean politicians are beginning to recognize the importance of management in economic development.

Institutional Framework

An institutional framework for the promotion of a management culture in the Caribbean will have three minimal components: the academic component, the institutional component and the outreach component. The academic component would address the philosophical issues of management. It would have responsibility for the identification of problems, the formulation of concepts, and the development of theories of management appropriate to the Caribbean situation. It would research issues arising from current problems, including ethics. It would also generate case studies and other instructional materials for management institutes. The instructional component comprises the various layers of educational programmes for the teaching of managerial concepts, principles and techniques. These range from the doctoral programme to vocational classes in computer operations and simple accounting. The functions of the outreach component are analagous to those of the extension services in agriculture. It ensures that the latest thinking on management and the most modern managerial techniques reach operators in the field.

The institutional framework which we adopt must accommodate these three components and maximize their efficiency. Because our target comprises the entire society, and since many elements of these components already exist, it would be most efficient for us to share the tasks and responsibilities as widely as possible. The obvious location of the academic component is the University. The University will also share in the instructional activities and, indeed, in the outreach programmes. The existing institutes of management, the community colleges and the polytechnics will be important centres of instruction, as will the business enterprises themselves. The management institutes and the corporations, as well as the relevant government departments, are the most natural providers of extension services.

But to provide the focus, the dynamism and the leadership needed for the effective promotion of a management culture, we will need to identify a single organization. I am not speaking of an institution for the centralized direction or even the coordination of such a programme; merely one which serves as a fountainhead, an inspiration, and a point of reference. The University is the logical locus of such an institution. We need, however, not a faculty of management, but a full-fledged school of business, drawing on the intellectual resources of the University, but with the operational autonomy which dynamic institutions require. The school of business, in turn, would serve to project the University into the business community and motivate the increased financial support which it so desperately needs. There is no substitute, in my mind, for a Caribbean school of business, independently funded and operated, but with its academic standards guaranteed through association with the University.

Delivered at the Conference on Management Education and Regional Development: An Interactive Relationship, Barbados, March 13–15, 1989

Note

1. Peter Drucker, *Management: Tasks, Responsibilities, Practices* (New York: Harper & Row, 1973), 13.

2. Courtney N. Blackman, 'The Economic Development of Small Countries: A Managerial Approach', *Contemporary International Relations of the Caribbean*, ed. Basil A, Ince (St Augustine, Trinidad and Tobago: Institute of International Relations, 1979).

3. Erwin Rommel, *The Rommel Papers*, ed. Liddell-Hart and Basil Henry (New York: Harcourt Brace, 1953).

18

THE CHANGING CARIBBEAN BUSINESS ENVIRONMENT

IMPLICATIONS FOR CARIBBEAN BUSINESS ENTERPRISES

Your generation is living in probably the most rapidly changing and turbulent period in human history, brought about by revolutionary developments in computers and telecommunications which have made possible the processing, storage and instantaneous transmission of information across national borders, and rendering distance almost unimportant in the conduct of multinational corporate operations. Indeed, Walter Wriston coined the term '*borderless economy*'[1] and Frances Cairncross spoke of '*The Death of Distance*'[2] — as we are now demonstrating in this distance learning exercise.

Simultaneously, we have seen the rebirth of the 'free market' ideology that lay dormant during the three decades following World War II when the doctrines of John Maynard Keynes prevailed. 'Free market' economists believe that economic outcomes should be determined almost entirely by the operations of the 'free market', and that government should involve itself as little as possible in economic activities. Keynes had argued that it was sometimes essential for government to intervene into product and financial markets in order to maintain stability and full employment in capitalist-type economies.[3]

Market fundamentalism is currently in the ascendancy, with 'free market' economists now holding the highest positions in the universities and ministries of finance of advanced industrial countries, and at the major Washington international financial institutions (IFIs) — International Monetary Fund (IMF), World Bank, Inter-American Development Bank (IDB). These countries and the IFIs, in turn, push, and sometimes impose, 'free market' policies on the governments of developing countries — too often to their detriment.

'Globalization' is the term used to describe the simultaneous emergence of the new technologies and resurgence of the 'free market' ideology. Globalization therefore possesses both a technological and an ideological component. The technological component is *substantive*, that is, consisting of *facts*: computer networks, mobile phones, faxes, email, et cetera. The ideological component, however, is *subjective*, indeed largely *propaganda*. Together they shape environment in which Caribbean business enterprises operate.[4]

Since new inventions are constantly being made, the technological component undergoes almost continuous change, while political, economic, and even religious differences among nations and ethnic groups, continuously lead to shifts in ideological positions. It is the impact of these two components of globalization on our region which promote constant change in the environment in which Caribbean business enterprises operate.

In the remainder of this presentation I first describe the major trends affecting the environment within which Caribbean business enterprise operates. Secondly, I enumerate the main challenges to individual Caribbean enterprises deriving from the pressures of globalization. Third, I focus on the problems faced by business managers as they deal with the challenges of the changing global market place. In conclusion, I identify the managerial implications of recent changes in the Caribbean business environment.

The Caribbean business environment

The current Caribbean business environment is characterized by five persistent trends. (I have deliberately used the term 'trend' to convey the sense of constant situational change.) The first of these is the quickening pace of Caribbean economic integration. Under the leadership of the Barbadian Prime Minister, Rt Hon Owen Arthur, CARICOM is feverishly trying to bring the CARICOM Single Market and Economy (CSME) into being.[5] The CSME envisages a borderless Caribbean region, within which goods, services, capital, enterprise and human resources move freely. Indeed, there is already considerable movement of labour, and capital and skilled personnel within the region. Thousands of Guyanese migrants now fill jobs throughout the region, with an estimated 25,000 in Barbados alone. Trinidad and Tobago corporations have expanded throughout the region, and Barbadian professionals, architects, engineers, lawyers, et cetera are ubiquitous.

The second important trend is the accession of CARICOM states to an increasing number of 'free trade' agreements. In addition to their own Treaty of Chaguaramas, CARICOM states, as a bloc, participate in trade agreements with the European Union (EU) under the Lomé Convention, with the US under the Caribbean Basin Initiative (CBI), and with Canada under CARIBCAN. To cope with task of negotiation of these numerous trade negotiations, CARICOM has established the Caribbean Regional Negotiation Machinery (CRNM). The CRNM is also currently negotiating on behalf of CARICOM in the Doha round of WTO negotiations, targeted for conclusion by January 1, 2005, an Economic Partnership Agreement (EPA) with the EU by January 2008, on the Free Trade Area of the Americas (FTAA), targeted for completion by January 1, 2005, bilateral negotiations with other countries, for example, Costa Rica, and with various trade blocs.

The chief feature of recent trade negotiations has been the insistence of advanced states on non-reciprocal agreements, and their reluctance to make concessions to underdeveloped and/or small states. The CRNM has its work cut out.

The third trend is 'financial liberalization', a programme involving the free floating of currencies, removal of interest rate regulations, exchange controls which, together with privatization, is the medicine most often prescribed by IFIs for economically ailing LDCs, no matter what their symptoms may be, and which, collectively, have come to be known as the 'Washington Consensus'. Almost every CARICOM state, occasionally of its own accord but often under the spur of IFI conditionalities, has undertaken liberalization programmes at some time. Jamaica, and Trinidad and Tobago, have experimented with some type of currency float. However, Barbados, Belize, and The Bahamas still operate a 'peg' against the US dollar, and have maintained exchange rate controls and restrictions on capital flows. A notable outcome of financial liberalization has been the sharp rise in cross-border investment, including mergers and acquisitions, in both the real and financial sectors. If the CSME comes into being, we will see the free movement of capital throughout the region.

Fourth, privatization, a tenet of the 'Washington Consensus', has gained considerable currency within CARICOM. Governments may privatize to raise additional funds, to bring an end to intolerable losses incurred by inefficient, and often corrupt, state-owned enterprise, and sometimes under irresistible pressure from the IFIs. For whatever reason, most CARICOM states have privatized national banks, public utilities, airports, and so forth; the trend now appears irreversible.

Fifth, and perhaps the most pernicious trend in the Caribbean business environment is an increasing tendency on the part of the most powerful nations to trample on our sovereign rights. For example, the Organisation for Economic Co-operation and Development (OECD) has moved unilaterally, outside the framework of international law and with the threat of savage sanctions, to exclude us from participation in the offshore business in which we possess a distinct comparative advantage. The Americans have imposed on the commercial banks of small states anti-laundering disclosure procedures which are illegal in the US.

Furthermore, through their various international institutions, in which the Caribbean has little or no voice — the Bank for International Settlements, the OECD, Financial Action Task Force, and the IFIs, the community of advanced nations have imposed on our governments financial and economic prescriptions that have brought us little other than grief. Even when acting within the framework of agreements to which we are signatory, First World countries may easily overwhelm us because of superior political clout — as in the infamous World Trade Organization (WTO) decision on bananas, which has laid low the Dominican economy. The net effect of these pressures from the First World has been to increase the cost of meeting the numerous regulatory requirements, as well as the uncertainty of not knowing what the next requirement will be.

Challenges to Business Enterprise in the New Environment

The Challenge of Change

The fundamental challenge to Caribbean enterprise in the new environment is the challenge of change. According to Peter Drucker, the world's foremost management guru,

> It is therefore a central 21st century challenge for management that its organization become a change leader.[6]

He continues,

> The only policy likely to succeed is to try to make the future … to try to make the future is risky. It is less risky, however, than not to try to make it.[7]

Business leaders must therefore be attuned to changing trends, and be ready at any time to make adjustments accordingly.

In small enterprises, this will be the responsibility of the CEO himself; in larger corporations, the CEO must ensure that his senior executives keep abreast of technological, economic and political developments in the firm's environment. In the largest businesses, there might be an entire department dedicated to scanning the environment and designing new strategies to deal with the implication of these new developments.

The Global Marketplace

The new trade agreements into which Caribbean states have entered, or with which they will of necessity be involved, typically require the opening of domestic markets to regional and extra-regional competition. This means, as Peter Drucker warns us:

> All institutions have to make global competitiveness a strategic goal. No institution, whether a business, a university or a hospital, can hope to survive, let alone to succeed, unless it measures up to the standards set by the leaders in its field, any place in the world.[8]

Let me illustrate: In my own wardrobe, I have quite similar shirts made in England, the US, Hong Kong, China, Indonesia, Singapore, Egypt, Mexico, Salvador, Honduras, the republics of the former USSR, and others. Alas, not many from CARICOM. In other words, I purchase my shirts in a global marketplace.

This means that calls for regional governments to protect local production will increasingly fall on deaf ears. Caribbean enterprises will therefore have to search the international marketplace for potential niches, design their products accordingly, and then market them aggressively.

The Global Workshop

The flipside of the global marketplace is the global workshop. For example, the more than 1,000 parts used in the manufacture of automobiles may be sourced from more than 20 countries, depending on the capacity of a producer to meet competitive prices and quality requirements. Similarly, Caribbean enterprise smust learn to source inputs from throughout the region or beyond, and to produce the final products in the most economic location. Since Guyana, Jamaica and Dominica, say, have the cheapest wage rates, inputs with a high labour content might be produced there, while the more sophisticated processes might be completed in Trinidad and Tobago or Barbados. Or skilled workers unavailable in Barbados, and Trinidad and Tobago may be introduced from Guyana and Saint Lucia. Indeed, the recent construction boom in Barbados would hardly have been possible without artisan skills from Guyana and the Windward Islands.

The Challenge of Politics

The responsibilities for resisting untoward pressures from the environment on our business environment, and for shaping trends to our national advantage, rest squarely on our political directorates. However, the business community must play its part by feeding its special inputs into the decision-making process. This can be done by exerting pressure on governments through various business associations, or by airing issues that affect business operations. Only recently, Dr Richard Bernal, Head of CRNM, called on CARICOM businessmen to make their views on trade negotiations known to the CRNM. In this way CRNM negotiators would be in a better position to protect the interest of Caribbean enterprises in the course of negotiations with foreign states. Of course, it would be best if businessmen themselves played a more active role in politics; if they continue to shun politics, they will get the quality of politician which their neglect of political activity deserves.

The Managerial Imperative

In the rapidly changing Caribbean business environment, only the best managed companies will survive — I call this the 'managerial imperative'. Successful Caribbean enterprises will be first to market, and will respond promptly to changes in market conditions. They will put consumer satisfaction first on their agenda, and will be constantly innovating in keeping pace with changes in consumer needs and tastes. By getting it right the first time around, they will create products of high quality and reliability, so that customers will be prepared to pay premium prices for their brand — one that delivers consistently high quality anywhere on earth.

To achieve the above outcomes, Caribbean top management must:

- Make maximum use of the new information technologies in their internal operations and, especially, maintain continuous communications with their customers.
- Speed up responses to changes in technology and market conditions by decentralizing their decision-making process, and push authority further down in the organization.
- As a corollary of decentralization, locate knowledge and authority in the same place.
- Noting that knowledge has superseded financial capital as the most important factor of production, employ well-educated staff, and then train and empower them.
- Recognize that operational control is achieved by setting specified goals, establishing performance benchmarks, providing for timely feedback of operational performance, and taking decisive action when results are unsatisfactory.

Finally, top management must accept ultimate responsibility for the performance of the enterprise. Too often Caribbean CEOs complain about a 'weak middle management' and 'lazy workers'.

In fact, if middle management is weak, it is because top management is even weaker! And how do 'lazy' West Indian workers transform themselves on migration to the US into the most hard-working and ambitious employees? They say that fish rot from the head down; so do enterprises destined to fail!

Presented at the Eastern Caribbean Institute of Banking and Financial Services, Basseterre, St Kitts-Nevis, September 14, 2004

Notes

1. Walter Wriston, *The Borderless Economy: The Twilight of Sovereignty* (NJ: Replica Books, 1997).

2. Frances Cairncross, *The Death of Distance* (Boston: Harvard Business School Press, 1997).

3. John M. Keynes, *The General Theory of Employment, Interest and Money* (New York: Harcourt Brace & World, Inc, 1964).

4. See Chapter 10, 'The Free Market in the Context of Globalization: Myth, Magic Or Menace'.

5. Arlette King, 'Understanding the CSME', Bank Notes, Central Bank of Barbados, vol. 8, no. 1 (June 2004).

6. Peter Drucker, *Management Challenges for the 21st Century* (New York: Harper Collins, 1999), 73.

7. Ibid., 93.

8. Ibid., 61.

19

THE ECONOMIST AS ADVISER

This paper shares with would-be economic advisers my observations on, and lessons from, more than 40 years of serious study of the discipline of Economics, 14 years as a senior national economic adviser, and another 15 years as an economic consultant to central banks, governments and international institutions.

Two recent experiences have prompted my choice of this topic, 'The Economist as Adviser'. The first was an invitation by the Eastern Caribbean Central Bank to address a group of young central bank and government economists; the second was my deep dismay that half-a-dozen American Nobel laureates, including this year's awardee, Professor Edward Prescott, could whole-heartedly support President Bush's fiscal programme that refunded one and one-half trillion dollars to taxpayers, with the wealthiest two per cent receiving about 60 per cent, which has led to record fiscal and current account deficits and a collapsing currency, and has thrown the US economy out of kilter.

As a former central banker, I have been particularly distressed that the Chairman of the US Federal Reserve Board, Dr Alan Greenspan, who had been a fervent champion of budget surpluses during the Clinton presidency, and who had initially recommended using the fiscal surplus to pay down the national debt, could so quickly be transformed into a full-fledged supporter of President Bush's massive deficit-inducing tax cuts. I therefore resolved to share the fruits of my training, experience and reflection in the expectation that a significant number of you will one day serve as economic advisers in governmental organizations, and will hopefully behave in a more responsible manner than your American counterparts. On second thought, US economists might benefit even more than you from the following remarks!

The paper first defines the discipline of Economics, distinguishes among various categories of professional economists, and zeroes in on the role of economic adviser. This is followed by a description of the tools of economists. Third are musings on the optimal academic and practical preparation of the economic adviser. Fourth, we identify the three most common pitfalls in the path of the economic advisers, especially those in the Caribbean: ideology, politics and mathematics. Fifth, we focus on two areas of particular concern for an economic adviser in developing countries: strategic planning and programme implementation. I conclude with general advice to the prospective adviser.

What Economists Do

It is difficult to define 'Economics' in one sentence; my favourite definition is therefore double-barrelled:

- Economics is the study of how men and women go about the provision of their livelihood.
- Economics has to do with the allocation of scarce resources among competing ends.

The first part of the definition establishes unequivocally that economics is concerned with the welfare of people; the second part directs our attention to the technical aspects of the discipline.

The basic paradigm of economists is the Market, and Price Theory is their primary tool. Adam Smith, the founder of the discipline of Economics, identified the Market as the central institution of a capitalist economy. He explained how buyers and sellers, even as they selfishly seek the best deals in the marketplace, unwittingly promote the efficient production and allocation of goods and services. He saw in this process an 'invisible hand'. In fact, he had discovered what modern systems theorists call a self-organizing process that minimizes the need for conscious human intervention once a minimum regulatory framework is put in place. (Note that there is no such thing as a 'free market'.)[1] In the appropriate institutional setting, then, the Market is a most effective and inexpensive allocator of resources. In addition to Price Theory, the economist, like other aspiring scientists, must make use of mathematics and statistical methods, especially in the construction of econometric models.

There are basically two categories of economists: theoretical and applied. Theoretical economists are concerned with elaborating the market paradigm and refining the various techniques of economic analysis. They mostly inhabit universities, and many of them shy away from advising on real-world problems. Alfred Marshall, the leading economic theorist of the nineteenth century, received two questions from the Chancellor of the Exchequer in 1903: his immediate response was to send the Chancellor a copy of a paper he had written in 1890, but as late as 1909, he had not addressed the specifics of the 1903 request. During the Great Depression of the 1930s, Columbia University's Wesley Mitchell, the father of business cycle theory, declined to offer advice on how best the Depression might be overcome. These days, however, theoretical economists too often descend from their ivory towers to advise LDCs. Their interventions usually do more harm than good. The collapse of the former Soviet economy at the hands of American academics advising a 'cold turkey' transformation from a command, to a 'free market', economy is the most egregious case in point.

Applied economists, on the other hand, apply price theory, and employ the tools of mathematics, statistics, and econometrics towards the solution of real-world economic problems. A real-world economic problem is one that requires that a decision be made, especially in circumstances where an inappropriate choice could have serious consequences. (Note that a decision to do nothing is also a choice.) This paper is primarily concerned with economists who advise ministers of government on various macroeconomic issues. For the sake of simplicity I have used the terms 'adviser' and 'minister' as metaphors to represent, respectively, economists who advise the political directorate and members of the political directorate themselves.

The Making of an Adviser

Ideally, a prospective economist ought not to study economics at the undergraduate level, but should instead obtain a firm grounding in the three major pillars of that discipline: history, mathematics and philosophy. He might then push on to a master's or PhD degree. Unfortunately, we do not live in a perfect world, and few have followed such a path. For example, I did not study economics at the undergraduate level but read modern history, a little philosophy and no mathematics at all! We cannot turn the clock back, and so we must simply try to fill in the gaps in our knowledge as we proceed.

History

We need to study history because economies exist in time as well as in geographic space. It is not surprising then that almost every economic statistic we use is time-related. We speak of GDP per annum, quarterly corporate profits, monthly salaries and hourly wages, of 2- to 4-year Kitchins and Juglar short-wave business cycles, and of Kondratieff long-wave 40- to 50-year cycles. We simply cannot speak meaningfully about economies except in their historical context.

Moreover, no significant economic phenomenon can be explained without reference to the past, since the arrow of time moves from the past to the future and causes always precede effects. Actuarial forecasts, in particular, depend heavily on historical demographic data. For all the above reasons, an economist called upon to advise in his own or in a foreign country should study diligently the history, culture, and even the literature, of that country before attempting to make economic recommendations.

There are two awkward features about history: first, it is constantly being rewritten as new research uncovers new historical 'facts', and as previously accepted 'facts' are shown to be erroneous; secondly, the body of historical facts, like the cosmos, constantly expands as the future unfolds. There is, in fact, no 'end of history', as Francis Fukuyama would have us believe, not even of the history that has already happened.[2] History is always a work in progress.

Mathematics

By its very nature, economics is concerned with the collection, classification and analysis of quantitative data so that the use of mathematics is unavoidable. First of all, mathematics facilitates the construction and manipulation of economic models, although it is rarely indispensable for that purpose. (Words, algebra and graphics can take economists quite a long way.) Through what Kenneth Boulding called 'the orderly loss of information', the economist transforms masses of data into knowledge for policy making.

The generation and publication of economic statistics is the task of specialists, and does not occupy economic advisers in their day-to-day work. However, an early grounding in mathematics, statistics and other quantitative methods enables the economist to judge when statistics have degenerated into 'damn lies'. Mathematics has some practical benefits as well: it helps students of economics to cruise through courses in price theory, macroeconomics and econometrics, facilitates communication with other economists, and widens the range of accessible technical journals, which are too often generously sprinkled with mathematical symbols. Another reason for studying mathematics at the undergraduate level, or even earlier, is that it is a subject most readily grasped by the young. Indeed, the greatest mathematicians usually do their most original work before the age of 30!

Philosophy

Economists, in the normal course of their work, utilize conceptual models — verbal, graphical, mathematical and econometric — in their search for knowledge. Knowledge may be described as a set of reliable propositions about reality. According to the *Pocket Oxford English Dictionary*, 'Philosophy is the study of the fundamental nature of knowledge, reality and existence', and epistemology is 'the branch of philosophy that deals with knowledge'. The usefulness of economic models therefore rests on the validity of the methodology we use in the derivation of propositions about reality. The three basic epistemological tools available to economic theorists are measurement, the logical method and the scientific method. All three of these tools are flawed, and will certainly never lead us to absolute truth.[3] However, a firm grounding in epistemology could certainly alert economists as to the limitations of their models. As Oskar Morgenstern nicely puts it, 'We must carefully distinguish between what we think we know and what we really do and can know.'[4]

It is quite remarkable that epistemology is so neglected in departments of economics everywhere, seeing that it addresses the very foundations of the discipline. I have argued elsewhere that the errors of the Caribbean New World group of economists of the 1960s and 1970s, brilliant as they were, lay in their weak grounding in epistemology, and I have been campaigning for the past two decades for the establishment of a faculty of philosophy at the University of the West Indies. There is something anomalous about a university that does not have a faculty of philosophy. Indeed, every university student should be required to take a basic course in philosophy before he or she is allowed to graduate.

Experience

Since the adviser is concerned with the solution of real-world problems, he must familiarize himself with the real world. Not surprisingly, those advisers do best who have participated in practical affairs, and are truly interested in the everyday problems of people. John Maynard Keynes, the greatest applied economist of all and economic adviser extraordinaire, was a worldly man, dabbling in the world of art, diplomacy, investment, publishing, and even farming.

Knowledge of the real world is only accessible at the workplace, both in the private and the public sector, by interesting oneself in various activities of civil society, by foreign travel, and if at all possible, through stints at major international organizations. (The last is a useful antidote against unwarranted respect for foreign advice.) It is particularly important for the adviser to respect the opinions of those who have had practical experience in the matter on which he is advising.

If at all possible, the adviser, even when well established in his profession, should try to take sabbaticals of three months or more during which time he should read anthropology, sociology, psychology, or anything but economics, so as to increase the range and variety of insights on which he may base his models. I think it was Nobel Laureate Paul Samuelson who said, 'He knows not economics who only economics knows!'

Pitfalls for the Adviser

There are three dangerous pitfalls in the path of an economic adviser. The first is ideology; the second is politics; the third is an overemphasis on mathematics and quantitative data.

Ideology

The most treacherous pitfall for the adviser is the trap of ideology. An ideology is a system of ideas about how the world works. It purports to explain an extremely large area of reality, and usually incorporates a teleological programme of action. Marxism, for example, claims to explain the workings of history and, indeed, almost every aspect of human experience. Similarly, adherents of 'free market' ideology, like Karl Brunner, believe that price theory can be used 'to explain the whole range of social phenomena', and that the outcomes of the free market cannot be improved upon.[5]

Socialist ideology exerted considerable influence over some CARICOM governments in the 1960s and 1970s. However, since the collapse of the socialist bloc in the late 1980s, the region has come under even greater pressures from the neo-liberal school, which now dominates the international financial institutions (IFIs) that impose structural adjustment and other programmes under the brand name of the 'Washington Consensus'. The economic progress of CARICOM member states over recent decades is an inverse function of official subscription to either of these two ideologies.

The trouble with the ideologue, that is, the true believer, is that since his ideology is universally applicable, and since the outcome of his programme of action is predetermined, there is no reason to distinguish among cases, or to revise strategies in the light of new information. A most egregious example of commitment to ideology is the failure of IFIs to distinguish between the well developed financial markets of developed countries and the imperfect markets of emerging economies. Acceptance of the spurious 'efficient market' hypothesis has led to the treatment of markets as homogenous for all practical purposes. In spite of the ravages of the Mexican 'Tequila' and Asian financial crises of the 1990s, and the more recent Brazilian and Argentine crises, neo-liberal economists still do not recognize the important macroeconomic role of financial markets in absorbing risks emanating from turbulence in the global financial system. As a result, they continue to urge freely floating exchange rate regimes and unfettered capital flows on LDCs, whose embryonic financial markets readily collapse when hot money makes a speedy exit.[6]

The ideological approach is the antithesis of the scientific diagnosis of disease and treatment of patients by modern physicians. Doctors begin by running a battery of standard tests — partly to protect against malpractice suits — but they also review the medical history of the patient, and design prescriptions that take into account the patient's current health status. They prescribe treatment for a specific patient, not the same treatment for every patient. It is highly unlikely that decisions and policies rooted in ideological preconceptions will prove effective in real-world conditions.

How does the Caribbean adviser avoid the pitfall of ideology? In a certain sense, each of us possesses an ideology that informs our daily conduct. But we need not be ideologues! First, the programme implicit in our ideology need not be teleological; secondly, if we remain open to new information we will be prepared to make adjustments as circumstances dictate. But most important of all is the perspective from which we approach the problems facing our society. As Lloyd Best has tried to teach us over the past four decades, our ideology should be home-grown, rooted in our history, culture and values, not taken off the Marxian, neo-liberal or any other shelf. And if we are called to advise a foreign country, we should then adopt the perspective of that country as best we can. Even so, we must at all times be prepared to review both our underlying strategy and our tactics in the light of new data and knowledge.

Politics

Politics is perhaps the most seductive pitfall of all for the economic adviser. If, as Lord Acton observed, power corrupts, political power certainly threatens the professional integrity of the adviser. There are three basic circumstances in which the adviser may be called upon to advise the minister:

As a civil servant, he is mandated by law to give his best advice to the minister, and then, to the best of his ability, assist him in carrying out policies approved by Parliament, whether they are agreeable or not. He must, of course, at all times operate within the law — that is why security of tenure for civil servants is so important.

The adviser may also be employed as a private consultant to advise the minister. In such a case he has neither legal nor moral responsibility to provide political support, and he enjoys the security of a legal contract.

Sometimes the adviser is legally mandated to advise the minister, but is not required to, and indeed, ought not to give political support. The situation of a central bank governor is an excellent case in point; as a former governor I will have something further to say on this matter.

The adviser who is also an open supporter of the political party in power is not covered here.

A potential source of conflict between minister and adviser is a clash of personalities. The minister typically possesses a huge ego, and has strong views on the subject of his portfolios. If he did not, he would not be very successful in politics! Secondly, in small societies, like those of CARICOM, the minister often demonstrates a tendency towards omniscience and omni-competence, and frequently takes on responsibility for the most minute administrative details. It is extremely difficult to advise someone who knows everything, and how to do anything. The same may also be true for a minister in a large country but is not so important in practice. Whereas a minister of health in a small Caribbean island may easily succumb to the notion that he is most qualified to manage the sole general hospital, the Minister of Health in Great Britain, with hundreds of hospitals under his responsibility, is unlikely to labour under the same illusion.

It is important that the adviser maintain a cordial but formal relationship with the minister. Cosy relationships sow the seeds of misunderstanding. Ministers, in both small states and large, nurture a burning desire to remain in office and regard advice that appears to threaten their re-election as hostile, if not downright malicious The adviser should therefore proffer advice in a clinical manner. At the same time, he must subdue his own ego and keep his emotions under control.

It is important that the adviser focus on the areas where his technical skills and experience are relevant. In this respect he would do well to heed the warning of Sir Henry Haskins, a British World War II general: 'Do not give advice that has not been seasoned by experience.' Above all, he should refrain from giving political advice. At any rate, the minister knows politics better than the adviser — that is why he is minister! Moreover, to the extent that an economist dabbles in politics, in the same proportion do his technical skills decline. One cannot be an economist and a politician at the same time; it is instructive that even the best lawyers do not defend themselves in law courts. I recall once participating, along with other senior technocrats, in a meeting with Barbadian Prime Minister, Tom Adams. To my horror someone ruled out a certain course of action on the grounds that the date of the next election had not yet been fixed. 'Mr. Prime Minister,' I quickly retorted, 'it is no concern of mine when you hold the election; that is your prerogative. I will give you my best technical advice. If you don't like it, I will give you my second-best solution, and so on, and so on.'

The relationship between a central bank governor and minister, under Caribbean conditions, is much more delicate than that between civil servant and minister or freelance adviser and minister: the civil servant enjoys security of tenure; the minister does not, and the freelance adviser is protected by contract; the governor, on the other hand, who is required by law to give honest advice to the minister, may be, and has been, summarily dismissed by the minister for doing what the law requires of him! I have elsewhere argued that Caribbean governments should follow the example of Germany, Austria and the European Union and strengthen the job security of the governor, thus allowing for the central bank to disagree openly with government on policies deemed detrimental to the economy.[7]

Whatever the level of his/her job security, the effectiveness of a governor will depend to a significant degree on at least the cordiality of the minister. This requires a certain degree of diplomacy on the part of the governor. He/she must be a 'politician with a little "p"', as I used to term myself. As such, I followed a few simple rules. First, I ignored controversial but inconsequential issues, keeping my powder dry for issues of real importance. Secondly, though never failing to tell it as I saw it, I would deliver bad news as kindly as I could, sprinkling such correspondence generously with 'Sir' and concluding with 'Your obedient servant' instead of the usual 'Yours faithfully'. Thirdly, I would get my views on important but politically contentious issues into the public domain well before the political debate commenced. Finally, I maintained my silence on government policy with which I disagreed.

Mathematics

Given the proliferation of learned journals with papers written almost completely in mathematical symbols, it is easy for economists to become enamoured with the quantitative aspects of the discipline. This reflects a long association between mathematics and science. An influential voice in this development was that of William Stanley Jevons in the mid-nineteenth century. 'Economics,' he posited, 'if it is to be a science at all, must be a mathematical science.'[8] In fact, it is not mathematics that defines science, but adherence to the scientific method. Millions of our innumerate ancestors were unconscious scientists in their development of new mechanical and agricultural implements: they began with a hypothesis, tested it through experimentation, and drew conclusions from their findings. Indeed, Marshall and Keynes, both splendid mathematicians, were most economical in the use of mathematics.

The truth is that economies, that is, groups of people trying to make a living, are far too complex to be readily captured in mathematical or econometric models. The construction of any model involves an abstraction of a limited number of features deemed to be crucial, and the omission of the most numerous aspects of reality. Yet, forgetting that the model is not the same as the reality, many economists neglect to take into account aspects of reality excluded from the model. (In a tall building from which the air has been evacuated, a hundred pound lead weight and a feather, if dropped simultaneously from a hundred feet, will hit the ground at the same time, but not if they are dropped from an airplane at 10,000 feet.) For this reason, Professor Eli Ginzberg, who lectured me at Columbia University, argued that the more susceptible a human problem to quantification, the less important it was.

Another area in which the adviser must exercise extreme caution is in the usage of statistical data. He must especially avoid what Morgenstern calls 'specious accuracy':

> Specious accuracy is often found in providing information down to several decimal points when no conceivable use can be made of

such detail — even if the data, given to this degree, should be entirely free from error, which is usually impossible.[9]

Morgenstern reminds us that the vast majority of statistics are in fact estimates, so that economists have a duty to disclose the attendant margin of error, and not convey a false impression of precision. Ever since reading Morgenstern, I cringe whenever the GDP of an underdeveloped economy, with woefully inadequate statistics, is reported to have grown by 3.27 per cent in the previous year, when it might well have grown by six per cent or declined by as much as three per cent.

Above all, Morgenstern reminds us of the importance of qualitative data:

> All economic decisions, whether private or business, as well as those involving economic policy, have the characteristic that quantitative and non-quantitative information must be combined into one act of decision. It would be desirable to understand how these two classes of information can best be combined. Obviously, there must exist a point at which it is no longer meaningful to sharpen the numerically available information when the other, wholly qualitative, part is important, though a notion of its "accuracy" or "reliability" has not been developed.[10]

This quotation recalls for me the occasion in July 1975 when Barbadian Prime Minister, Errol Barrow, asked my advice on the rate at which the Barbados currency should be pegged to the US dollar. 'The economy,' I told him, 'will adjust to any value between the range of US\$1.00 = BDS\$1.80 and US\$1.00 = BDS\$2.40. Only the Almighty knows what the correct rate is, and he has been so far silent on the matter. But since the rate, US\$1.00 = BDS\$2.00 is easiest for the tourists, let's make that the rate.' 'Okay,' he replied, 'then two to one it is.' The fact that this peg has held firm for three decades confirms that qualitative data can in some circumstances be even more important than quantitative data.

Nor must our adviser allow mathematics and statistics to obfuscate rather than illuminate his recommendations. He should keep in mind that advice is best given in concise reports written in clear English and accessible to the intelligent layman. I shall let Alfred Marshall have the last word. He once wrote to an acquaintance:

> I have a growing feeling that a mathematical theorem dealing with economic hypotheses is very unlikely to be good economics, and I go more and more on the rules: 1. Use mathematics as a shorthand language rather than as an engine of inquiry; 2. Keep to them until you have done; 3. Translate into English; 4. Then, illustrate by examples that are important in real life; 5. Burn the mathematics; 6. If you can't succeed in 4, burn 3. This last I do often.[11]

Core Competencies

The two most important areas in which our economic adviser is expected to demonstrate technical competence are national planning and programme implementation. These are also areas in which the performance of CARICOM governments has been weakest.

National development plans (NDPs) were reasonably useful in the 1950s and 1960s when economic change was gradual, the structure of industrial production stable, and the geopolitical parameters fixed by the realities of the Cold War. From the 1970s, the usefulness of NDPs rapidly declined. The turbulence of the transition from the Old Industrial Age to the New Information Age rendered projections and forecasts more and more unreliable, and made government policy making accordingly more problematic. Whereas 1955 was not too dissimilar from 1950 or 1970 from 1965, the breakdown of the Bretton–Woods Agreements in 1971 and the oil shocks of the 1970s made 1980 vastly different from 1975, while the collapse of the Soviet Union in 1989 created a totally new geopolitical reality. As Paul Valery nicely put it: 'The trouble with our times is that the future is not what it used to be.'

Writing about development planning within CARICOM, Professor Andrew Downes concluded:

> Several assessments of development plans suggest that they have been largely ineffective; that is, many of the goals specified in the planning documents have not been achieved.... Development planning in the region was largely abandoned in the 1980s.[12]

However, the new Age of Uncertainty does not eliminate the need to plan for the future; indeed, it makes planning even more important. However, it calls for a different kind of planning — strategic planning. Some CARICOM governments have declared their intention to shift from development to strategic planning. It is therefore important for our adviser to understand what strategic planning is about.

Strategic Planning

Strategic planning is necessary because of future uncertainty. A strategic plan is a set of mutually consistent policies for the achievement of a specified goal, usually within a specified time period. The minister must share his vision of the future with the adviser, and determine the goal and term of the plan. The question facing the strategic planner, writes Peter Drucker, is 'What do we have to do today to be ready for an uncertain tomorrow?'. The question, he reiterates, is not what will happen in the future, but 'What will not get done unless we commit resources to it today?' He continues:

> There are plans that lead to action today and these are true plans, true strategic decisions. And there are plans that talk about action

tomorrow; these are dreams, if not pretexts for non-thinking, non-planning, non-doing.[13]

In short, he insists, strategic planning is concerned, not with future plans, but with the futurity of today's decisions.

The purpose of the strategic planning exercise, then, is the identification of those critical areas where hard decisions must be taken today if we are to have a fighting chance of attaining tomorrow's goal; its outputs are a strategic agenda, that is, the list of hard decisions that have to be taken today. The strategic agenda of government will constitute the basic framework of the NSP, within which the various ministries and government agencies formulate their own sub-strategies and programmes towards the attainment of the national goal. The social partners — business and labour, other non-governmental organizations (NGOs) as well as individual citizens — should also be encouraged to participate in the strategic planning process, and to devise for themselves programmes which are supportive of, and consistent with, the NSP.

The climax of the strategic planning exercise is the commitment of resources today. Only then can work commence towards the achievement of the national goal. The commitment of resources is also a clear indication of resolve on the part of the executors of the NSP. Since resources are almost always scarce, their commitment to the goals of the NSP will involve reallocation from uses deemed less critical. This will create discomfort for the deprived and anguish for the strategic decision maker. Indeed, the greatest task facing the adviser on strategic planning is to convince the minister that a plan which causes no pain is, by definition, not strategic. Again, 'No pain, no gain!'

Implementation of an NSP will also involve what Drucker terms 'the sloughing off of the past'. This involves the abandonment of bureaucratic procedures from our colonial past that were designed to maintain the status quo rather than promote progress, and which were predicated on the backwardness of the natives. As Drucker reminds us, 'Business — and every other organization today — has to be designed to treat change as the norm and to create change rather than react to it.'[14] The adviser should make it crystal clear that the responsibility for change is that of the political directorate, not of his subordinates.

Programme Implementation

The fulfilment of a strategic plan involves the implementation of various programmes. Governments in the Caribbean region have generally assumed that once the appropriate legislation has been passed, and institutions established and headed by politically sympathetic persons, implementation will take care of itself. In fact, programmes dissolve into numerous tasks whose execution requires the attention of suitably qualified and motivated managers. That is why Peter Drucker argues that 'the developing countries are not underdeveloped, they are under-managed.'

The responsibility of management is to manage the operations of an entity in such a way that the value of its outputs exceeds the value of its inputs. There is strong evidence that Caribbean countries have failed quite miserably in this respect. In a recent presentation, 'Stabilization, Debt and Fiscal Policy in the Caribbean', Ms Ratna Sahay of the IMF reported that economic growth in the region has been disappointing in recent years, while public debt has risen rapidly, so that by the year 2003, 14 of the 15 Caribbean countries ranked in the top 30 of the world's highly indebted emerging market countries. This debt burden, she rightly warned, is unsustainable.[15] The fact that our debt, especially our foreign debt, is so high indicates that substantial resources have been injected in regional government programmes; however, the lack of a corresponding increase into economic output suggests the poor management of our national resources.

At the same time, CARICOM is, by all indications, exceptionally well endowed in respect of the critical production input, namely the human resource. Five Caribbean member states rated in the UNDP High Human Development Index, rank in the category of 'high human development', seven in the 'medium development' category, and only Haiti in the 'low development' category. The problem must lie in the management of our human resources, for management is essentially the direction of the efforts of people.

Civil Service bashing is a popular Caribbean sport. In fact, the public service within CARICOM includes a higher proportion of highly educated personnel than does the private sector. However, public servants are severely burdened by bureaucracy and grossly obsolete practices. It is to these concerns, especially to the sloughing off of the past, that the adviser should direct the urgent attention of the minister.

Conclusion

The role of adviser is by no means glamorous and can be a quite frustrating and thankless one. He certainly should not expect the minister to accept his advice at all times. For one thing, his advice may not always be correct, and the minister may sometimes have quite sound political or other reasons for rejecting it. Hopefully, he will accept some advice that is useful, and other advisers following will move the process a little further. If the adviser's recommendations are accepted and prove right, the kudos will go to the minister; if they prove wrong, the responsibility will most likely attach to the adviser.

It may take many years before even the soundest advice is accepted, for as the late Israeli diplomat, Abba Eban, once observed, 'Governments never adopt the right policy until they have exhausted all available options.' In 2003, a seminar was convened at the Cave Hill campus of the University of the West Indies marking the tenth anniversary of the establishment of a 'social contract' between government, business and labour, an approach I had proposed two decades earlier.[16] There were on that occasion quite a few claimants to parenthood of the 'social contract'. Fortunately, I had lived to attend the seminar, and was able to remind the participants that, in cricketing parlance, I had at least rolled the pitch.

But the most unfortunate outcome of all would be if the adviser gave the advice he thought the minister wanted to hear; in which case the minister would have been misled and, worst of all, the professional integrity of the adviser, his most precious qualification, would have been irreparably compromised.

Prepared for the XXXVI Annual Monetary Studies Conference (2004) Central Bank of Trinidad and Tobago, November 1–4, 2004; November 2, 2004

Notes

1. For a fuller discussion see Chapter 10, 'The Free Market in the Context of Globalization: Myth, Magic or Menace'.

2. Francis Fukuyama, *The End of History and the Last Man* (New York: Free Press, 1992).

3. For a fuller discussion see Courtney N. Blackman, *The Practice of Persuasion* (Bridgetown, Barbados: Cedar Press, 1982), 5.

4. Oskar Morgenstern, *On the Accuracy of Economic Observations*, Second edition (New Jersey: Princeton University Press, 1963), vii.

5. Karl Brunner, interview by Arjo Klamer, *Conversations with Economists* (New Jersey: Rowan & Allenhold, 1983), 183.

6. See Chapter 9, 'Factors in the Choice of an Exchange Rate Regime: With Special Reference to the Caribbean', 177–204.

7. Courtney N. Blackman, *Central Banking in Theory and Practice: A Small State Perspective* (Trinidad and Tobago: Caribbean Centre for Monetary Studies, University of the West Indies, 1998).

8. William Stanley Jevons, *The Theory of Political Economy*, 5th edition (New York: A.M. Kelley, 1965), 3.

9. Morgenstern, *On the Accuracy of Economic Observations*, 62.

10. Ibid., 3.

11. As quoted by Paul Omerod, *Butterfly Economics: A New General Theory of Social and Economic Behaviour* (New York, NY: Basic Books, 1998), 60.

12. Andrew S. Downes, 'Long Term Planning: International Action and Restructuring in the Caribbean', (unpublished, October 2000).

13. Peter F. Drucker, *Management: Tasks, Responsibilities, Practices* (New York: Harper & Row, 1989), 125–27.

14. Ibid., 14.

15. Ratna Sahay, 'Stabilization, Debt and Fiscal Policy', (paper written for a High Level Seminar, Development Challenges Facing the Caribbean, co-organized by the Central Bank of Trinidad and Tobago, and the IMF, June 11–12, 2004, Port-of-Spain, Trinidad).

16. See discussion in Chapter 7, 'The Balance of Payments Crisis in the Caribbean: Which way out?'

SECTION V

The Barbados Experiment

20

ECONOMIC STRATEGY AND GROWTH IN BARBADOS

FROM COLONIAL TIMES TO THE YEAR 2000

Pre-colonial experience

This paper reviews critically the economic strategies pursued by successive Barbadian administrations and their outcomes, dating back to colonial times. Until 1937, the year of the riots, the goal of the Colonial Office was the promotion of conditions conducive to the orderly cultivation of sugar cane. This entailed upkeep of a minimal infrastructure, such as a safe water supply, passable roads, public health, fairly widespread access to primary, but limited access to secondary, education. Above all, there was a determined maintenance of law and order.

The issue of economic development did not arise. The colonies were seen as sources of raw material, exclusive markets for UK exports, and lucrative job opportunities for colonial civil servants and adventurous young Englishmen. At any rate, the prevailing economic theory of 'laissez-faire' did not condone government intervention into the market; it was assumed that if profitable investment opportunities arose, entrepreneurs were sure to recognize and exploit them.

In response to the abominable colonial conditions that caused riots throughout the West Indies in the late 1930s, and no doubt as a public relations measure to promote support of the war effort, the Colonial Development and Welfare (CD&W) Act was passed in 1940, allocating £5 million (sterling) to the colonial empire over five years. During World War II the emphasis was on 'welfare' rather than 'development', but with the increase of funding to £150 million in 1945, the CD&W programme took on a more developmental aspect.

In its publication, *The Economy of Barbados, 1946–1980*, the Central Bank of Barbados estimated the per capita income of Barbados for 1946 at US$188, placing it in the category of 'low income countries', using the current World Bank criteria. The population was then 196,200 with a labour force of 90,200, of which 11 per cent were unemployed.

Immediate post-World War II period

The 1946–56 plan represented Barbados's first venture into formal development planning. The plan allocated $50,000 to the development of minor industries and $10,000 to tourism. According to Michael Howard, in *Public Finance in Small Open Economies: The Caribbean Experience*, 'development plans of the 1950s were merely extensions of colonial budgets to include the planning of capital expenditure.'[1] They were financed by revenue surpluses and CD&W grants, and were focused mainly on the sugar industry.

The move to full ministerial status in 1954 permitted government to shift to loan financing of capital expenditure, especially through foreign borrowing. In the 1955-60 plan, CD&W grants and foreign loans accounted for 42 per cent of total planned expenditure. Howard sums up: 'Apart from the emphasis on infrastructural development ... the economy remained largely underdeveloped.'[2] Nevertheless, by the end of the decade, the political preconditions for economic development had been well and truly laid.

The Sixties

It was in the 1960s that the first generation of politicians and bureaucrats familiar with the work of development economists like Sir Arthur Lewis and Walt W. Rostow came on the scene to put in place the preconditions for economic 'take-off', to use Rostow's terminology. Using the degrees of freedom provided by internal self-government in 1961, and independence in 1966, government made soft bilateral loans from the UK and Canada, and tapped the foreign capital markets to fund infrastructural projects. Investments in the airport and harbour expansion helped to launch the tourism industry, and, through generous incentives and intensive promotion, foreign investment was attracted to drive manufacturing for export. Barbados declined to adopt socialist 'occupation of the commanding heights of the economy' through nationalization of foreign-owned industry and massive investment in state enterprises. In particular, Barbados neither nationalized, 'indigenized', nor forced out branches of foreign commercial banks, thus sparing itself the subsequent bank failures and, in some cases, the collapse of entire indigenous banking sectors, experienced by Guyana and Jamaica.

However, government did practise limited state entrepreneurship intended to 'jump-start' key industries. For example, to seed the tourism industry it built the Hilton Hotel; to support agriculture it made a major investment in the Pine Hill Dairy; and it entered into a joint venture arrangement to establish the flour mill. The Barbados Development Board (later the Barbados Industrial Development Corporation, and now the Barbados Investment and Development Corporation), and the Barbados Tourist Board were also established to support the two new pillars of the economy: manufacturing and tourism.

By far the most important economic policy measure of the 1960s was the launching of a programme of massive government expenditures on education — a strategic initiative in Barbadian history second only to the introduction of sugar cultivation in the late 1630s. In this decade the main pillars of higher education were put in place: the Cave Hill campus of the University of the West Indies, the Samuel Jackman Prescod Polytechnic, the Barbados Community College, and free secondary and, for the most part, free tertiary education. Successive Barbadian governments have typically spent one-fifth of their budgets on education. Accumulated expenditures, in nominal values, sum to BDS$4.8 billion for the 34 years following independence; if allowance is made for inflation, the value in today's dollars would exceed BDS$30 billion, or US$15 billion, a remarkable investment in human capital that explains Barbados's outstanding economic progress and its high ranking on the UN Human Development Index.

The Seventies

The basic development strategy of the 1960s continued into the 1970s. Government ran fiscal surpluses on current account and supplemented them with soft loans from the World Bank, Inter-American Development Bank (IDB) and Caribbean Development Bank (CDB) to finance ongoing development projects. It also made occasional Euro-dollar loans to fill balance of payments needs.

After a slow start, both tourism and manufacturing picked up in the second half of the decade, but sugar weakened. Manufacturing export receipts rose from BDS$61.0 million in 1970 to BDS$337.3 million in 1980, and tourism expenditures from BDS$80.7 million in 1970 to BDS$415.0 million in 1980. The volume of sugar exports and price per tonne fluctuated widely: exports of sugar and molasses (132,000 tonnes) were highest in 1970 and lowest in 1975 (72,937); export earnings of BDS$107.4 million were highest in 1975 and lowest in 1971 (BDS$29.9

million), but the sugar industry entered a spectacular decline from which it would not recover.

Excessive taxation of the 1975 windfall sugar earnings hastened the decline of the industry, but other factors, both domestic and external, made the outcome inevitable. Firstly, the labour-intensive industry could no longer attract the increasingly well-educated school-leavers; secondly, the New Information Age, which, as we now know from hindsight, had its beginnings in the 1970s, led to the sharp reduction in the value of commodities worldwide, and the sugar industry became increasingly dependent on preferential prices which did not always cover costs. Even the price of oil is lower today in real terms than before the two oil shocks.

An important institutional addition, indeed an innovation, was the establishment of the Central Bank of Barbados in 1972. With the demise of the Sterling Area in 1974, the Barbados dollar was pegged to the US dollar in July 1975 at the rate of US$1.00 = BDS$2.00. The maintenance of that peg would become the main tenet of Barbados's economic policy in the face of deep disapproval on the part of Washington IFIs. The Central Bank, with its power of money creation, replaced the local branches of foreign commercial banks as the source of short-term liquidity for government, greatly improving the efficiency of public sector financial operations. At the same time, the door was opened to excessive fiscal deficits and consequent balance of payments disequilibria. In Howard's judgment, however, 'Although the (Central) Bank contributed significantly in 1977 and 1979, Central Bank money creation before 1981 did not cause a serious problem for the balance of payments.'[3]

The 1970s also marked the important regional development of the Caribbean Community and Common Market (CARICOM). Barbados's Prime Minister Errol Barrow had taken the lead in the establishment in 1968 of CARIFTA, a free trade association including Antigua, Barbados and Guyana. The Caribbean

Development Bank (CDB) followed in 1970, and would become an important source of soft development finance for Barbados. CARIFTA would in 1973 grow into CARICOM.

With the establishment of the Caribbean Multilateral Clearing Facility (CMCF) by regional central banks and monetary authorities, intra-regional trade expanded rapidly, with Barbados putting in an unexpectedly strong performance; exports to CARICOM as a proportion of our total exports rose from 24.3 per cent in 1971 to 27.3 per cent in 1982. Exports of furniture and garments to Trinidad and Tobago were especially buoyant, as the citizens of the twin republic spent their petrodollars profusely on Barbadian imports, real estate, and tourism services.

But the most remarkable phenomenon of the post-War period was the sharp increase in productivity registered throughout the Barbadian economy. Dr Delisle Worrell, in his essay, 'An Economic Survey of Barbados 1946–1980,' in *The Economy of Barbados 1946-1980*, reports:

> Productivity increases in all sectors could have been of the order of 300 per cent between 1946 and 1979. Value added per worker rose 100 per cent in tourism between 1960 and 1970, and in manufacturing increased by a factor of five between 1960 and 1978. Even in the lagging sectors, output per worker was up substantially; the increase for agriculture between 1960 and 1978 was 100 per cent.[4]

By 1980 Barbados ranked among 'middle income' developing countries, with a per capita income of approximately US$3,000. With respect to health, education and public utilities, standards approached those of a developed country; and most importantly, the economy of 1946, in which agriculture contributed 52 per cent of GDP, had been transformed into one in which services supplied over two-thirds of GDP, with industry accounting for one-fifth, and agriculture only ten per cent. Barbados had clearly entered Rostow's third stage of economic development — 'take-off into sustained economic growth' — and was being held up as a model for other developing countries to emulate.

The Eighties

The 1980s were testing times for the Barbadian economy. The start, midpoint and end of the decade were marked by fiscal excesses related to political electioneering, so that most of the decade was spent on damage control rather than on issues related to economic growth. There were, however, one or two saving graces.

Howard describes the year 1981 as 'a turning point in Barbadian fiscal management'. He observes: 'Prior to 1981 the deficit was reasonably well managed and was financed by domestic and foreign sources.'[5] However, against a background of recessionary conditions in the world economy, government undertook massive capital expenditures which resulted in a record deficit of BDS\$181.0 million, more than half of which, Howard notes, 'was financed mainly by foreign borrowing and by money creation.'[6] (Actually, the Central Bank financed only a modest BDS\$21.9 million.) The economic situation was exacerbated by the short but sharp 1981–82 downturn of the US economy, which forced Barbados into its first IMF stand-by agreement during 1982–84. But the Barbadian economy, weakened by the fiscal events of 1981, was slow to recover from recession.

Barbados's difficulties were compounded by the protectionist policies of Trinidad and Tobago following the passing of Dr Eric Williams. Furthermore, Guyana's default led to the suspension of the CMCF in 1983, with US\$65 million owing to Barbados. It would be almost a decade before Guyana resumed substantial repayments on that debt.

The economy suffered an even more severe blow in 1986. In fulfilment of election campaign promises, the incoming DLP administration experimented with the Reaganesque 'supply-side' economic policy, and cut taxes sharply. The result was a succession of three huge annual fiscal deficits: BDS$164.0 million in 1986, BDS$189.8 million in 1987 and BDS$146.2 million in 1988. These deficits were financed primarily by foreign loans: BDS$107.9 million in 1986, BDS$154.3 million in 1987, and BDS$77.4 million in 1988. The overall national debt, which at year end 1980 stood at BDS$493 million, had risen to BDS$1,880.1 million by year end 1990; more seriously, the foreign element of the debt had risen from US$82 million at year end 1980 to US$408 million at the end of 1990. At the decade's end Barbados found itself in deep balance of payments difficulties.

The most positive development of the 1980s was the emergence of Barbados as a recognized 'off-shore' business and financial centre. New legislation had been passed in the late 1970s, following the declaration of the incoming Adams administration in 1976 that it would transform Barbados into a 'supplier of business services to the rest of the world'. A second positive development was the push to develop 'infomatics', that is, the export of information-related services. Export earnings from these two initiatives, currently estimated at BDS$60 million, now exceed receipts from sugar exports, and have effectively added another supporting pillar to the economy.

The Nineties

The 1990s started badly for Barbados. In the run-up to the 1991 elections, the incumbent administration ran what is still the largest fiscal deficit in Barbadian history: BDS$244 million. Once again, fiscal intemperance coincided with a US recession, mercifully brief and not as severe as in 1982. With its foreign credit exhausted, the administration turned to the Central Bank for credits of BDS$172 million. The secondary effect of this money creation was the virtual exhaustion of the island's foreign exchange balances, forcing government to sell off its holdings in Barbados

Telecommunications to Cable and Wireless in order to pay off a maturing Japanese yen 'bullet' loan. Government was also forced into an IMF programme from a much weaker bargaining position than in 1982.

During the early years of the 1990s Barbados laboured under the stern IMF conditionalities in a programme of 'structural reform and macroeconomic stabilisation', which involved higher taxes, reduced government expenditures and savage cuts in government personnel. The IMF also forced the monetary authorities to align their financial operations more in keeping with the 'free market' principles of the 'Washington Consensus.' However, the devaluation of the Barbados dollar, demanded by all Washington IFIs as a quid pro quo of financial assistance, was barely averted by a commitment to reduce public sector salaries by eight per cent.

In its weakened state, the Barbados economy recorded a decline in average GDP of almost five per cent for 1991 and 1992, and by 1993 almost a quarter of the workforce was idle. Mercifully, the island escaped the external 'debt trap' which would crush so many developing countries, including Jamaica and Guyana; and except for a few months in 1991, when net international reserves fell below US$20 million, the Central Bank of Barbados was generally able to provide foreign exchange to the public for essential foreign payments.

The first task of the incoming Arthur administration in 1994 was to complete the macroeconomic stabilization of the economy and restart the process of economic growth; it quickly restored the confidence of both domestic and foreign investors. Riding the early waves of the longest US economic expansion in history, the Barbados economy took off on its most robust economic upswing since independence. Construction, especially in the hotel and housing sectors, and tourism expenditures, especially by UK visitors, were the star performers. As a result, the unemployment rate fell to 12.3 per cent in 1998, and to under ten per cent in 2000, slightly lower than in 1946.

The two decidedly strategic initiatives taken by the new administration were the introduction of a value added tax (VAT) in 1997, and the contracting of a loan of US$89 million from the IDB for EDUTECH 2000. The first considerably expanded the national tax base and made for more efficient tax collection; the second is a programme intended to make the current generation of Barbadian youth computer literate.

There was a third outcome of great significance. The Barbados National Bank, which had bled red ink for more than a decade, moved into massive profitability. This performance confirmed that a public enterprise, if given a clear mandate (in this case profitability), and relieved of political shackles, could deliver the goods, as indeed, the operationally autonomous ICB has done for over two decades.

The establishment of the World Trade Organization (WTO) in 1995, and the launching of negotiations in 1995 by the US and 33 other American states towards a Free Trade Agreement of the Americas (FTAA) by the year 2005, together represented the most radical transformation of Barbados's external trading environment since the abolition of imperial tariffs by the UK in the early twentieth century. They effectively ended the era of non-reciprocal trading arrangements.

But even the travails of the early years of the decade yielded valuable fruit. The close brush with devaluation impressed upon the national psyche a deep appreciation of the importance of the fixed exchange rate peg against the US dollar, and the efficacy of 'wage restraint' in the maintenance of the overall stability and health of the economy. The institution of the 'social partnership' between government, business and labour for establishing the parameters of national wage increases is now held up as a model for other developing nations.

Barbados in 2000

The profile of the Barbadian economy as we enter the twenty-first century is pleasing. A per capita income of approximately US$8,000 places us in the World Bank ranking of 'upper middle income' countries, and foreign exchange reserves are at record high levels — nearly US$500 million. According to UN development reports from the late 1980s through 1999, Barbados has been first among developing countries on the Human Development Index, and in the top 30 of all UN member countries. In 1999 the Standard and Poors Credit Rating Agency awarded Barbados an A2 rating. Indeed, the remarkable economic growth recorded by Barbados since the Second World War, and its resilience in the face of the oil shocks, successive international business cycles and the global financial crises of the 1990s, suggest that the economy has 'taken off', and is now poised to enter Rostow's fourth stage of economic growth: the 'drive to maturity'.

Prospects

However, there are some dark clouds lurking on our increasingly murky horizon. According to Central Bank forecasts, the weakening US economy could slow the Barbados growth rate from its recent three to five per cent range; sugar appears to be on the way out and manufacturing is no longer competitive. Moreover, recent OECD initiatives on 'money laundering' and 'harmful tax competition', designed to blunt our competitive advantage in offshore financial business, still threaten. Mr Owen Arthur, Prime Minister of Barbados, has played a leadership role in the fight against these unilateral OECD offensives. Nevertheless, never in its history has Barbados been as well positioned to face the uncertainties of the future.

Notes

1. Michael Howard, *Public Finance in Small Open Economies: The Caribbean Experience* (Westport, CN: Praeger Publishers, 2002), 153.

2. Ibid., 152.

3. Ibid., 28.

4. DeLisle Worrell, 'An Economic Survey of Barbados', *An Economic Survey of Barbados, 1946–1980*, ed. DeLisle Worrell, 39–40.

5. Michael Howard, *Public Finance in Small Open Economies*, 28.

6. Ibid., 28.

21

THE BARBADIAN ECONOMY SINCE INDEPENDENCE

A GLANCE BACKWARD AND A LOOK AHEAD

Back in 1973 I visited with the legendary Masai warriors in a remote part of Tanzania. I recall the deep sympathy I evoked from one tribesman when he learned through an interpreter that I possessed but one wife and no cows at all. In years gone by, a male adolescent Masai achieved manhood, not merely by survival to some predetermined age, but through the demonstration of prowess in the slaying of a lion.

By analogy, the Barbadian economy can claim maturity, not merely because our nation has survived for 21 years, but through the resilience it has demonstrated during one of the most turbulent periods in modern economic history. Not long after we achieved independence, the Bretton–Woods Agreement, which had provided exchange rate stability to the world international trading community for a quarter century, collapsed in 1971; 1973 saw an explosive rise in inflation; 1974 brought us the first oil shock when the price of oil quadrupled, leading to the recession of 1975, and in 1979 the price of oil quadrupled once again, setting off the 1981–82 world recession, the most severe since the Great Depression of the 1930s. The US stock market collapse last month was the icing on the cake.

These vicissitudes have overwhelmed many nations much larger and better endowed than Barbados. African and Latin American countries, with hardly any exceptions, have been devastated by rapid inflation, frequent currency devaluations and a horrendous debt burden, which have forced most of them to seek rescheduling of their foreign liabilities, and driven others into default. Meanwhile, Barbadians, admittedly at the cost of higher unemployment and a greatly increased foreign debt, have enjoyed a virtually uninterrupted improvement in our living standards and have not defaulted on any of our overseas financial obligations.

I propose to use the twenty-first anniversary of our nation's independence as an occasion for sober reflection on the state of our economy. This will involve, first of all, a review of our economic performance since independence and a critique of our economic management to date. This will enable us to get a fix on our current economic situation. We will then look into the future to see what challenges await us and what opportunity beckons. This will make possible the formulation of effective strategies and policies for the years ahead.

Finally, I will share with you my vision of how the Barbadian economy might look as the nation approaches middle age. My address will not be of the kiss-and-tell variety; it will be concerned about economic policy, not about party politics or personalities, and the chips will fall where they may.

Economic Performance since Independence

The three conventional measures of economic performance are real per capita growth in gross domestic product, that is, growth after allowance is made for inflation; price stability and the level of unemployment. As an index of development, rather than simple growth, I shall add a fourth criterion of performance — structural economic change.

According to World Bank estimates the Barbadian economy has grown at an average annual rate of about two and a half per cent. This estimate, in my view, is understated but still compares favourably with the performance of industrial market economies.

The corresponding rate for the United States was about two per cent, for the UK one-and-a-half per cent and about five per cent for Japan. Over the entire period most upper middle-income countries, into which category the World Bank places Barbados, recorded slightly higher growth, but in recent years most of them have suffered sharp economic decline. However, with a per capita income of $4,630.00 (1985 US dollars) Barbados ranked 34 of the 142 countries reporting to the World Bank in 1987. In respect of per capita GDP growth I would rate our performance as solid.

Barbados scored high points for price stability. The average annual rate of price increases since 1966 was slightly over ten per cent. By comparison, the US came in at about six per cent, the UK at about ten per cent, Japan at about seven per cent, and West Germany under five per cent. Over the past few years, however, we have enjoyed remarkable price stability, with inflation falling below two per cent in 1986. When you consider that the openness of our economy forces us to import inflation from our major trading partners, our performance in respect of price stability since 1966 has been most respectable. It looks even better when compared with developing countries that have suffered from numerous devaluations. Chile held the record for the period 1965–1980 with an average annual inflation rate of 129 per cent, while Bolivia achieved at the astounding average annual rate of inflation of 569 per cent from 1980 to 1985.

Our performance in the area of unemployment must be deemed unsatisfactory. Unemployment statistics are most unreliable before 1976, but it does seem that between 1966 and 1973 the unemployment rate was usually around 12 per cent — an apparently acceptable rate in the Barbadian social context. The year 1975 was an exceptionally bad year, with over 20 per cent of the labour force out of work. From 1978 through 1981 unemployment levels hovered around the 12 per cent level. Since 1982 the unemployment rate has seldom fallen below 15 per cent and has averaged 18 per cent since 1985. It is cold comfort that unemployment has proven almost as intractable a problem in developed countries, with rates in the UK, France and West Germany rising at times above ten per cent, and that rates of 30 per cent or more are quite common in the Third World. On the credit side, our economy was able to provide jobs of higher productivity in tourism and manufacturing to replace more than 10,000 lost in agriculture.

The Barbadian economy has undergone welcome structural change since 1966, when it was essentially a monoculture with sugar as king. Sugar accounted for 25 per cent of GDP in 1966 and 80 per cent of our exports, employed 25 per cent of the workforce and earned about 40 per cent of our foreign exchange. By 1986, both tourism and manufacturing had overtaken sugar in all the above departments. Manufacturing improved its contribution to GDP from four per cent in 1966 to 12 per cent in 1986 and lifted its exports from $50 million in 1966 to $368 million in 1986. Tourism raised its share of GDP from three per cent in 1966 to 12 per cent in 1986, and its foreign exchange earnings from less than $30 million to over $600 million. Also encouraging has been the growth in non-sugar production, whose contribution to GDP now rivals that of sugar. In recent years we have seen the beginning of a promising offshore business sector. This broadened production base explains much of the resilience demonstrated by the Barbadian economy in the recent years of economic turmoil.

Economic Management

To assess the quality of our economic policy making, we will have to examine the data more closely. The last 21 years divide logically into four periods that coincide, more or less, with the international business cycle. The first period, 1966–1970, saw the economy expand at an average rate of four per cent per annum. During the second period, 1971–1975, which included the first oil shock and the recession of 1975, the economy contracted at an annual rate of negative 0.5 per cent. In the third period, 1976–1980, we enjoyed our greatest prosperity, with the economy expanding by more than five per cent per annum. During the most recent period, 1981–1987, the economy has been generally flat. Because economic policy during this period has had the most serious implications for our current situation, I shall deal with it separately in the next section.

Generally speaking, Barbadian economic policy makers score high marks in the first three periods, that is, from 1966–1980. Essentially, they redistributed buoyant earnings from sugar and, later, tourism and manufacturing, towards social overhead capital, either through government investment in our harbour, airport and other infrastructure, or by guaranteeing foreign loans for the upgrading of privately owned public utilities. An attractive investment incentive programme and vigorous overseas promotion led to rapid expansion of our manufacturing and tourism industries. The national policy makers also enhanced our human capital through generous expenditures on education, health and social welfare services. Our modern infrastructure and highly educated workforce have contributed to sharp increases in national productivity, and have provided the basis of a new and promising offshore business industry.

Most commendably, successive administrations imparted a distinctly populist bias to their economic policies. Highly progressive tax rates ensured that the lion's share of our national income gains went to the more disadvantaged classes. This has made Barbados one of the most egalitarian societies in the world. Moreover, the level of our social indicators — households with electricity, telephones, running water and motor cars, infant mortality rates and life expectancy — gives us the profile of a highly-developed country. This has transformed Barbados into an essentially middle-class society of considerable social cohesiveness — our most important economic asset. In fact, the policy of progressive taxation was maintained for too long, so that the managerial and professional classes were unable to accumulate enough liquid funds for sundry employment generating investments. The 'alternative budget' of 1986 represented an abortive attempt to correct this situation in one fell swoop, and the April 1987 budget had to take back some of the earlier gains.

Above all, our economic policy makers must be complimented for avoiding the traps that lured so many developing countries, including some of our Caribbean friends, into economic disaster. They eschewed nationalization as a policy and limited their excursions into state enterprise. They rejected the fashionable path of 'self-reliance' and adopted the export-oriented policies to which developing countries are now turning in droves. They stuck to a regime of stable exchange rates, and refused to experiment with devaluation as a policy tool. They pursued liberal exchange control policies, thus promoting public confidence in the currency. Finally, by keeping import restrictions to a minimum, they avoided bureaucratic waste and stimulated industrial efficiency.

There are two areas where the national policy makers get failing marks. The first is in agriculture. Here, they failed to override a deeply ingrained social bias against the sugar industry. Punitive taxation, especially in 1975, and crushing trade union wage demands, deprived the industry of the resources needed for research and reorganization. Furthermore, support institutions, such as the Marketing Corporation, the Agricultural Development Corporation and the Agricultural Division of the Barbados National Bank, have never been made to carry out their strategic roles. A comprehensive strategy for agriculture must be developed before it is too late. This will involve the establishment of a separate and well capitalized Agricultural Credit Bank. Subsidies to agriculture in recent years are puny in comparison with those enjoyed by farmers in the industrial countries.

The second failing grade is in the operation of statutory corporations. Here, successive administrations have simply refused to separate business operations from political considerations. With few exceptions, the management of statutory corporations lacks the financial incentives and the freedom from political intervention required to attract, develop and retain high-class executive talent. Indeed, many top managerial positions are more frequently vacant than filled. The weakness of key statutory corporations over the years has imposed an intolerable burden on the public purse, and has blunted the effectiveness of well formulated government initiatives.

Current Economic Situation

With the possible exception of 1982, the Barbadian economy is weaker now than at any time since 1966. All three of our major foreign exchange earners are under severe pressure. Sugar prices have improved, but output is down; manufacturing exports are one half what they were a year or so ago; tourism buys its increased numbers with sharp price discounts, and unemployment remains at socially dangerous levels. Meanwhile, the foreign debt, which was just over US$80 million in 1980, has quadrupled and required debt service payments of almost US$50 million in 1986.

Our economic difficulties derive largely from the turmoil prevailing in the world economy. As indicated earlier, most developing countries are on the verge of bankruptcy and a few, like Haiti, Guyana, Zaire and Bolivia, are in a state of economic collapse. Indeed, there are very few countries that are not experiencing some form of economic malaise. However, some of our economic wounds here in Barbados have been self-inflicted as our policy makers departed from the path of fiscal prudence in their excessively populist zeal to sustain rising living standards. But unless output is rising, living standards can rise for only as long as foreign exchange reserves and national creditworthiness hold.

The Central Bank's 1980 Annual Report, in its 'Prospects for 1981', spoke of the combination of far-reaching income tax concessions and wage increases, well in excess of the rate of inflation, which had occurred in 1980. These triggered our current troubles. The report also cautioned that 'because of recessionary conditions in North America and slow economic growth in Europe, no significant increase in tourist arrivals is expected.' It also warned of reduced sugar receipts for 1981. Nevertheless, government's current expenditure increased by almost one quarter and its capital expenditure by over three quarters, leading in calendar 1981 to a record overall deficit of $181 million — three times as large as the deficit of the previous year, and double the previous record of 1977.

To make matters worse, the world recession of 1981–1982 turned out to be far more severe than expected, dragging us down into negative GDP growth. Our tourism and sugar earnings failed badly, and heavy foreign borrowing was necessary in 1981 to sustain our foreign exchange reserves. In October 1982 we entered into an 18-month IMF standby arrangement. The IMF standby agreement imposed a much-needed discipline, and the fiscal deficit was reduced by half during 1982, and even further in 1983. Unfortunately, the recovery from world recession did not lift the Barbadian economy as we had expected. Sugar prices, for one, remained in the basement, and our Trinidad export market collapsed.

The economy was flat in 1983 and raised its head briefly in 1984 when it grew by four per cent. It lay down again in 1985 and it was only under the artificial stimulus of the alternative budget that real GDP rose again by five per cent in 1986. GDP growth in 1987 is feeble once again. The consequent weakness in our balance of payments position warranted further deficit reductions but, with the IMF gone, our policy makers resumed an aggressive fiscal policy and the deficits began to widen once again. The supply side alternative budget of July 1986 pushed the 1986 deficit to $164 million, the second highest on record, and we are heading for another deficit over $170 million in 1987. This succession of fiscal deficits has required repeated foreign borrowing to deal with their balance of payments consequences.

The failure to institute an effective incomes policy during the period following 1980 has been our most unfortunate national policy failure. Throughout this period of economic stagnation, both private and public sectors yielded meekly to trade union pressures for wage increases that bore no relationship to productivity gains. In 1981, looking forward to a gloomy winter season, the hoteliers gave a wage increase of 35 per cent. They have never recovered.

Real GDP was virtually the same in 1986 as in 1980; yet, in that period, the overall index of wages rose by 45 per cent in the government sector and by 56 per cent overall. The sharp increase in the wages rate, unaccompanied by productivity gains, has had a deleterious effect on employment and the international competitiveness of our goods and services. Local enterprises have cut back drastically in the labour-intensive sectors. Two of our three department stores ceased operations, foreign investors were deterred from investing in Barbados, and some of our most important guest companies took their leave. As our recent Task Force on Employment has demonstrated, it's much easier to eliminate jobs than to create them.

A Glance Ahead

Most sociologists now accept that the turbulence of our times stems from the fact that we are, in the words of John Naisbitt, experiencing 'a megashift from an industrial to an information society.[1] The unprecedented acceleration in the rate of social and economic change was producing what Alvin Toffler describes as 'Future Shock', and was throwing the affairs of mankind into disarray.[2]

Recently, the international economy has become even more volatile and unpredictable, climaxing on October 19 this year with the fantastic collapse of the US stock market that sent shock waves through the world's financial markets. Traditionally, economists have thought in terms of tendencies towards equilibrium or regular cycles of behaviour. However, some scholars now perceive current economic phenomena as increasingly erratic rather than orderly, and are looking to the 'theory of chaos' for new insights and approaches.

It appears that the virtually instantaneous transmission of information across the world is producing patterns of social, economic and political behaviour never experienced before. Neither our common sense nor available analytical tools seem capable of apprehending them. The Science of Chaos is a fast growing interdisciplinary exploration of complex systems and offers innovative techniques for unravelling disorder.[3] I am suggesting that our future economic environment will not merely be complicated and volatile but could be chaotic as well.

Peter Drucker believes that our future will be shaped by what he calls 'discontinuities', that is, decisive breaks with previous trends. He sees major discontinuities in four areas: 'First, revolutionary technologies will create major new industries and render major industries obsolete.'[4]

A task force set up by the Rockefeller Foundation to study these technologies described their implications for developing countries as 'not a welcome view of the future'. I quote further from a commentary on that report:

> It is even possible that as a result of advances taking place in the research laboratories of the richer countries, the poorer countries could lose the few comparative advantages in the world economy that they now enjoy. Automation could reduce the need for cheap labour; the new materials science could produce substitutes for natural resources found in developing countries: genetic engineering could significantly alter markets for the products of tropical farms and plantations.[5]

Second, from being an international economy, we are becoming a world economy with a global factory and a global marketplace, as multinationals obtain their supplies from the cheapest sources, manufacture their goods in the cheapest production centres and sell them in the most lucrative markets — without reference to national boundaries. Similarly, fantastic volumes of capital funds now move with electronic swiftness from one international financial centre to another in search of the highest rate of return. Years ago, Marshall McLuhan prophesied the coming of the global village. Later Ernest Dichter would speak of the global market. In the 1960s Peter Drucker invented the expression 'production-sharing', and spoke of the global shopping centre. Today, Robert Grunwald is talking about the global factory.[6]

Third, knowledge has become the most important form of capital, and knowledge workers our most crucial resource. The technologies which underpinned the major industries of the late nineteenth and the first half of the twentieth centuries were the work of what one author describes as 'gifted tinkers': Edison and Farraday in electricity, Marconi in wireless, Bell in telephony. The new technologies — computers, fibre optics in telecommunications, materials science in space engineering, and biotechnology in agriculture, animal husbandry and pharmacology — are grounded in abstract scientific theory, and evolved in the elaborate laboratories of universities and multinationals. What is worse, the tasks of non-knowledge workers are increasingly carried out by computers. At a recent conference where I met him for the first time, my guru Peter Drucker observed that computers are now capable of carrying out 50 per cent of the tasks that people can do. By the year 2000, they will be able to carry out 75 per cent. The remaining 25 per cent will have to wait for the twenty-first century.

Fourth, the wide diffusion of educational information is undermining centralized authority. Societies are becoming more and more pluralistic with interest groups of all varieties, for example, homosexuals, youth groups, women, springing up in the most unlikely societies. Furthermore, the disastrous experiments in state ownership in the west, and here in the Caribbean, have convinced intelligent governments of the necessity for decentralization. In the United States and the United Kingdom the watchword is privatization and deregulation — though frequently for unintelligible reasons. It is the recognition of the growing ineffectiveness of centralized authority which is driving Mr Gorbachev to 'Glasnost' and Mr Deng Xiao Peng to a more market-oriented system.

Governments which refuse to take these new trends into account are soon rendered irrelevant by their people. We have an excellent case in point right here in the Caribbean. Guyana has the most highly centralized form of government in the Caribbean, controlling almost 80 per cent of the official economy. However, Professor Clive Thomas, Guyana's most distinguished economist, estimates that the unofficial economy, also known as the 'black market', is at least as large as the official economy. Its participants carry on their import, export and foreign exchange operations as if the government did not exist. They have their own rules of commercial business conduct but, of course, pay no taxes.

A Strategy for the Future

I warned on leaving the Central Bank eight months ago, that the immediate economic problems facing us were quite formidable. My judgment was confirmed with a vengeance by the US stock market crash of October 19, 1987. I doubt very much that it will precipitate a world depression as did the crash of 1929, but we should brace ourselves for a recession in 1989. In these circumstances, I commend the advice given by the Prophet Mohammed to the camel driver who, on the approach of the sandstorm, asked the holy man whether he should pray to Allah or tether his camel. The Prophet replied, 'Pray to Allah and tether your camel!'

The most pressing item on our agenda is to correct the current fiscal and external imbalances in our economy. This will involve a sharp reduction in the fiscal deficit. In particular, we must put the axe to rising government expenditure as we have been promising to do for some time now. (A study of recent fiscal developments in the US would be most instructive.) It may even be necessary to take back some of the 'give-backs' of the alternative budget. A smaller fiscal deficit would reduce the need for foreign borrowing. It would also reassure the international financial community and enhance our chances of raising the US$50 million or so that we will need to borrow annually for the next three years.

Having lost hundreds of billions of dollars in loans to the Third World, the international financial institutions are most diligent students of our economy. But they will go a long way with countries whose economic policies make sense. I cannot stress too strongly the need to maintain control over our balance of payments situation. To lose it would be to surrender the management of our economy to the IMF. I can think of few worse fates. This requires that we restore our foreign exchange reserves to levels that provide for a wide margin of safety. My definition of hell is when you have run out of foreign exchange reserves.

But the long-run economic future of Barbados will depend largely on the quality of the response of our national policy makers to the discontinuities in our world environment that Peter Drucker has identified. First, we must be aware of new technological developments all around us and be ready to adapt them to our own needs whenever advantage is to be gained. We must especially keep our public utilities in a state-of-the-art condition. Other candidates for technological update are the Royal Barbados Police Force, and the law courts. Their facilities need to be as modern as those of the Central Bank.

The first discontinuity which challenges us is the technologies of the computer and of telecommunications. Professor John Kemeny, the third Sir Winston Scott lecturer (1978), argues that the computer has restored developing countries to the same starting line as the developed.[7] Taiwan and South Korea may have proved him right. I was most concerned sometime ago at government's declared policy to halt the proliferation of computers. In fact, we should be doing the opposite, not least of all because computers are becoming less and less expensive. Thirteen million Americans now use the computer in their daily work. New jobs are generated, not so much in the manufacture of computers as in the new services and products they make possible. We Barbadians have no chance of solving our unemployment problems except through the use of the computer.

The second discontinuity is the globalization of production and marketing. Here, we have no choice but to integrate our own economy into the global production and marketing systems. Such a policy involves cooperation with multinational and other foreign corporations. We should push our businessmen in that direction. They should stop wringing their hands over the loss of the Trinidad market and reconcile themselves to the fact that the local market is far too small to support a viable manufacturing industry.

We should, of course, exploit any opportunities provided by membership in CARICOM, especially through the combination of intra-regional resources for the penetration of extra-regional markets. In this respect, it is important that we maintain the competitiveness of our exports. For years I have warned about wage restraint; Barbadian labour costs are now so far out of line with those of our competitors, for example, Jamaica and Mexico, that it may well be time to consider wage freezes and wage cuts, as the US and Curacao have done.

The third discontinuity is the emergence of knowledge as the most important capital resource. Our national instincts in this area should serve us well. However, we will have to pay increased attention to the quality of our tertiary institutions, especially the University, since they are our most important producers of knowledge. I would particularly like to see a faculty of philosophy added to the university curriculum, for it is through philosophy that we gain new knowledge. Recently, I chided Sir Hugh Springer and Sir Philip Sherlock, lovingly of course, for failing to establish a faculty of philosophy from the inception of the University of the West Indies. I was more severe on Sir Hugh, since he is one of the most knowledgeable West Indians in this field. They were both appropriately penitent.

I appreciate that the government budget is already strained to provide adequate funding for higher education. Free university education was instituted when the per capita income of Barbadians was a quarter of what it is today; isn't it time that students whose parents can afford it should make some contribution? Others might make some contribution to their education through loans repayable after graduation, as is the case in the United States. Isn't it also time that private enterprise channel some of its profits to the endowment of the University? Wouldn't it be nice if by its fiftieth anniversary the University is obtaining the major portion of its funding from its own endowments? He who pays the piper calls the tune; our University will never be fully mature as long as governments pay the piper.

The fourth discontinuity, the erosion of centralized authority, presents the most difficult challenge for a small society. It is easy for politicians in small societies to delude themselves into believing that they can control every minute detail of economic activity. In the early stages of our economic development, massive investment in infrastructure require highly centralized planning, legislative and administrative processes, and calls for a strong central government capable of imposing the heavy taxation needed to execute major projects. As development proceeds, government must disengage from microeconomic activities and allow for the proliferation of decision centres in the society. This would permit economic advance on a broad front. Drucker goes even further. He contends that modern governments have no choice in the

New Information Age but to disengage from activities which the private sector can accomplish, leaving themselves free to concentrate on tasks which they alone can carry out, for example, maintenance of law and order, public health, public education and foreign affairs.

The decentralization of our governmental apparatus will require the enlightenment of our electorate. We need to escape from the notion that government is there to do things for us. This attitude must be replaced by the proposition that government is there to help us do better the things of which we are capable. Politicians would then no longer feel constrained to promise, for example, that they will provide jobs for everyone overnight. As a matter of fact, job creation occurs primarily in the private sector and involves the commitment of retained profits to marketing and investment activities. Even the considerable capital expenditures by government in 1981 and 1986 made hardly a dent in the unemployment level.

Decentralization will involve pushing decisions now made by ministers further down in the civil service and statutory boards. This will free ministers to carry out the task that they alone can perform, that is, policy making. Such a strategy would involve a much greater emphasis on training in the civil service so as to promote the highest standards of professionalism. I have already spoken of the need to separate politics from operations in the management of statutory corporations. The era is over when all roads should lead to the Prime Minister. The nation has come of age and its citizens are mature enough to share in the management of our society.

My Vision of the Future

As the Chinese proverb says, 'Prediction is always difficult — especially in respect of the future.' As I have suggested, the world around us is changing at an accelerating rate and in most perplexing ways. I have two visions of the future Barbadian economy: if we select the wrong strategy, I see Haiti. I need not describe it. I will give the vision contingent upon the premises and strategy I have suggested. My crystal ball is cloudy, but I will tell what I see.

Today's three key productive sectors will still exist, but their operations would not be recognizable to those present this evening. Let us look at each sector separately.

Manufacturing

Manufacturing establishments will be integral parts of multinational production-sharing systems operating in Barbados because of relatively lower wages than in Europe or the US, but with very high quality technical, professional and managerial staff. Some factories will be part of CARICOM enterprises drawing their inputs and financial resources from around the region. Most of the manufacturing processes will be automated, and staff will typically work at video display units.

Agriculture

We will probably be producing more sugar than we do today but, through the use of new laboratory-produced strains, we will require much less land. Only a fraction of our cane output will be for sugar; the greater part will be used in new products, special plastics perhaps, and much more for rum. Much of the cane will also be combined with molasses to feed cattle of the highest quality that will yet have three times the milk productivity of our present herds. We will produce much more of the food we eat, and a variety of new fruits and vegetables for the local and overseas seasonal markets. Production will be highly mechanized, and will be supported by a top class research establishment. The category of agricultural labourer will disappear; only technicians and professionals will work on the farms.

Tourism

Most tourists will still visit our shores to enjoy sand, surf, sun and fun. However, many will come primarily to visit relatives employed in the manufacturing and financial services or to take advantage of high-class educational and medical services which will attract large numbers of students and scholars. CARICOM citizens will also come to Barbados to take in numerous artistic presentations, including shows at the Frank Collymore Hall.

Offshore Business

State-of-the-art telecommunications linking Barbados with the financial markets of the world, together with modern public utilities and amenities, will support a thriving offshore service industry. It will be manned by an army of lawyers, accountants and financial analysts with support staff all using computers. They will be highly efficient, and lawyers will actually service their clients within the time promised.

Maintenance

An army of highly trained technicians will maintain our ultra-modern infrastructure and high-rise office buildings, and keep computers and other electronic machinery in working order.

Gee! I must have been dreaming!

A lecture delivered at the Frank Collymore Hall, Bridgetown, on November 26, 1987, to mark the 21st anniversary of the independence of Barbados

Notes

1. John Naisbitt, *Megatrends* (New York: Warner Bros. Inc, 1982)

2. Alvin Toffler, *Future Shock.*

3. James Gleick, *Chaos* (New York: Viking, 1987).

4. Peter F. Drucker, *The Age of Discontinuity* (New York: Harper & Row, 1968).

5. 'Rockefeller Foundation in the Developing World' (New York: Rockefeller Foundation, 1986).

6. Robert Grundwald, *The Global Factory* (Washington, DC: The Brookings Institution, 1985).

7. John Kemeny, 'Man and the Computer' (Third Sir Winston Scott Memorial Lecture, Central Bank of Barbados, 1978).

22

THE BARBADOS MODEL

I have frequently been asked by foreigners: 'How is it that so small an island, with so few natural resources, can provide so high a standard of living for its citizens?' By the mid-1980s the Washington international financial institutions (IFIs) were full of praise for the 'skill and acumen' with which we had managed our economic affairs, and were recommending the 'Barbados model' as one to be emulated by other developing countries — the feature of fiscal discipline in particular. In recent years the question directed most frequently to me on the *'Breakfast Club'*, a radio talk show in Kingston, Jamaica, has been, 'Why has Barbados's economic performance so far outstripped that of Jamaica in spite of the latter's larger population and superior natural resource base?' It would be false modesty to deny that Barbadians have done well. With a population of less than 270,000 we boast a per capita income approaching US$7,000, placing us in the World Bank's category of upper middle-income countries, and a literacy rate as close to 100 per cent. A life expectancy of 73 years, and an infant mortality rate of less than 15 per 1000 — maternal deaths during childbirth are a rarity — give us the demographic profile of a developed country. Indeed, the latest UNDP Human Development Index, based on the three criteria of national income, education and health, places Barbados 25th of the more than 150 countries surveyed, and first among developing countries.

Moreover, the Barbadian dollar which, on my advice as Governor of the Central Bank, was fixed at BDS$2.00 = US$1.00 on July 5, 1975, retains the same value today. Barbadians enjoy a rare quality of life, with income more equitably distributed than in most countries. We possess a highly developed infrastructure of highways, seaport and airport, electricity, water and telecommunications; a well-developed national security safety net for the disadvantaged; a relatively low crime rate, and a remarkable absence of social and political unrest. At the same time, civil and democratic rights, irrespective of religion, ethnicity or gender, are deeply entrenched in Barbadian society. Indeed, Freedom House in New York City has year after year ranked Barbados among the freest of free nations. I have frequently described Barbados as the world's most successful predominantly black nation. How do we explain the 'Barbados model'?

The Science of Chaos

Casting around for an explanatory model of the development of our island civilization, I gained great insight from the new science of 'Chaos', invented by the mathematician-meteorologist Edward Lorenz in the 1960s. John Gleick, in his bestseller, *Chaos: Making a New Science*, explains the concept:

> In science as in life, it is well known that a chain of events can have a point of crisis that could magnify small changes. But chaos meant that such points were everywhere.[1]

This feature of chaotic systems came to be known as the 'Butterfly effect', after Lorenz's celebrated paper, 'Predictability: Does the Flap of a Butterfly's Wings in Brazil Set Off a Tornado in Texas?'[2] What is more chaotic, I thought, than the history of our nation? We have suffered from foreign wars, a mini-civil war between Royalists and Roundheads in the 1640s, slave revolts, riots, droughts, epidemics, hurricanes, mass migrations, and the effects of technological change, all occurring in an unpredictable manner! This led me to search for those historical accidents that collectively have conspired to produce the fortunate features of our civilization, the 'Barbados model', to borrow the nomenclature of the Washington IFIs. Not all of these accidents seemed 'fortunate' to contemporary Barbadians immediately affected by them — least of all those of African descent.

Seven Fortunate Historical Accidents

The first and most enduring of Barbados's fortunate historical accidents is its geography. Standing aloof from the Eastern Caribbean chain 100 miles into the Atlantic, Barbados would become the first port of call and a springboard for further British penetration of the West Indies and North America, especially the Carolinas where in 1670 Barbadians founded the charming city of Charleston. Geography was also an important military advantage. In the days of sailing ships, its natural barrier of coral reefs and Atlantic breakers made Barbados virtually unassailable from the east, while the strong prevailing north-east trade winds made it difficult for French warships stationed in Martinique or Guadeloupe to attack our island from the north-west. This largely explains why Barbados is the only Caribbean island never to have changed hands during the European conflicts of the seventeenth and eighteenth centuries in the region, thus permitting the uninterrupted development of the island.

The second fortunate historical accident reinforced the first. While their motive for occupying other colonies in the region was territorial acquisition or absentee economic exploitation, the English came as settlers to Barbados in 1627 with the intention of making a second start in the New World. The total absence of an indigenous population spared us the historical trauma of genocide experienced by other Caribbean societies where the Arawaks and Caribs were virtually wiped out by colonizing Europeans. In 1655 there were 23,000 English settlers on the island and only 20,000 slaves. The English settlers would put down deep institutional roots: they founded the second oldest parliament in the New World in 1639; they dotted the island with Anglican churches; for 'the education of poor white boys'; they established in 1733 my own high school, Harrison College, which in time would benefit poor black boys as well; in 1875 they transformed Codrington College into the region's first institution of higher learning; they transplanted to the island the English Common Law and, above all, the game of cricket, which has flourished even more luxuriantly on our island than in the country of its origin. Sir Garfield Sobers, a Barbadian, is universally accepted as the greatest all-round cricketer of all time.

The commitment of Barbadian settlers to parliamentary government was especially strong, leading them to declare independence from Great Britain in 1651. Indeed, the cry of 'No taxation without representation' was heard in Bridgetown before it was in Boston! Their revolt was fortunately quelled by the arrival of Cromwell's fleet, but the 'Articles of Capitulation', signed at Oistins with Sir George Ayescue in 1652, actually reinforced the representative form of government on the island, and came to be known as 'The Charter of Barbados'. I tease my English friends that it is unclear from the 'Articles' who capitulated to whom! The struggle for parliamentary government would be successfully fought again in the 1870s, when the British government threatened the imposition of crown colony government; that is, direct government from London through a governor and non-elected council. A compromise with the British narrowly averted crown colony government in Barbados, but this retrogressive regime would stunt political development in the rest of the British Caribbean. It would not be until the post-World War II era that representative government would be restored or established in other British Caribbean colonies.

The third historical accident was the early accession of the free coloured to political and civic rights. Stimulated by the recent success of the Haitian Revolution, Barbadian slaves in 1816 plotted the massacre of 'bad' masters. This discriminatory policy aroused suspicion among the 'good' masters who sounded the alarm. The price of this civility was the death, in battle or by hanging, of nearly 400 slaves.

Ironically, it was the free coloured militia who first took the field to put down the revolt. So impressed were the white planters with that display of solidarity that by 1820 they had lifted most of the remaining civil disabilities from the free coloured,[3] and in 1831 extended the franchise to them, albeit under qualifications unattainable by the vast majority of them. In 1841 Samuel Jackman Prescod, a champion of the recently freed slaves, became the first coloured member of the House of Assembly; Sir Conrad Reeves, architect of the constitutional compromise with the British in the 1870s, would become in 1884 the first black Chief Justice of Barbados and the first black knight of the British Empire.

Because of their deep passion for liberty, their indomitable courage in battle, and the dignity with which the condemned faced their execution, the rebellious slaves have been justly hailed as heroes. Paradoxically, however, the early enfranchisement of the free coloured, who participated in their defeat, must from the hindsight of almost two centuries be seen as a providential outcome for descendants of the slaves. At best, a successful revolt would have replicated in Barbados the history of Haiti; at worst, it would have resulted in a blood bath as British imperial forces wrought revenge for the death of their kith and kin — as they would with such ferocity in suppressing the Indian mutiny 41 years later.

The fourth, and probably most important, of the fortunate accidents was the early exposure of Barbadian slaves to education. As early as 1710 Christopher Codrington, a rich white planter, died and bequeathed his estate to an Anglican missionary organization, the Society for the Propagation of the Gospel (SPG), for the purpose of educating and making Christians of the slaves. Less than ten years after the fall of apartheid in South Africa, it is heart warming to recall that a white Anglican, Bishop Fleetwood, preached in 1711 that blacks were equally the workmanship of God with (the planters) 'with the same faculties and intellectual powers ... and bodies of the same flesh and blood, and souls certainly immortal.'[4] Education went hand in hand with Christianity. By the end of the eighteenth century many slaves had become literate. In 1818 a public primary school was established for instruction of the children of blacks and coloured people; of the first 89 pupils 32 were the children of slaves. The first public primary school for coloured girls would follow in 1827. Ever since then the instinct has been ingrained in the minds of black Barbadians that education was the most reliable means of upward social mobility and political liberation. Moreover, the remittances from educated Bajan emigrants have been an important foreign exchange earner over the years — priests, teachers and policemen to the wider Caribbean; nurses and transport workers to London; nurses and sundry university graduates to the US.

The fifth historical accident of the island's small size has worked to our advantage in many and counter-intuitive ways, but never so much as in the decades following Emancipation, which came partially in 1834 and finally in 1838, when the Apprenticeship Act was repealed. In those Caribbean colonies where lands remained unsettled; for example, Guyana, Jamaica, and Trinidad, the former slaves left the sugar plantations to become peasant farmers or artisans. By 1847, almost half of Trinidad's former slaves, and two-thirds of Jamaica's, had abandoned the plantations to establish free villages. To maintain sugar production the planters were forced to introduce indentured labour from India and, to a much lesser extent, from China. With the island already totally occupied, Barbadian freedmen were forced to remain on the plantation as wage labourers, to accommodate to the ways of the white planters and, in the process, absorb English values and attitudes over the next century.

More importantly, as British society became more liberal, so did the Barbadian.

However, I reject Lawrence Harrison's characterization of Barbadians as 'black Englishmen',[5] even as white Barbarians would reject the sobriquet of 'white Africans'. The English settlers were also influenced by the black slaves, and from their interaction blacks and whites have developed a unique civilization — both kinder and gentler than that left behind in either England or Africa. Confinement to the plantation, or its shadow, must have been a bitter pill for contemporary freedmen to swallow, but it has paid off magnificently for subsequent generations. Ironically, the Jamaican freedmen who became an independent peasantry were to pay a high posthumous price in the illiteracy of their descendants.

The sixth of our fortunate accidents must be the *noblesse oblige* of the coloured and black elites in the years immediately following Emancipation — and to the present day. In contrasting the Barbadian coloured elites with their Haitian counterparts, Lawrence Harrison observed, 'Whereas before they (the Barbadian black elites) in no way identified themselves with the slaves, after emancipation they assumed a tutelary responsibility for the blacks.'[6] F.A. Hoyos adds that 'they took the recently liberated slaves under their wing and persuaded them to accept their habits, their lifestyle and their philosophy.'[7] Coloured leaders like Samuel Jackman Prescod, Anthony Barclay, Joseph Thorne, Nat Roach and London Bourne, fought with great determination to promote the civil rights and welfare of the former slaves. They would be followed by a succession of political leaders from among the rising black elites, who based their political power on the expanding constituency of working class blacks.

Ever since then, the politics of Barbadian coloured and black elites has been 'populist'. Following the climactic riots of 1937, we were especially fortunate to throw up a succession of three leaders who would have been outstanding in any nation: Grantley Adams, Errol Barrow and Tom Adams, son of Grantley. Moreover, they arrived in the right sequence: the wily Grantley played the British Colonial Office off against the local white plantocracy in leading us to self-government; the aggressive Barrow launched us on the path of economic development and on to full independence, and cool Tom steered us adroitly through the turbulence of the late 1970s and early 1980s. They all spent lavishly on education and the social services, placing a sturdy floor under the welfare of the least advantaged. At the same time, they managed the economy pragmatically, and were not seduced by the alien ideologies that have wrecked the economies of so many developing nations, including some within CARICOM. Most amazingly, they accomplished the transfer of political power from the white oligarchy to the black majority without physical violence, and with a minimum of personal discomfort to the former. It was indeed a glorious revolution!

Whenever a new general was recommended to him, Napoleon's first question was, 'Is he lucky?' The seventh fortunate accident is a composite of a number of breaks that I have subsumed under 'economic luck'. I should add that some of this luck has been manufactured, to the extent that Barbadians have seized the opportunities presented to them. By the time that Barbadian tobacco, the first cash crop of the settlers, had gained the reputation as the foulest on the market, the Dutch had introduced sugar cane from Pernambuco in Brazil, a region which I visited for the first time this year. When subsidized beet sugar production in Europe threatened the sugar industry in the late nineteenth century, the economic disruption caused by the insurgency under José Marti reduced the supply of Cuban sugar and lifted prices on the international market. And when a strange fungus threatened to wipe out the Bourbon cane, the mainstay of sugar agriculture in the region, the path-breaking cane breeding experiments of John R. Bovell, a white superintendent at Dodds Plantation, St. Philip, led to the development of new and disease-resistant varieties which literally saved the cane sugar industry from extinction.

And when all seemed lost, sugar prices would rise sharply during, and in the years immediately following, the First and Second World Wars. In the 'hard times' of the early twentieth century, thousands of Barbadians would find work on the construction of the Panama Canal, and during the Second World War in the oil refineries of Aruba and Curacao. In the 1940s and 1950s thousands would also emigrate to London to staff the public transport system and national health hospitals. The advent of the commercial jet-liner in the 1950s would launch the tourism industry, which now earns a gross US$600 million in foreign exchange for the island, while technological advances in telecommunications have made possible the establishment of our offshore financial sector and the marketing of 'infomatics' services, which promise to be our new growth industries.

Conclusion

The question remaining is whether the Barbados model is sustainable in the turbulent environment occasioned by the transition from the old Industrial Age to the New Information Age. Chaos Theory tells us that we cannot be certain that one, or a series of, unfortunate accidents will not overwhelm us as in the case of several other developing countries. We must certainly stick to those fundamentals that have served us so well in the past; for example, investment in education, democracy, the rule of law, maintenance of our infrastructure, tolerance, and compassion for the disadvantaged. But we must also adjust to the forces of globalization. Prime Minister Owen Arthur has warned Barbadians again and again that the days of preferences and non-reciprocal trade agreements are numbered, and that we must become competitive in the world markets. We must also pray that most of the accidents that befall us in the future will be as fortunate as they have been in the past, though less ironic or paradoxical.

Feature Address to the Caribbean and Latin American Student Association of Pittsburgh, and the Caribbean Association of Pittsburgh on the occasion of their XVII Annual Caribbean Night – 'Focus on Barbados', November 8, 1997

Notes

1. James Gleick, *Chaos: Making a New Science* (New York: Viking Penguin Group, 1987), 23.

2. Edward Lorenz, Address at the annual meeting of the American Association for the Advancement of Science in Washington, December 29, 1979.

3. Karl Watson, *The Civilized Island Barbados* (St George, Barbados: Caribbean Graphic Ltd, 1979).

4. William Fleetwood, S.P.G.'s Annual Sermon in 1711, as quoted by F.A. Hoyos, *Barbados: A History from the Amerindians to Independence* (London: Macmillan, 1978), 84.

5. Lawrence E. Harrison, *Underdevelopment is a State of Mind* (Boston: Madison Books, 1985), 93.

6. Ibid., 95.

7. F.A. Hoyos, *Barbados: A History from the Amerindians to Independence* (London: Macmillan, 1978), 135.

INDEX

Printed in the United States
78061LV00001B/1-66